THE NEW TECHNOLOGY OF
FINANCIAL MANAGEMENT

WILEY FINANCE EDITIONS

THE NEW TECHNOLOGY OF FINANCIAL MANAGEMENT

Dimitris N. Chorafas

JOHN WILEY & SONS, INC.

New York • Chichester • Brisbane • Toronto • Singapore

"Men accept Change only through Necessity.
And they see Necessity only in Crisis."

Jean Monnet (1888–1979)

658.155
C55n

Copyright © 1992 by Dimitris N. Chorafas.
Published by John Wiley & Sons, Inc.

Library of Congress Cataloging-in-Publication Data

Chorafas, Dimitris N.
    The new technology of financial management
/ by Dimitris N. Chorafas.—Wiley finance editions.
        p.   cm.
    Includes index.
    ISBN 0-471-57402-3 (cloth : alk. paper)
        1. Foreign exchange—Data processing.   2. Options (Finance)—Data
processing.   3. Information technology.   I. Title.
    HG3851.C474   1992
    658.15'5—dc20   92-1023

Printed in the United States of America

10 9 8 7 6 5 4 3 2 1

Printed and bound by Courier Comnanies. Inc.

Foreword

Over the past 15 years, the globalization of markets in general, and of banking and finance in particular, has provoked a revolution in the use and application of high technology. Expert systems are no longer the exclusive domain of nuclear physicists or the military, but have become the essential tools of the successful banker. Constant evolution in systems is therefore a fundamental requirement for those institutions that wish not only to survive but also to prosper in the mainstream of today's changing marketplace.

It is widely accepted that one of the symptoms of this changing market environment is the fact that many banks operating independently today will be overwhelmed by their competitors over the course of this decade. Major takeovers and mergers are announced almost every few weeks. Some estimates say that as many as 75 percent of today's banks will be unable to remain independent until the year 2000.

As we embark upon the last decade of the millenium, this is obviously not the time to sit back and reflect. Diversification and innovation in quality services remain the rules of the day, particularly in the treasury, forex, and securities spheres—the engine room of banks, where astute planning and market perception can be brought to fruition with the aid of skilled guidance in the application of new technological methodologies.

In this book, Dr. Chorafas presents the reader—both technologist and financial professional—with not only such vital guidance but also a vision of technology as a friend rather than a foe in the challenges that institutions face.

v

I have had the pleasure of working with Dr. Chorafas on several projects in financial services, and, having experienced first-hand his innovative insight into the subject, I am certain that it will remain an essential work of reference for many years to come.

RANJIT DE ALWIS
Director of Product Management and
Member of the Management Board
CEDEL
Luxembourg

Preface

As the financial environment of the 1990s unfolds, the changes that it represents are deep-rooted. Some of the factors affecting this environment include the following:

- Evolution of the workforce
- Redistribution of wealth
- Advent of high technology
- Effect of the knowledge society as a whole

A wave of change is being driven by international economic factors in the capital markets, money markets, and foreign exchanges. The future bank is the *knowledge bank* — a leader in forex, securities, investment advice, and treasury operations. The same is true of financial operations in manufacturing and marketing.

But even if the present picture is a far cry from what treasury functions used to be only 10 years ago, this picture, too, could change. Managers and professionals of financial institutions must be alert to the dynamics of the market and eager to investigate the dominant direction of evolutionary developments.

A sound analysis of business opportunity should not exclude any reasonable possibility in the way financial services will be shaping up. Experimentation is the keyword today, and it can be successfully performed through simulators and knowledge engineering constructs. Algorithms and heuristics are cornerstones of successful treasury and foreign exchange operations, as are distributed databases, market data filters, profile analyzers, and, most importantly, intelligent networks.

These are the issues this book addresses. It is designed for professionals who want to be at the top of their business and stay there, whether they come from a treasury, forex, and securities background or whether they have been trained as technologists.

The focal point of Chapter 1 is the organization that is necessary to support treasury operations. For this reason, it starts with a job description of treasury duties, emphasizing the importance of strategic planning in getting results, and ends with technological developments as well as the effects of automation on the treasurer's job.

Chapter 2 discusses the common infrastructure needed for treasury, foreign exchange, securities trading, and investment advice. It does so in a comprehensive manner, from the design of new financial products to the evaluation of the effects of taxation.

Successful trading needs both technology and knowledgeable people to use it. Chapter 3 takes a detailed look at the forex room, the steady evolution of its technological infrastructure, and the types of investments that are necessary in forex operations.

Some of these investments will be made in analytical tools. Chapter 4 goes into considerable detail in explaining what this approach involves, emphasizing the role of distributed heterogeneous databases, the need for seamless access to them, and some of the foremost solutions, exemplified by DAIS and MIA.

Trading in national and international markets requires increasing data flows, which are today sold for a price by information providers. The problem is not one of lack of data but rather of being snowed under by large data volumes pumped through monitors all day long. Chapter 5 describes the best approach to market data filtering.

The information that we buy, collect, and store in our databases must be examined not only critically but also analytically. Chapter 6 explains how this can be done, and brings the issue of interactive computational finance into perspective.

In a comprehensive manner, easy to follow for non-mathematicians, Chapter 7 explains the contribution of knowledge engineering and simulation. Chapter 8 underlines the fact that technology-based solutions are for the enduser. Therefore, they must involve agile human-machine interfaces.

The timely comprehension of market trends is one of the domains where technology can be most helpful. Chapter 9 focuses on intelligent charting and pattern recognition but, as Chapter 10 suggests, new tools require a new culture in order to be used in the most effective manner. The book concludes by placing emphasis on telecommunications and their significance in modern financial operations.

- Chapter 11 discusses the role that networks play in the globalization of financial products.

- Chapter 12 explains how networks should be designed for trading and for better client service.

- Chapter 13 introduces the concept of an intelligent network, ou‡lining the services that it can offer.

Because of globalization, deregulation, and fast-moving technological evolution, we have no time to lose and no place to hide. A financial institution has no alternative but to master its technology.

No bank, no brokerage, no treasury business today has an inventory of large and stable profit-making sectors permitting it to hang on to its old connections. In fact, it has very few areas to depend on, and these are challenged all the time by the bank's own larger customers, who have now become its competitors. We have to develop new sources of income.

I feel indebted to a great number of bankers, corporate treasurers, forex operators, securities brokers, and technologists who contributed ideas as well as reviewed and commented on many parts of this book. The brilliant brains behind many of the leading concepts in this text have been Edmond Israel of the Luxembourg Stock Exchange, Heinrich Steinmann of Union Bank of Switzerland, André Lussi of CEDEL, Carmine Vona of Bankers Trust, Colin Crook of Citibank, and Gordon Macklin of NASD. To Eva-Maria Binder goes the credit for the artwork, typing, and indexing.

DIMITRIS N. CHORAFAS

Valmer, France and Vitznau, Switzerland
July 1992

Contents

1

Developing the Organization and Technology to Support Treasury Operations

It is illuminating to look back to the Middle Ages or, for that matter, to the twentieth century's communist regimes. One of the characteristics of both epochs was that *conformity* was rampant. Another negative quality was almost total *intellectual stagnation* — and we can appreciate why the two go together and in the process stifle innovation.

One thing a chief financial officer cannot afford is intellectual stagnation in the operations under his or her control. Organization and structure in treasury operations should, of course, match the management style of the chief executive officer and of the board, but this should not be done at the expense of ingenuity in managing the finances.

With steadily changing financial markets the need to seize the moment is always present. At the same time, the treasurer of a bank or industrial corporation must make sure that the firm's financial staying power matches its market appeal, its product cycles, and its human capital requirements. This is necessary to ensure continuing profitability.

What sort of company needs treasury services the most? The First World currently features four types of enterprises:

1. Manufacturing and commercial multinational companies that are held by stockholders and that constitute a major part of the backbone of today's industrial, financial, and economic structure.

1

2. Financial industry organizations: commercial banks, investment and merchant banks, and insurance companies. These organizations may be publicly held, or may be partnerships, and they act as financial intermediaries performing many different tasks.

3. Manufacturing firms or financial institutions in the nationalized sector, which, in countries such as France, Italy, and England, control a major part of the economy.

4. The small-to-medium industrial and financial organizations ownership of which is divided between the public and private sectors. These organizations play a role in regard to the larger entities and their well-being, but are at the same time conditioned by the larger entities.

In all these organizations, the treasury function is critical. The treasurer's position is absolutely indispensable in the first type of organization; very important in the second type, though the position may be shaped in a different manner; tends to be confused with the making of the national budget in the case of the state super-market in the third type of enterprise; and identifies itself with the ownership in the fourth type.

TREASURY FUNCTIONS

If all desired long-, medium-, and short-term funds could be borrowed from one lender, and all deposits handled in one only currency at one financial institution, the treasurer's function might be fairly simple. This is what some banks propose to industrial corporations through project financing, but this is not necessarily what the manufacturing or merchandising company should do.

The reason for the existence of the treasury is to provide the organization with an in-house means to optimize its global finances. This requirement highlights the importance of both the traditional and the more recently invented treasury functions:

1. *Financial planning.* This function includes planning the company's capital market investment program, as well as planning borrowing requirements. Other financial planning functions include forecasting cash receipts and disbursement, advising on dividend payments, and reporting financial results to the officers of the company.

2. *Cash management.* This comprises opening accounts and depositing funds in banks, administering money market instruments, paying company obligations through proper disbursement procedures, managing petty cash and bank balances, and maintaining records of cash transactions.

3. *Foreign exchange operations.* This requires keeping accounts in all major currencies, hedging to protect the company from exchange rate fluctuations, hedging with interest rate swaps and forward rate agreements, and investing in options and financial futures.

4. *Credit management.* This function includes determination of customers' credit risks, orderly handling of collections, management of cash discounts and terms of sale for prompt payment, and so on.

5. *Security flotations.* The treasurer must negotiate with investment bankers; evaluate and recommend types of securities most desirable for the company's borrowing requirements; and correlate these terms with the company's long-term ability to retire bonds, to make switches in capital market borrowing, and to repurchase or sell stock.

6. *Custody of funds and securities.* This duty encompasses provision of trustee functions, compliance with governmental regulations, handling of transfer agents, stockholder relationships, disbursement of dividends, relation with pension funds, and portfolio management.

7. *Other financial functions.* These include asset and liability management, income and cash flow estimates, hedging in futures and options, new financial instruments, links to clearinghouses, financial networking, trust management, custodian reporting, and contracting of loans and income.

The treasury must also keep balances; sign checks, contracts, leases, notes, bonds and stock certificates, mortgages, deeds, and other corporate documents; and collect, endorse, and deposit checks.

Because these job descriptions come from the practices of several corporations (banks as well as manufacturing firms), and since the treasury business is not standardized, some of the points overlap.

There is no single best way to organize the treasury function; actual organization must reflect a company's policies and practices. Yet all treasuries have common elements. One of the most basic is the operational and reporting requirement for funds management, shown in Figure 1.1.

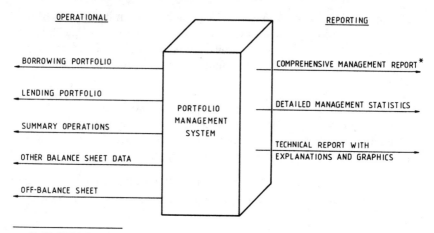

OPERATIONAL

BORROWING PORTFOLIO

LENDING PORTFOLIO

SUMMARY OPERATIONS

OTHER BALANCE SHEET DATA

OFF-BALANCE SHEET

PORTFOLIO MANAGEMENT SYSTEM

REPORTING

COMPREHENSIVE MANAGEMENT REPORT*

DETAILED MANAGEMENT STATISTICS

TECHNICAL REPORT WITH EXPLANATIONS AND GRAPHICS

* TO BE PRESENTED IN ORDER OF MAGNITUDE, BUT WITH JUSTIFICATION.

Figure 1.1 Operational and reporting requirements for funds management.

FREEDOM OF DECISION REGARDING FINANCIAL ISSUES

The treasurer must be ready to discuss the practicability of his[1] financial program at any time. He must also be able to work out plans that will steadily improve the corporation's financial condition. Given the complexity of the goal that he is asked to reach, the treasurer is often given a large amount of operating freedom in financial issues—but such freedom of decision means greater responsibility.

With the sufficient information at his disposal, the treasurer is expected to make basic analyses and study consequences before determining financial policies:

- Is the business in satisfactory financial condition?

- If not, why not? What should be done about it?

- If yes, how stable is the present situation?

- If the business is in satisfactory financial shape, what policies got it there?

[1]The author recognizes that both men and women hold positions of all types in modern business organizations. For convenience, however, the masculine pronoun has been used in this book.

- Can the company continue such policies under changing market conditions?

- What may necessitate a change in plans?

Whether the financial condition of the corporation is healthy, unhealthy, or affected by endogenous and exogenous factors, the treasurer should expect frequent audits. Treasury is the area in which both the mercantile credit manager and the banker investigate, although they will use different methods and widely various degrees of thoroughness.

The treasurer should also understand that sometimes such analyses miss the true underlying situation; traditional figures may show good yearly earnings, but the company might be headed downhill for the crash of bankruptcy. This can be recognized in only two ways:

1. By performing fundamental analysis of the relationships among strategic goals, yearly balance sheets, and off–balance sheet items.

2. By using simulation and heuristics to unearth hidden issues and their details, which often escape attention because of the layer of cosmetics put on financial statements.

It is rather unusual for an annual report to stockholders to contain sufficient information for a comprehensive financial analysis; that is why astute creditors require much more basic information. They want both supplementary data and details, and they have available the software and computer power to submit them to scrutiny.

The treasurer must also be personally experienced in the game of utilizing figures to the greatest possible advantage. And he would need both algorithms and expert systems to help him understand the limitations and inadequacies of financial data in their classical presentation form.

If the treasurer is also the chief financial officer, then an integral part of his duties is supplying the infrastructure for factual and documented financial services, appropriately planning and controlling expenditures, and obtaining financial results as points of pivotal importance. This includes the following duties:

1. Forecasting the financial consequences for the company, given current and projected top-management decisions

2. Appraising the financial results of ongoing operations of each division and the benefits received from expenditures

3. Evaluating proposed budgets for the next financial year as well as in the shorter term

4. Establishing medium-range and longer-term financial plans

5. Elaborating principles and methods of keeping accounting control active and focused

6. Improving on procedures for the receipt, banking, custody, and disbursement of money

7. Conducting external financial relationships, including the determination of tax liabilities

8. Authorizing credit and collection of money due

9. Disposing of surplus assets and handling relations with fiduciary agents

10. Obtaining insurance coverage for all classes of assets and associated risks

The treasurer's degree of freedom will be much greater with more sophisticated information systems at his disposition, permitting both overseeing of and experimentation on costs and benefits in the several operating divisions of the firm. Experimentation should be coordinated with the results of internal audits, overseeing activities, and the preparation of accounting and statistical reports.

Each of these functions involves multiple steps that generally have to be tailored to the prevailing conditions. As an example on general procedure, Figure 1.2 presents an account hierarchy regarding collection of money due, the eighth item in the preceding list.

The functions of the chief financial officer and that of the treasurer should not be confused with the mission given to the *controller*. The controller is responsible for *internal audits* and for the interpretation of control data. He must also provide basic information regarding managerial control through formulation of accounting and costing policies and their associated standards and procedures.

Once again, the exact description of functions varies from one company to another. In the general case, however, specific control activities include evaluation of the following items:

- Primary and subsidiary general accounts

- The company's finances

- Loans given or taken

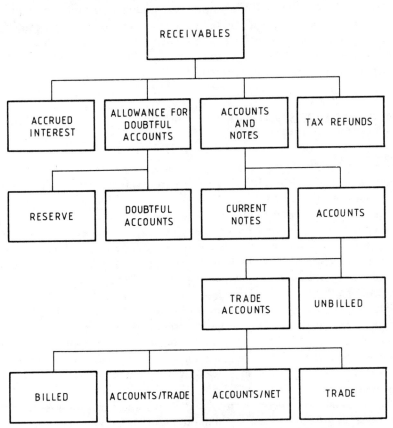

Figure 1.2 An accounting hierarchy for receivables.

- Invoices and accounts receivable and payable
- Cash payments and receipts
- Payroll accounts and fringe benefits
- Plant and equipment records
- Cost accounting activities of the various management functions

A primary responsibility is that of defining discrepancies or malpractices. The auditor's office engages in the interpretation of regular financial reports and statements, and of the inventory of assets. One of the main activities is auditing taxes and associated payments.

The highlight of the controller's duties is usually the provision of adequate protection against loss of the company's money and property. The prescription of appropriate systems for risk management is sometimes included in the mission; this activity extends the original audit concept, which includes only verification of the propriety of expenditures.

THE IMPACT OF STRATEGIC PLANNING ON TREASURY OPERATIONS

The key factors that affect treasury operations are so dynamic that, in their steady change, they leave little margin for error. This is as true of the choices the treasurer should make as it is in terms of seizing the moment and capitalizing on the opportunity.

To position himself and his company against the forces of the coming years, the chief financial officer needs to formulate a *strategic plan*, which is in itself a challenge. Strategic planning is vital in helping to ensure an *integrated approach* to resource management—from human resources to financial, marketing, technological, and product-oriented assets.

Strategic planning is a prerequisite for technology investments. In its absence, a great deal of money will be spent on nonessential items, and the company may fail to focus on future business opportunities to gain an edge against competitors. Strategic planning provides the reference ground for new product development as well as for other fields such as treasury operations.

For example, a corporation may find it necessary or desirable to raise additional funds. It may borrow them on a short-term note, on a long-term mortgage note, through bonds, or by issuing additional stock. It is usually regarded as good business management to borrow on short-term notes only if such funds are needed for current operations, and if the current operations will produce the cash with which to repay the loan.

If the necessary funds are to be used for plant additions or other permanent investments, they should usually be obtained by issuance of long-term securities in the form of stocks, mortgage notes, or bonds. There are, however, other key variables to be taken into account:

- The state of the economy in the countries in which the company operates

- The prevailing interest rates by country of operations

- The trends that exist in the financial markets and associated forecasts

- The tax laws permitting deduction of the interest paid on different types of securities and loans

- Cross-border legislation making it feasible to spread a financial commitment and optimize in a network sense

Each of these references underlines the wisdom of a well-tuned strategic plan within which all operations including those of the treasury, will be integrated. Successful financial enterprises have this ingredient in common: clear strategic perspective and detailed plan of action that is flexible enough to be adjusted as opportunities develop.

When Judy Lewent became vice-president of finance and chief financial officer of Merck and Co., *Business Week*, in its April 30, 1990 issue, published an article stating that its 500-person staff must be, in effect, a group of in-house investment bankers. These in-house treasury officials are showing how advanced finance practices can bolster the bottom line:

- They use a computerized foreign-currency options program for hedging, important in Merck's increasingly global operations.

- They also have developed and currently use a simulation program called the Drug Research Uncertainty Game (DRUG), designed to teach new Merck managers about the riskiness of drug development.

In years past, these two examples were not critical treasury functions, but times have changed. Today, a financial plan should not look at a single firm in an isolated mode; it should instead work in synergy with the market forces. A key strategy in financial industry growth is developing close relationships — extending the treasury's reach without increasing its size.

Provided that the concept fits within the perspective of the strategic plan, the treasury must take a careful look at the financial effect of *strategic alliances*. Strategic alliances and partnerships are a potent way to do more with less:

- They permit the company to stay lean, controlling costs while gaining access to new markets.

- They make feasible flexible alternatives to expansion or acquisition.

- They may also mean an inordinate commitment of financial resources.

If they are carefully worked out, strategic partnerships blur the boundaries between organizations, permitting them to take advantage of one

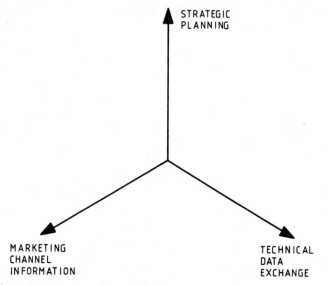

Figure 1.3   Three axes of reference for a strategic alliance.

another's capabilities only if they coordinate their activities for mutual benefit. However, such coordination requires an unprecedented degree of financial information sharing.

It is not only the external ally who must get more information but also
the managers in one's own organization. Management must have greater
knowledge in order to be an active element in an effective partnership,
which must create multiple links. This should be the case along three lines
of reference as Figure 1.3 demonstrates.

- Joint planning at the strategic level

- Technical data exchange at the professional level

- Marketing channel information at the distribution and service level

The common ground is finance. This is also the frame of reference necessary
to ensure successful financial products and is, therefore, a valid conceptual
approach for the corporate treasurer to follow.

New financial products include futures and options, floating rate instruments, caps and collars, interest rate and currency swaps, mortgage-backed
financing, and adjustable rate preferred stock, as well as derivatives of all of
these. The frame of reference remains valid even when traditional financial
services are packaged differently.

INNOVATION IN TREASURY FUNCTIONS

Market drives can be reflected onto investments through a continuously rebalanced portfolio based on dependable securities and their underlying instruments. But repackaging requires models and computers for study and experimentation. Options, for instance, are volatility instruments exposed to interest rate risk. Risk calculation enables investors to take direct positions, examine alternatives, and optimize solutions—the goal of financial engineering.

The effective promotion of new products rests on the technology that assists the hand of professionals in:

- Capturing opportunities as they arise

- Ensuring that good ideas do not slip away

- Making sure that new ventures are ready to join the mainstream business

Every one of these points involves treasury expertise as well as a close collaboration between financial wizards and operating departments. Successful banks and industrial organizations ensure that their chief financial officer is able to shake up the existing conservative, self-satisfied culture of the finance department—insisting that every person is able to innovate in the way his or her work is being performed.

The need for innovation in the treasury function must be thoroughly discussed. An R&D spirit should be applied selectively, but, where it is applied, it should be implemented well. Innovation gives more people at more levels the opportunity to develop and lead projects.

Every professional should feel that innovation is part of his job, although nobody should depend only on the lucky break of an innovation's spontaneity. The organization as a whole should create channels to speed the flow of new ideas, turning them into saleable products. Because cash is necessary to any transformation, the treasurer is an integral part of such an effort.

Speaking of innovation, for instance, in its treasury and forex applications, Barclays Bank in London demonstrated that *up to 20 sensitivities*[2] may be required in order to correctly evaluate a proposed transaction. To gain a fast response, the institution has to use either a dedicated $5 million mainframe or low-cost high technology such as supercomputing.

---

[2]Sensitivities are issues crucial to the evaluation of a treasury transaction that should be properly analyzed and accounted for in realtime in relation to one another.

A stand-alone PC is not the answer because it will need about 100 hours of processing time, which is not a practical proposition. A fast-moving, deal-driven environment *must* be cost-effective. The analytics, the software, and the hardware are all subject to innovation, permitting us to position ourselves properly against the market forces.

Whereas many financial organizations today feature a bureaucratic treasury management that inherently seeks self-preservation, an approach based on high-grade professionalism will be fundamentally opportunity-seeking.

- The major concern of bureaucracy is to administer a known routine uniformly, guided by past experiences.

- The key aim of a professionally oriented business is to exploit opportunity wherever it occurs and however this can be done, regardless of what the organization was doing in the past.

Bureaucracy tends to be position- and grade-centered: the four-star general or field marshal syndrome. Its authority derives from position, status, and rank. Professional organizations tend to be expertise centered, with authority coming from better know-how, wherever it lies. Bureaucratic management is repetition oriented, searching for efficiency through doing the same thing over and over again. In a professionally oriented organization the focal point is creativity, seeking innovation for efficiency reasons.

- In a bureaucratic financial institution, management stresses *rules* and *procedures*, rewarding adherence to them.

- By contrast, an institution run by innovative professionals is *results oriented*, rewarding outcomes rather than the strict observance of procedures.

Bureaucracies tend to pay for status, with pay being position based. Positions are arrayed in a hierarchy, and greater rewards come from attaining higher positions. Professionally oriented financial institutions tend to pay for contributions, for the value the person (or team) has added to the results that were obtained.

The fact that the treasury deals with large sums of money is no reason why it should be stiffened through an undue reliance on past procedures. Experimentation through simulation and knowledge engineering is the answer—all the way from forecasting to planning, operations, and control action.

These are the concepts that should underline the strategic plans of the 1990s, as well as their execution. Far from adopting an approach leading toward uniformity—hence, ossification—the aim should be that of finding opportunities through these mechanisms:

- The expansion of information

- Its experimental evaluation

- The ability to maximize all possible communications links

This is an innovative approach, which contrasts with bureaucracies that operate through formal structures designed to channel and restrict the flow of information.

Although the reference to professional-type organizations is generic, the treasury function is one of the best frames of reference from which to visualize what I have discussed. For instance, examine the position of the chief financial officer, noting the ways in which he deals with the general complexity of the job as well as the ways in which he faces specific uncertainties, intentions, and contradictions, even the variety of languages used within the operation.

As every expert treasurer knows, uncertainty and complexity often lead to multiple problems involving uncertainty, whereas we can treat with confidence well-structured knowledge. From this point springs the wisdom of starting with the strategic plan. Such a plan deals with fairly sophisticated subjects:

- Cash flow

- Different currencies

- Assets and liability management

- Changes taking place every minute in the financial markets

Treasury people must always use easily explicable approaches, the most successful being those that are simple at the start. They must reconcile this factor of simplicity with the fact that new knowledge means *discovery*, and discovery requires much know-how as well as a great deal of imagination.

There is a lesson to be learned from this dichotomy: Professionally oriented financial institutions tend to minimize stereotypes and maximize options. They encourage continuous regrouping of people, functions, and products, steadily focusing on market trends and financial realities. They keep costs low and, as often as possible, employ thoroughly studied means to achieve corporate goals, deriving power from access and involvement rather than from tight control.

TREASURY FUNCTIONS AT CITIBANK AND THE QUOTRON CONTRIBUTION

Having given a brief description of treasury duties, it is proper to look into structural issues. Structures necessarily vary because no two companies have exactly the same organizational dependencies; each adapts the definition of treasury functions to fit its particular profile. For instance, Citibank in the UK is organized into three divisions: *marketing, treasury,* and *operations.* Five departments constitute the treasury function, which employs among itself about 100 people, of which half are dealers and the other half supporting personnel:

1. *Foreign exchange* is the first department, its main mission being inter-bank financial transactions.

2. *Commercial forex* is another department, with its goal being efficient handling of the larger commercial customers.

These two departments work closely with one another—hence the need for an effective information transfer, which in 1981 was met through personal computers and local area networks, one of the first successful applications of its kind.

3. A third department is *money markets—international.*

4. Yet another is *money markets—domestic.*

These two departments cover the broad area of British and international money markets, and, just as forex does, they operate in collaboration.

5. The last department is *treasury management operations.*

This function involves planning, market research on functionality, marketing, technology implementation, financial control, and personnel. The technology specialists of this department were instrumental in establishing Citibank's workstation and local area networks solution, and they steadily contribute to sharpening the information systems in order to support treasury goals.

Commercial and trade activities fall under the label of *marketing.* This category includes loans, letters of credit, money transfers, bills, and check processing. A steady effort is being made to improve the profitability of each channel by weeding out manual labor and instead automating at a state-of-the-art level through networks, computers, and artificial intelligence (AI).

This is particularly true of the operations division, which performs back-office support functions for the treasury through its production services department. Other departments focus on management of premises, communications (integrating telephone and data communication systems), software development, and production.

The aim of treasury support services is to process all transactions handled by the dealers. From reconciliations to accounting, the bulk of the work is done by computer, with software designed to match as closely as possible the activities of the treasury division through a logically integrated functionality.

Apart from keeping its own treasury house in order, Citibank addresses the needs of the treasurers of corporate clients through its Quotron subsidiary. Let's first take a brief look at Quotron as an information provider, and then we will focus on treasury reports.

Through about 90,000 of its desktop terminals in brokerage offices, Quotron provides stock quotations and other financial data. Citibank participates in the stockmarket through its trust department and the foreign brokerage houses it owns—but Quotron operates as an independent unit, having, among other clients, Merrill Lynch and Shearson Lehman Hutton.

Since its acquisition of Quotron, Citibank has been busy designing new products for its subscribers, coming up with novel ways to master the information-providing business. Today, Quotron subscribers not only get quotes on stocks, but they also obtain a comprehensive global report. Its marketing is worldwide and it focuses on multinational corporations rather than banks because multinationals have the most cross-border requirements.

The global report is designed to serve the treasurer *as a person*, not the company in the abstract. Hence, it addresses itself to the personalized requirements of corporate treasurers who like to

- Have options and be informed about them

- Be independent decision makers rather than linked to any one bank

- Be able to make up their own mind about final decisions

- Take their own risks after being informed about the market

The way Citibank sees it, this underlines the need for a global report that integrates all information; in addition to doing this, however, it focuses on the specific problems addressed by the treasurer at the specific moment he signs on the service. Expert systems are used to help in attaining this goal through profile analysis.

In the background of this approach is the fact that every corporate treasurer has his own decision style and wants to be properly positioned to make learned choices prior to commitment. The Global Report helps him reach this goal.

To solve the treasurer's problems in an able manner, and with the necessary flexibility, the design of this financial reporting system starts with the customer profile: Who is the customer? What are his preferences in terms of financial and other information? In which sequence would he like to see them presented? Visualized? These are the key questions and they are answered online through knowledge engineering.

The way Citibank's Quotron looks at this subject, the corporation is *not* the enduser. The enduser is a person—the treasury executive with distinct personal characteristics:

- His way to interpret goals

- His need for communications

- His decision style

- His personal information requirements

Even within the same firm, such information needs vary from one treasurer to another, sometimes quite substantially. They also grow with time and change with the market mood. Citicorp aims not only to personalize the service but also to add more functionality to the menu. For instance, it wants to sell information focused by industry sector: packaged goods, health care, insurance, and travel—in all cases personalizing the way the presentation is done.

The provision of actual information enriched with practical knowledge is of great importance to the treasurer, as well as to other functions in the company. Queries are becoming increasingly ad hoc; they are no more clearly defined than they ever were. The challenge lies in the ability of the system to respond to *fuzzy queries*. This requires even greater attention to artificial intelligence.

Because 80 percent of a financial institution's profits come from 20 percent of its customers, and because these typically are professional and sophisticated people, bank management must be very careful with the technological content of the services that it provides; among other things, such content will determine the fees that it asks. Like product marketing, pricing must rest on *value differentiation.*

- Is the information provider answering all of the treasurer's needs in an increasingly focused manner?

- Is the service enabling the treasurer to face market challenges ahead of competition?

Every treasurer worth his salt is interested in finding policies that will improve the financial condition of his corporation in the long run. But at the same time, his day-to-day activities require him to ascertain whether his short-term decisions are fundamentally sound and adequately secured, or whether changes in the condition of the business today might jeopardize the soundness of what he did yesterday.

A structured presentation alone, even the best that could possibly be conceived, will not meet this need—and sometimes it may be counterproductive. The right structure is important, but just as vital is a steady stream of distilled personal information and the proper knowledge to interpret it for decision support purposes.

TECHNOLOGICAL DEVELOPMENTS AND THE EFFECTS OF AUTOMATION

Treasurers and investors willing to take a bet on their market views do so by taking risks. At the same time, those who are uncertain or risk averse try to hedge their positions—which does not mean that they escape risks altogether, but that they may balance them better.

Precisely because treasury activities involve a fair amount of uncertainty, *risk management*[3] models are used to select portfolios with specified exposure to different types of risk. At the same time, to optimize the assets under their authority, treasurers practice financial engineering. They construct and employ financial instruments targeting specific market segments and taking advantage of arbitrage opportunities.

To handle these requirements in an able manner, treasury information must be rapid, credible, easy to understand, and simple to use. Decision support systems put at the disposal of the treasurer must be enriched with AI, be able to handle management by exception, and provide for flexible but homogeneous presentation, which is done online interactively.

The message of these preceding three paragraphs is applicable to the treasury function both in a bank and in a large financial organization. Significant advancements in technology have made it easier for treasury departments, with an edge on the state of the art, to exploit opportunities to their

[3]See also D. N. Chorafas, *Risk Management in Financial Institutions* (London: Butterworths, 1990).

competitive advantage. The most striking improvements have been visible in analytical studies and telecommunications.

Technology has speeded transmission and manipulation of information, which in turn drives the speed of transactions and the timetables for new product development. The increased quantity and speed in flow of information and the improved access to worldwide resources, from exchanges to databases, have created a world of new financial products. The latter range from the use of AI in the management of funds to the refinancing of mortgages and other debts through securitization.

By providing an efficient infrastructure, technology makes the financial officer face outward. Banks push their paper out and bring in computers and optical media. They do so to modernize operations but also to achieve greater competitiveness, as they turn their branches into sales offices.

For more than 30 years, financial institutions at large, and the treasury function in particular, concentrated their technological effort on the processing function, which is the easiest to computerize. Now attention is being paid to the part of the bank that receives and initiates *customers' business*—where an estimated 70 percent of the banking industry's costs are incurred.

Citicorp is automating the opening of its accounts by using expert systems. These distill the experience of managers into a computer program that asks customers questions that vary according to the answers being received.[4] As banks load their computers with more information, expert systems can cross-check the customers' replies more effectively and provide the professional staff with assistance in its daily business.

Most significantly, the implementation of AI is not done in a detached manner, but in synergy with other technologies. For instance, according to a Bank Administration Institute survey of 413 U.S. banks, financial institutions are beginning to count voice response systems among their strategic customer service tools.

Voice-processing devices that convert computer data to a digitized voice over telephone lines have moved forward as the favored instruments in retail banking services. The number of voice response systems implemented to let customers perform inquiries and transactions over telephone lines is growing rapidly along a diverse cross section, as shown in Figure 1.4, and it is in combination with such applications that expert systems give the best results.

There is no shortage of applications domains. Developed by one of the foremost companies, an expert treasury system executes program trad-

---

[4] *The Economist*, March 25, 1989.

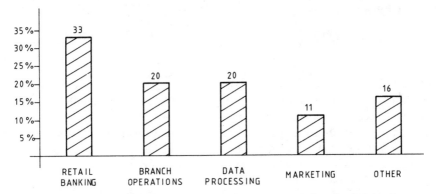

Figure 1.4   Usage of voice response systems by department.

ing, arbitrage, spotting, and technical analysis of 90-day futures. It also does charting as well as stochastic and heuristic evaluations of different hypotheses concerning key treasury functions.

No excuse can be found by treasury officers or other bank executives for failing to take the proverbial long, hard look at technology. The challenge is one of summing up all of the costs and the benefit involved in sophisticated solutions. And reference material from weapons systems does suggest that costs are not necessarily only in the software and hardware. In the military, as the cost of airplanes escalated, the flying class itself became exclusionary:

- Expensive modern aircraft are crewed by officers, who receive near-private-sector pay and handsome reenlistment bonuses.

- Easily overlooked in aircraft price calculations is the cost of training a modern combat pilot, which stands around $7 million.

In finance, too, *computer literacy* is so important an issue that overlooking or downplaying its role ends by vastly subutilizing a technological investment. I have spoken of the role of expert systems in financial activities. A similar case can be made about multimedia networks.

The emphasis on intelligent networks[5] comes none too soon. Like the ancient inhabitants of Easter Island, treasurers and other financial officers find that production is faster than transportation, which becomes the bottleneck. The global size of operations makes first-class networking mandatory.

[5]See also D. N. Chorafas and H. Steinmann, *Intelligent Networks* (Los Angeles: CRC/Times Mirror, 1990).

- Citibank has 2,500 branches in 97 countries.
- Standard Chartered features 2,000 branches in 60 countries.
- Barclays' operates in 83 countries.

Another bottleneck to squeeze through is the currently very expensive and error-prone practice of handling paper-based payment documents. The answer is *image technology.*

"As we move into the future," said a cognizant financial executive, "it is very important to master image processing and integrate it into our operations." This is seen as a key area in increasing productivity in the banking industry as well as in manufacturing and commercial organizations. All prominent companies are aiming at deploying knowledge about image handling throughout their organizations.

The point being missed in some cases is that image technology is inseparable from artificial intelligence implementation. The approach taken in image automation can be divided into two groups:

1. Payment documents, particularly of a check processing nature
2. Office imaging, with emphasis on the back office

Figure 1.5 shows the main layers of optical disk usage from an application at the Union Bank of California. This procedure is fairly similar for payment documents and office imaging, but the attention to detail is quite different.

The effective automation of payment documents through photonics is vital; during the last four years, roughly 50 to 55 billion checks were processed by banks in America every year, at a cost of around $30 billion. Foremost financial institutions now believe that image processing could rapidly reduce these costs.

Imaging software and hardware permit photography of checks and other vouchers, changing the images into a digital stream to be stored in and retrieved from optical disks. These digital images can be transmitted down fiber-optic cables for processing and switched around the clearing system through the automated clearinghouses operated by the Federal Reserve Board.

Volume will ensure that the amount of savings is tremendous. Security Pacific, one of the top five check clearers in America, processes an average of 6 million checks a night. It estimates that it would save between $25 million and $50 million a year through such a system—or more than that amount by earning fees through processing business from smaller banks that have to offer their clients a state-of-the-art service but do not have the volume of business to justify the investment.

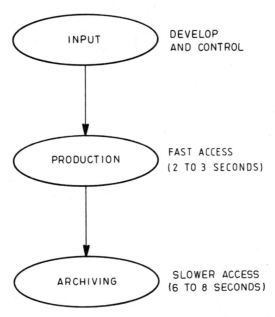

Figure 1.5   Optical disk usage: Union Bank of California.

The principle is that, in a knowledge society, financial assets and the services necessary to manage them are much more sensitive to the effects of automation than the manufacturing and agricultural sectors have ever been. But only corporations that know how to manage their technology benefit from the spectrum of facilities that have become available, from knowledge engineering to workstations, supercomputers, databases, and networks.

2

The Common System:
Treasury, Forex, Securities

A financial institution, like a manufacturing organization, will be successful in selling innovative products if the selling is managed according to the requirements imposed by the products. Internationalization, product differentiation, and a large number of new deals are accompanied by increasingly complex problems that eventually end up in the treasury.

A good example is the whole field of 24-hour trading, increasingly characterized by transactions of a forward nature, the need for realspace operations, and the multiple risks that they involve. Risk is not an alien word in banking and in Treasury activities in general, but its nature and magnitude have changed.

Today there are three areas of high risk in financial operations: foreign exchange, securities, and treasury. These are the growth domains of the financial markets. They have profit potential and see new products being introduced, and, as a result, they confront management with an increasing amount of risk and uncertainty.

Innovation in financial products, treasury operations, foreign exchange, and securities dealing have a common frontier. The main elements are as follows:

1. *Taxation,* which by all likelihood in the 1990s will be high for companies

2. *Inflation,* expected to be kept relatively low but nevertheless fluctuating

3. *Interest rate changes*, which will most likely be significant and involve all major currencies

4. *Risk management*, which must be done in realspace fashion, covering all domains of trading and investment

We can build a solid foundation on which to base these supporting pillars if we have clear policies, the right organizational perspective, and a mastery of technology. In our efforts, we should do the following:

• Properly estimate *volatility*

• Pay attention to *liquidity* management

• Focus on a few *key currencies*

• Involve a controlled number of *commodities*

• Be sure to master the art of *arbitrage*—both in skills and in technological support

The essence of arbitrage rests on the ability to put together information from different sources, deciding according to the business opportunity that is developing. Much depends on proper *product design*, but the *infrastructure* must also be well built. These two factors work in synergy, as the following section will demonstrate.

DESIGNING THE FINANCIAL PRODUCT

The financial institutions that have traditionally been interested in actively exploring new products are the major insurance companies. They have a group of product designers, who concentrate on new offers, and product managers, whose mission is product promotion, including answering salespeople's queries on insurance policies to sell to different types of clients.

Banks have essentially been newcomers in product design, but today in insurance, banking, and the treasury function within a large manufacturing organization, the basic principles are clear enough. A dynamic product and service policy necessarily focuses on the market, the client, and the client's drives.

• *Banks that know how to succeed* plan their product and sales strategy systematically.

- *Banks that do not master the market* at the right time and do so effectively get customers that nobody else wants.

These two statements are just as valid whether securities, foreign exchange, or pure treasury function is discussed. Systematic planning means adopting advanced methods, like the Japanese do with their financial consultancy services. But the capable management of high-risk products has prerequisites.

Any bank would like to be the broker in financial dealings and thereby earn a fee. It would not like to be the speculator in major swings that take place in the market, outside its control—and thus lose its capital. Information that makes the product planner and the trader smarter is a vital hedging element. Knowledge should focus on exercising control over risks and enhancing the profit potential for the trader and for the organization as a whole.

Trading is a high-risk, high-reward profession that at first glance may appear unsuitable for an advanced technological solution, for the following reasons:

- The knowledge is fuzzy.

- No two experts seem to agree.

- For a system to offer significant benefit, a large volume of data must be analyzed in realtime.

But if this is the reaction at first glance, it is also a superficial one, because at least two of the three factors outlined (the first and third) are in the annals of artificial intelligence success stories, and there are solutions as well for the second issue.

Artificial intelligence approaches can be instrumental in helping define what gets integrated with what else and at what level. Logical constructs can help control overall exposure to treasuries and equities. Symbolic and analytic tools assist the treasurer, the trader, and the product manager in focusing on risk. This is the role that the logistics operation must offer the enduser: a steadily updated decision assistance.

There is a new class of specialists on Wall Street called the *rocket scientists*. Working with supercomputers and artificial intelligence, they have been given the mission of steady product innovation with controllable risk. Another mission should be to obtain fast results, using the most advanced tools technology makes available.

New financial products are not patented; there is no copyright in the banking business. As a rule, therefore, new products offer the financial

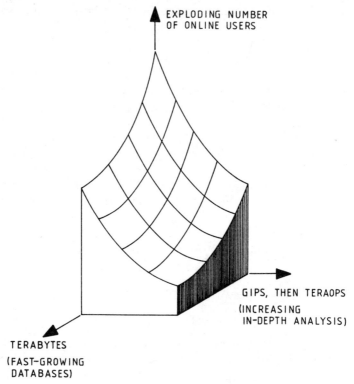

Figure 2.1   Three axes of growth for information systems development: online users, networking, and database infrastructure.

institution that developed them a competitive advantage only for a short time. Hence, opportunities to excel have to be steadily found and exploited without loss of time in bringing them from R&D to the market.

There are two prerequisites to achieving this goal: a well-informed top management and a range of tools. An infrastructure has to be put in place all the way from R&D to sales. It should be modular, and, as Figure 2.1 demonstrates, it should provide for future growth along three axes of reference:

1. The fast-growing number of users—both local and remote in the sense of the global network

2. A steadily increasing processing power, which is now counted in giga (one billion) instructions per second (GIPS), but by mid-1990s it will be in tera (one trillion) operations, or teraops

3. The ability to exploit through artificial intelligence a fast-growing database size, already counted in terabytes

The users of such a powerful infrastructure, which was unthinkable just five years ago, must all be highly computer literate. One cannot too often stress the need for computer literacy in treasury operations.

ESTABLISHING THE PROPER SYSTEMS SUPPORT

Market research in the financial industries has proved that, in selecting a bank, the customer not only pays attention to the pricing, image, and location of the bank, but also to the *person* who represents the financial institution. The customers who count most to a bank's profitability give tough critiques of the bankers they deal with, and capable treasurers are the best example of demanding clients.

To solve the financial problems of these sophisticated clients, one must approach them with abundant energy and singleness of purpose. One must leave nothing to chance—from the collection of information to experimentation and the packaging of the financial product, which will be given to the client as the solution.

To overcome corporate opponents and at the same time control the risk to which a bank is exposed, we must never consider an adversary to be petrified in his habits, thoughts, tools, and decisions—even if evidence says that it might be so. Unless we always keep our mind dynamic and our spirit open-eyed, the following crises might occur:

- Events unfavorable to our cause will crowd one upon another.

- Our products will fall behind those of competition.

- Risk will grow out of bounds, and profitability will deteriorate.

Unless we exploit the factors of *time* and *space* to our advantage, our forces will be ill balanced. Forces scraped together in a last-minute attempt have never obtained commendable results. This is synonymous to saying that, to effectively manage the innovative but high-risk banking products that form the common ground of treasury, forex, and securities, we must provide our bank with the necessary policies and high-technology infrastructure able to do the market integration work.[1]

[1]See also D. N. Chorafas, *System Architecture and System Design* (New York: McGraw-Hill, 1989).

- If we wish to survive, we have to have clear policies.

- If we wish to overtake our opponents, we must be much better equipped than they are.

- If we wish to control risk, we must *now* use the best tools technology makes available instead of waiting and falling behind.

Not only should we immediately implement artificial intelligence and supercomputers to our advantage, but we should also train our employees in their usage, as well as design our products to get the maximum out of the competitive advantages presented by technology. We must provide our employees with the following tools:

- Full interactivity and visualization

- Comprehensive experimentation tools for the evaluation of alternatives

- Information distilling at trader level through logical and analytical tools

- Fast media for discrepancy evaluation

- Integrative capabilities for immediate response

The right system will be designed around these concepts. It will feature distributed databases, workstations with expert systems focused on specific domains, and online access to supercomputers for opportunity analysis and risk management. A solution projected for treasury operations is shown in Figure 2.2.

The need for shaping the proper infrastructure does not stop there. Although the trader can see on video the day, hour, minute, and second the information is fed to him, he does not have a precise idea of when such information was created, say, at the stockmarket's floor. The resulting discrepancy between real and reported prices can be accentuated by the fact that computer programs typically stack incoming messages in a queue but do not feature a fine-grained timestamp.

There is much that can be done in terms of refining the way the system operates by capitalizing on what technology can offer. Not only is the timestamp absolutely necessary, but procedural changes are also due. For instance, the latest floor message should override older information without canceling it. The latter should remain in the database, available on request.

As we will see in the following sections, the electronic management for high-risk transactions has requirements that do not exist in other domains — for instance, in the now commonplace electronic mail, which has replaced

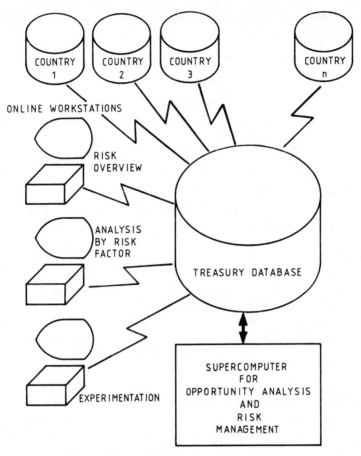

Figure 2.2   Distributed treasury database.

many phone calls, office memos, and telexes. The proper setting of a support system is instrumental in the success of financial products both new and old, but it is a determinant in the ability of the newer products to establish themselves and to compete successfully.

ELECTRONIC MANAGEMENT OF HIGH-RISK TRANSACTIONS

Put in practice through global networks, knowledge engineering, and super-computers, the electronic management of high-risk transactions is a complex concept to grasp at first glance. It is made up of a number of different programs that are interdependent in many ways. To simplify, let's think of such a process in four steps:

1. It begins with the very rapid collection of data as they occur in the marketplace, including timestamping.

2. These data are handled through the supercomputer for purposes of operational identification and classification, according to the financial activity to which they pertain.

3. The classified data are then fed into an analysis and fusion process for correlation, filtering, exploitation, and targeting. (The market data filter will be discussed further in Chapter 6.)

4. Targeted data are made available to the appropriate executive or dealer (or both) in realtime.

From this point on, cognizant decision makers at various levels evaluate the realtime information and take appropriate steps. The whole concept is based on *subsecond response time*. When high finance is at stake, we cannot afford delays; waiting amounts to increasing the probability of losses.

New technology can provide enormous leverage in relation to our financial capabilities. We should look at such projects as *force multipliers*, allowing users to employ their strengths with maximum efficiency. The main issue is to conceptualize the application without getting stuck in traditional data processing.

The plan for a high-risk transaction should be global, thoroughly covering the following topics:

- *Applications domain:* treasury, forex, securities
- *Type of trading:* spot, forward, options, currencies, equities, debt
- *Location of operations:* home office, branches at home and abroad, all major exchanges

Figure 2.3 suggests a hierarchy that demonstrates this type of multifaceted approach. Endowed with the appropriate software, AI and supercomputer power can be instrumental in correcting some of the problems that became apparent as the technology of processing trades failed to keep pace with the technology that generated them.

Because they must plan for the future, financial institutions, as well as the treasury operations of larger corporations, do their best to eliminate islands of aging, labor-intensive methods of executing trades. That is precisely where the system is overwhelmed every time there is a crisis, as in October 1987.

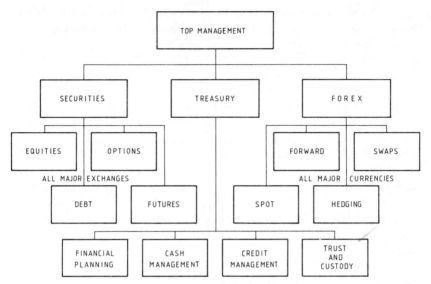

Figure 2.3   A frequently implemented hierarchy of treasury functions.

Some stockmarket experts, for instance, think that if buyers and sellers had been matched automatically by computers, there might have been less panic and less of a decline in the stock market on Black Monday. Automatic matching of trades in high-risk transactions, particularly in foreign exchange and securities, is indeed one of the promising areas of computer-supported financial trades. The irony surrounding this issue is that, although many investment houses, investors, and the exchanges themselves embrace state-of-the-art technology, implementation has focused on the more routine part of operations—not on the truly imaginative applications domain. To be served, the latter requires inference capabilities and a whole family of expert systems.

Such use of advanced technology is a far cry from past approaches, which mainly addressed themselves to the back offices, even if they had little success in automating them. It also involves new design concepts exemplified by image processing systems, optical disks, design automation, and other advanced implementations. The premise is as follows:

- If we can detect, locate, and capitalize on markets trends, then we will gain a *competitive edge.*

- If we can design fully automatic collection and situation-monitoring systems, thereby giving our managers and professionals pertinent information more rapidly, we can have a *time advantage.*

This is the essence of knowing the competition, and of getting better equipped than our corporate opponents. With the body of information that supercomputers and intelligent networks make available, there can be few surprises because strategies and tactics can be worked out well in advance and applied when necessary.

The latter statement rests on the concept of planning strategies in advance, permitting the chief of a major division (treasury, forex, or securities) to study the eventuality of a sharp uptrend or downtrend in the market. This being done, the next important component is experimentation.

Future financial systems capabilities will depend primarily on such computer-integrated developments to inform *our* managers and professionals— but also to confuse, delay, deceive, or disrupt potential adversary action. However, the current degree of technical knowledge of data processing personnel is insignificant when compared with the competence that is required for such an approach to become a financial institution's daily practice.

SUBJECTIVE OPINIONS AND PLAUSIBLE INFERENCES

The decision on whether or not our financial institution is moving in the right direction regarding its mastery of the markets and of technology is one that has to be made by the board. One should remember that banks that do not thoroughly understand the intricacies of supercomputers and networks will certainly be the losers.

Although in certain cases management may not even understand why or how it lost a certain lucrative part of the market, the underlying factor may well be that sophisticated customers judge the survivability of the financial institution they deal with on the following criteria:

- The quality of its human capital

- The technology tools being used

- Whether these tools are handled in a capable manner

These factors go hand in hand. Treasury functions, securities operations, and foreign exchange activities that are not capitalizing on high technology find it difficult to attract the top of the class in human capital. The persistent query that the top graduates today pose to their prospective employers is, "What is the level of your technology?"

This question is asked not only in terms of the investments made in hardware and software, but also in terms of R&D activities and of other brains who already work with the organization. The best of the newcomers are those with an affinity for learning; they are aware of the fact that if the environment to which they move is behind the times, they will soon lose their skills.

The implementation of realspace systems, of knowledge engineering, and of supercomputers are examples of an environment that is moving ahead. The same is true of the measurements and metrics that I discussed in Chapter 1.

The rocket scientists whom financial institutions and treasury operations now need on a steady basis know that in the natural sciences they are able to do direct measurements that permit description of physical magnitudes. Now they have to be taught that, in the financial industry, many dimensions cannot be directly measured, but can be computed from directly measurable quantities.

This idea is the root of the concept of *plausible inference*. Indirect measurements of derived quantities help to characterize objects and entities; and, as the rocket scientists know, mathematical computation and logic approaches can be instrumental in this regard.

Finance depends a great deal on the expression of opinions that are subjective, rather than objective, and do not lend themselves to direct measurement. However, for years we have quantified some of their characteristics by taking quotas or percentages, expressing projections, and doing time series, so we are well positioned to use newly developed tools such as possibility theory that offer a framework of plausible inference.

This framework of plausible inference is important to treasury, forex, and securities operations—and applicable to all of them. It allows us to interpret and combine the possibilities that arise from various comparisons. In other words, we are entering a new era of decision support characterized by *uncertainty management*. In office automation, this may concern the following issues:

- Type of document

- Logical structure

- Inference on contents

- Retrieval criteria

In subsequent chapters we will see how, why, and to what extent similar concepts are applicable to forex.

We have come to appreciate that uncertainty is a very important part of daily business, and we have the tools to use it to our advantage. Unlike the criteria that characterized past data processing chores, the electronic management of high-risk transactions requires strategies that make it feasible for the enduser to exercise ingenuity.

Because the competent operation of treasury, forex, and securities often depends on the same crowd, the software that we choose (or design) must ensure that the enduser is provided with common interfaces and that he sees a homogeneous approach to visualization, although, of course, the contents would vary by sector. There should also be control media for parameterizing system behavior layer by layer.

In a design sense, users should be given a choice of protocols, permitting customization without losing homogeneity. Among the problems to be solved, we distinguish the following:

- The establishment of a generic layer for initialization and system access

- The choice of a natural language and conventions specifically assisted through artificial intelligence

- Agility in human-machine communications and flexibility in the choice of applications programs

- Run-time configurability, also executed through knowledge engineering constructs

- Coexistence with established and operating implementation of data processing (DP), word processing (WP), decision support system (DSS), or other programs

A valid system integration framework necessarily involves homogeneous interfaces. Functional integration requires distributed databases and multimedia communications, not just traditional information management, which is based on incompatible systems, batch processing, and paperwork.

The list of requirements is quite long, but we should start with the fundamentals, paying attention both to the *big picture*, which will guide us further, and to the *details*, which will see our mission through. We should also be aware that even if we have today the most efficient solution, tomorrow it may be obsolete because the best of our competitors have moved ahead in implementing high technology.

DEVELOPING THE BASIS OF A COMMON SYSTEM

As a matter of policy, technological solutions must focus on the common areas among treasury, forex, and securities, accounting for the fact that, as shown in Figure 2.4, the same general group works in these areas. At the same time, forex and treasury as well as securities and treasury share the need for close financial coordination, and therefore depend on using a common infrastructure.

Such communality suggests the need for an orderly procedure regarding the necessary studies, and also advises the wisdom of setting priorities. An orderly approach not only will permit solution of all problems that treasurers, forex managers, and securities executives identify as being critical to their work, but also will integrate them into a coherent, comprehensive aggregate. There are three focal points for such a system: markets, financial products, and money rates.

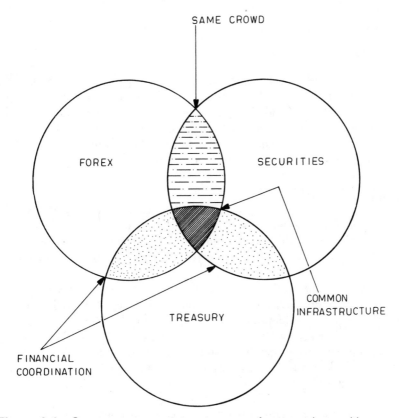

Figure 2.4   Common areas among treasury, forex, and securities applications.

Markets

Given second-by-second performance as reported by the financial information services, we should be able to instantaneously compare one international financial market to another.

Running 24 hours per day, like the network itself, expert systems should be doing *cross-market evaluations,* based on historical data including both private and public databases. For instance such systems should test key currencies and establish spread in foreign exchange by financial center. Having obtained such results, other knowledge-based constructs should provide solutions to specific problems. For example, in the forex domain there are three such constructs:

- Forward

- Spot

- Options

Testing with the intent of unearthing business opportunities requires the proper identification of critical factors, to be done in collaboration between knowledge engineers and domain experts. An intelligent solution of the markets module will permit attacking through the same methodology more specific issues such as exchange rates, always incorporating AI-based testing procedures to improve upon performance.

Financial Products

The object of this module, discussed during several working meetings with treasury experts, is that of weighing component currencies in a trading scheme, particularly emphasizing currencies that the trader chooses in his dealing.

Another example is the evaluation of composite currencies such as special drawing rights (SDR) and the European currency unit (ECU). Trading opportunities can be identified by testing the ECU against its component currencies. For instance, we can emulate the ECU through other currency transactions and bring realtime results to the dealer's attention, also creating an ECU database. Experienced traders believe that a dual goal should be sought after:

- Analytical orientation in realtime ECU transactions

- The ability to prepare for new composite currency approaches in the international financial markets of the ECU and SDR types

This concept is much broader and can be applied beyond foreign exchange into other trading domains. Once developed, this capability should be used in further treasury activities that have to do with composite currencies such as bonds, loans, and commodities.

This example further dramatizes the fact that a common system approach is made necessary by the very change in the world economy since the early 1970s, with the *flow of money* replacing trade in goods as the force driving exchange rates. As a result of the increasing integration of the world's financial markets, differences in national economic policies can affect present interest rates and expectations of future interest rates, calling forth huge transfers of financial assets from one country to another. These transfers swamp the flow of trade revenues in their effect on the demand and supply of different currencies, and hence in their effect on exchange rates.

Money Rates

Because they must execute operations involving bonds, loans, commodities or other issues on behalf of the company itself and its clients, traders need to know the best alternatives at each moment. As telecommunications technology continues to advance and because 24-hour corporate banking is in effect worldwide, transactions move faster and are more significant in size, making currencies even more volatile.

Figure 2.5 shows how a well-rounded system solution will look. It will operate in a realspace mode with profitability in the foreground and risk management in the background. To track and exploit changes in money rates in a realspace fashion, the system must rest on these precepts:

- An intelligent network

- Very high-speed computation

- The exploitation of a global database

- Pattern-oriented capabilities based on AI-enriched solutions

- Ad hoc analytical availability for every trader

- Synthetic presentation to management

- System-wide synergy to existing applications

A supercomputer-based solution should be running money exchange alternatives in parallel, giving the dealer a leading edge in telling the customer the best proposal. As I have already emphasized, subsecond response time

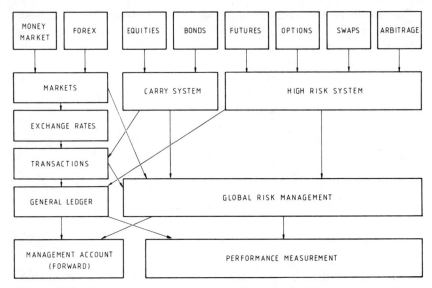

Figure 2.5 A money rates management system with performance
measurement, as initiated by a leading bank.

should be the rule, permitting the traders to present their best proposals
to their customers over the phone, as business is currently contracted.

In a money analysis sense, the input will be provided by the markets
module; the exchange rate module should focus on money transactions,
covered interest, securities, and options. The handling of the balance sheet
and all of the off–balance sheet business should be an integral part of the
application.

ESTABLISHING AND MAINTAINING SYSTEMS PRIORITIES

I have discussed the fact that a complex development such as the common
system for treasury, forex, and securities cannot be built in one attempt.
Priorities must therefore be established that reflect the need to do first
things first.

In one project that was undertaken along this line of reference, the director of foreign operations stressed that he did *not* want the money markets
and money rates modules to extend to covered arbitrage and covered interest. He had his reasons, of course:

1. An operation of the type that he identified would be mainly *forward*, hence reflecting only part of the work that needed to be done in these two domains.

2. There were booking limitations caused by the bank's own portfolio.

3. The goals of such operations are different from those of supercomputers, and knowledge engineering can serve best (at least in the director's opinion).

Covered arbitrage focuses on making large profits from few transactions rather than on small profits from many transactions. Covered arbitrage is served best through massively parallel technology. Another reason given for lower priority is that there are too many bid/offer propositions—and therefore acceptances and confirmations. Finally, a large margin of variation is associated with futures.

In contrast, other applications areas were identified as constituting a priority. It was thus suggested that, if these implementation fields find satisfactory solutions, and if the cognizant executives accept them as immediately operational, attention should focus on two further areas—*options*, for instance.

One of the peculiarities of options and futures is that most of the bank's clients have a strategy for options that includes the following points:

- Interest rates

- Forward

- Menus

The goal of an options module, according to this director, should be to emulate customer strategies, leading to a factual and documented offer to the client. Valid criteria for system design are quick response, calculation of risk in options, synthetic presentation, and solutions leading to the able management of options.

One should also notice the fact that, during meetings with cognizant executives and expert traders, emphasis was placed time and again on *client service*, where a leading edge can be achieved. However, let's keep in mind that only a few—in fact, the best—financial institutions truly take such an integrative approach when looking at forex, securities, and options as interconnected areas. This practice permits significant improvement service quality.

Treasury, forex, and securities are also domains where fuzzy reasoning is more prevalent than crisp, well-defined decision processes. The concept of crisp versus fuzzy decisions is also very important.

Fuzzy reasoning exists in many professions, not only in forex and securities trading—for example, in medical diagnosis. The doctor sees that the patient has a fever and that he coughs and has a headache. These are symptoms that can be measured independently, but they presumably have the same cause, although the nature of that cause is a matter of inference.

Something similar happens in forex trading when the dealer observes on the monitor the fluctuation of exchange rates. The monitor gives prices but not causes, with the exception of news flashes, which may be misleading. The causes have to be guessed by the trader, a process that is largely subjective:

- For an *objective* evaluation, we typically apply probability theory.

- For a *subjective* evaluation, we can use a new mathematical tool known as *possibility theory.*[2]

One of the advantages of using fuzzy sets and handling real-life situations through possibility theory is that this approach is closer to the trader's judgment, which is often intuitive. It also accounts for the fact that some symptoms can be measured and others cannot; inference therefore plays a key role.

A similar background characterizes trading in commodities: An AI-enriched project along this line should eventually cover all commodities, including gold, with primary emphasis on the interplay among financial instruments. Trading is a multifaceted subject; more and more loans seem to be moving away from dollar-denominated transactions to include commodities.

A fully developed commodities module could, for instance, involve possibility theory to judge movements in commodities prices, extending this forecast into projections regarding the price of the dollar and other currencies. A subset of the commodities module might address itself to balance of payments, as well as interest rates and the public's predisposition to save.

A simulator must also be constructed to relate the issues just discussed and to present a *synthesized picture.* Synthesis should be achieved through parallel processing; offered online in realtime, comprehensive patterns will enable the treasury, forex, and securities operators to *think in parallel.*

Provided that the proper analysis has first been done, a realtime synthesized picture can be presented to the traders (and to responsible managers)

---

[2]See also D. N. Chorafas, *Knowledge Engineering* (New York: Van Nostrand Reinhold, 1991).

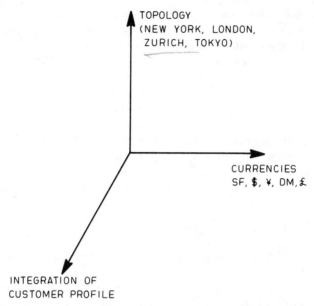

Figure 2.6 Three axes of references for a currency trading system.

along two, three, or more axes of reference, at each system user's discretion. Figure 2.6 shows a frame of reference that involves three elements:

1. *Topology of financial markets* (New York, London, Tokyo)

The model should permit the admission of more financial markets as requirements develop, even if the addition of more markets will result in greater complexity.

2. *Currencies* to be handled at a selected constellation of financial markets

3. *Customer profiles* based on past business and enriched by AI-assisted models

It is wise to have at least two expert systems specializing on customer profiles: one for corporate clients and another for institutional investors. The two are related. The first finds the money, and the second makes the funds available.

Just as important is the writing of a knowledge engineering module for *pricing and commission optimization*. Provided that the preceding models have been built in satisfactorily, that they have been accepted by the users, and that they are operating successfully, they should be enriched with a construct whose goal is commission optimization.

Different commissions by product line, as currently applied, should be mapped into this system. The commission database should be based on the prevailing commissions structure, but with negotiated commissions also included, down to customer detail and timestamp.

Another necessary component is a *customer mirror*, which permits management to clearly document the cost of customer transactions, the commissions obtained, and the resulting profit or loss.[3] Evidently, analytical costing is a prerequisite to this approach, as well as to interconnection of other currently operating data processing modules into a hybrid system.

CONSULTING ON TAXATION

As every treasurer will appreciate, advice on taxation is an integral part of money planning. Specifically applied to financial advising, the goal is to assist the corporation in managing net worth within the letter of the law. Solutions must be dynamic as laws change, and they capitalize on the fact that, despite their often confusing wording, laws are more or less crisp.

One of the "musts" in the treasurer's toolbox is a family of expert systems consulting on taxation. The approach is rather simple in one country, but for a multinational corporation the process can be fairly complex. The MNC must deal with the modeling of the factors that characterize a multinational corporation, the national and international tax structure, and the way corporate treasurers optimize tax issues.

One tax consultation expert system, built by the knowledge engineering group of Coopers and Lybrand, works along this frame of reference. It starts with five windows:

- Command menu

- Company graphics

- Country icon

- Company icon

- Detailed command presentation

This icon-based interactive approach permits building up a corporate structure and proceeding with tax calculation facilities. It suggests locations and

---

[3]See also D. N. Chorafas, *Bank Profitability* (London: Butterworths, 1989).

parent companies for new companies to be added to the corporate structure, in order to optimize taxation.

The expert system provides a menu that permits the user to specify a desired location for a new company. The computer supplies various financial details relevant to international tax. By feeding an estimated yearly business and expected gross profit, all other details may be calculated:

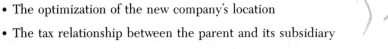

- The optimization of the new company's location

- The tax relationship between the parent and its subsidiary

The factors characterizing new subsidiaries may be optimized in a similar manner, and the tax expert system run by selecting the proper option from the command menu. The AI construct will make all the necessary international tax calculations, as well as the corporate tax calculations for each company in each country, based on business and profit parameters specified by the experimenter.

With every hypothesis advanced by the treasurer, the system sees to it that all the financial details relating to the taxation of the company have been updated.

- The corporate tax payable by the subsidiary

- The effect of the withholding tax (down to the dividend level)

- Various permissible tax deductions

- The payable dividend and tax credit that may be passed on to the parent company

The ownership of the new subsidiary may be changed by selecting as the new owner one of the other companies on the list of holdings. This allows experimentation with company structure and evaluation of the tax advantages or disadvantages of any alterations.

For instance, if ownership of the new subsidiary is transferred from the parent company to an overseas holding company and the taxes recalculated, the funds payable to the shareholders of the parent company may well be different from those computed for the previous corporate structure. The high tax paid by the company in one country can be offset by the low tax paid by another subsidiary in a second country. Thus, full advantage may be taken of the tax already paid when the funds are returned to the parent firm.

Besides doing international tax calculations, this expert system advises on various aspects of corporate structure. For example, if the parent company wishes to create a new R&D subsidiary but is not sure where it should be located geographically or how it should be parented within the group, the AI construct can help locate the R&D lab both geographically and within the corporate structure—in the optimum position for taxation. Other things being equal, the expert system will suggest locating the R&D lab in a country where the parent firm already has operations and that offers large tax incentives to R&D companies locating there. The expert system will also advise on the ownership of this company after having taken benefit of local taxation laws.

This AI construct knows about various company types and locations that best suit corporate management at headquarters. For instance, the low tax paid by the new company may be used to offset high taxes from other subsidiaries, thus optimizing the overall tax situation.

In this manner, every complex new investment can be given a location, with the expert system attempting to identify the optimum parent within the corporate structure. Alternatively, a second corporate structure could be provided and the computer would search for the best location in the corporate structure as either a new branch or a new company added into the existing corporate hierarchy.

Such an approach provides a powerful tool for evaluating the effects of mergers and acquisitions as well as the financial results of such operations. In this sense, the international tax planning expert system makes it feasible for policymakers to optimize and evaluate their corporate organization from a variety of different viewpoints. Other modules are used for the following purposes:

- Analyze corporate loans

- Examine interest payments and royalties

- Advise on personnel issues

- Experiment with transportation

- Provide a basis for evaluating securities as well as foreign exchange

The lesson to be learned is that AI can ensure an excellent level of support in tax advising. For this reason, Japanese financial institutions are very active in this domain; their expert systems successfully cover a wide implementation area from inheritance problems in portfolio management to a range of other applications vital to a financial business.

In Japanese financial institutions, AI constructs for taxation began to gain popularity in the domains of investment management and in loans. In the beginning, these AI constructs emulated support provided in other fields, for instance, insurance. Taxation is looked at as an advisory service based on screening characteristics, and, as the Japanese have demonstrated, expert systems can be very effective in treasury operations as well as in handling client queries regarding the trust function.

A good example of a tax advisory expert system in banking is one that consults on inheritance. It was developed jointly by the Nishi-Nippon Bank and Hitachi, and it can provide more than 100 types of consultation on the delicate and subtle problems of transition between generations. Included in its structure are family references, value of asset, and intentions of the person who seeks advice.

The Dai-Ichi Kangyo Bank provides another example of expert systems for taxation. Its construct covers both inheritance tax and all other aspects of sound consulting assistance to the client. The object is optimizing taxation and providing well-rounded advice.

A sophisticated expert system on taxation developed by the Mitsubishi Research Institute (MIRI) has a corporate orientation and modules that address three domains:

- Acquisitions

- Partnerships

- Inheritance taxes on a corporate basis

The first module advises how to lawfully reduce taxes by reducing assets, for instance, early retirement of personnel. In essence, this expert system is a legal tax consultancy optimizer. It requires data on a company's structure and liabilities. The input must be precise in order to provide advice that is acceptable to the customer but that is also properly documented and legal.

To produce this expert system, MIRI wrote the complex Japanese tax law in rule form. For one of the banks using it, this made feasible handling the work done in each of its 350 branches that in the past was done only in the central office, thus removing the associated delays and costs. The same goals prevail at the treasury, and, although the AI construct may not be needed in so many locations, it can prove its value where it is used.

3

The Forex Room

In its way, the foreign exchange dealing room has become the heart of the bank: Here the global marketplace takes on real substance, and the banker can sense the market's pulse. From his desk, the trader can imagine the sun rising and setting around the world. Networks ensure that he is never far from the forex room of his counterpart, even if he is at the antipode.

There are more than ten thousand forex dealers around the world. They come from different nationalities, and nearly all of them are under forty: the strain is too much for older people, and there is talk of breakdowns, psychosomatic complaints, and burnouts even among the younger.

These young forex traders are hawks; they take no prisoners. They are not bound by the past, and they are not afraid to take risks. In short, they are a new breed of bankers who need new, more powerful tools to do the job that is expected from them.

According to the forex culture, the instantaneous availability of worldwide information—and the knowledge to handle it—defines whether a bank is global or not. I do not mean dealing rooms containing computer equipment with superhuman intelligence, but rather networks enriched with expert systems putting their users in a position to visualize opportunities, evaluate current risk in a range of positions, and get immediate assistance in generating the underlying buy and sell orders.

Experimentation is essential, and advice must be provided interactively, at subsecond speed, reflecting historical patterns, last-minute news, and the day's performance of the dealer himself. The work that has already been done in this field identifies the benefits derived from global networks, rich databases, and artificial intelligence; we must not only focus on lessons learned but also define the direction of future trends.

Computer support in foreign exchange operations should go beyond the simple automation of trading activities to include the ability to deal simultaneously in many currencies with a number of corresponding banks and financial marketplaces; to obtain full details on spot and forward; and to have available both detailed and summary commitments. Among the many support elements that forex software should provide is a steady appreciation of cash flow.

One of the requirements of a dynamic trading environment is that of integrating different information-providing services: ensuring access to public databases, connecting forex to other in-house applications, and providing full visualization support. Just as important is getting assistance from analytical tools and expert systems, a subject examined in detail in Chapter 4.

GENERATIONS OF INFORMATION SYSTEMS FOR FOREX OPERATORS

Forex operators trade currencies for a living. It is a tough job, but it is also enormously influential and can be lucrative. The collective might of the world's currency traders has simply overwhelmed the power of central banks to control the course of any currency.

The Federal Reserve, the Bank of Japan, the Bank of England, Germany's Bundesbank, and other reserve banks of the First World have often engaged in an effort to lower this or that currency (or, alternatively, to support it). But they have been steamrolled by large institutional buyers who, through their traders, can move billions at the stroke of computer keys. These are, in effect, shadow central bankers, anonymously moving exchange rates every day, and therefore affecting the economic lives of people and companies all over the world.

The frequent inability of central banks to stem a tide comes from the fact that they simply do not have enough money to fight the will of the markets. All the reserves of all the reserve banks together do not add up to the daily turnover in currencies taking place in the financial markets of the world.

Power and *knowledge* blend through *trading*. Traders feel able to influence the fate of a world currency: The few top dealers can affect the market for a few days. As currencies fluctuate, the dealers speculate about the outcome. Oil is one of the currencies; its price is also an indicator. Whenever an oil shortage is imminent, the banks quickly sell yen and buy pounds or dollars.

Most, though not all, sudden changes in currencies are not caused by any political event, but by technical factors. A multinational corporation may switch a huge sum from dollars into Deutsche marks, bringing down the dollar rate. Is this move made on information or foresight, or is it just a gamble? Many large deals between currencies are surrounded by guesswork:

- Who is buying?
- Who is selling?
- Who is moving from yen to dollars or from dollars to Deutsche marks?

Big transactions can reverberate through every bank as well as the international monetary system. In the electronic marketplace, the most powerful currency can still depend on the whims of a few large corporations and institutional investors, and the mobility of money is encouraging all the big financial organizations to become global.

As the currency markets have expanded and as corporations have become multinational, trading has evolved into a split-second game in which a day's profit or loss can be made in minutes. As trading grows, it plays a large role in reflecting worldwide reaction to financial news and to economic policy. This is what justifies major investments in technology.

Three system objectives are topmost within this dynamic and steadily evolving environment of forex trading:

- The best possible online dealer support
- Efficient back-office automation
- Front- and back-office integration

It is not enough to provide computer-based assistance to the dealer. We must also make feasible simultaneous access to public and private databases, agile human-machine interfaces for queries, supercomputer-based experimentation along with the necessary models. Our solution should as well permit fast trader interaction.

From deal capture and position keeping to experimentation, simulation, and exposure management, there is plenty of work to be done in shaping up the computer room. Breakthroughs can be achieved by blending high technology with efficient procedures, thus responding to the ever-growing dealer requirements in a competent manner. Knowledgeable readers will appreciate that I am talking about an electronic market whose support requirements have radically changed.[1] In the 1970s the electronic market was

[1]See also D. N. Chorafas, *Electronic Funds Transfer* (London: Butterworths, 1988).

characterized by centralized batches; stand-alone, back-office-oriented operations; nonintegrated systems; a multiplicity of screens and keyboards; and a general incompatibility of formats and input media.

These approaches were computer-based but were also promoted by old-school data processors (EDP-ers). As a result, dealers got little or nothing in real support from the computer, and they were really never involved with the development of the application as such. Figure 3.1 shows a stereotypical system solution that characterized the late 1970s: partly batch, partly realtime, but nothing exciting. Several banks still live and operate with antiquated 1970s forex systems—and they are the losers in the trade.

In the seventies, the majority of applications were mainframe-based, though a number of dedicated minicomputers were used by more clear-eyed financial institutions. Personal workstations were not yet available, but they did come into the forex room by 1979 as stand-alone machines—often nicknamed "gorilla computers" because they came, so to speak, from the window, against the will of the centralized (and ossified) EDP department.

The more advanced financial institutions started the 1980s by installing in the forex room a personal computer for every dealer. These machines were

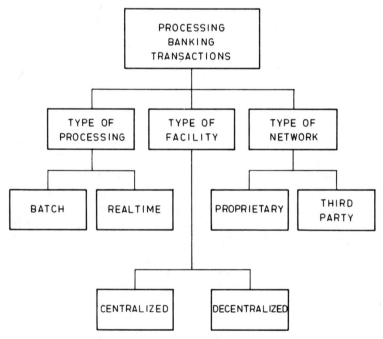

Figure 3.1 Typical electronic banking system in a bank of the 1970s.

then interconnected and, with gateways and file servers, began accessing local area networks (LANs). Realtime assistance and enduser orientation, including decision support and graphics and color in interactive presentation, began in the 1980s. Integration of information services was beginning, as well as reduction of the variety of screens and keyboards, with emphasis on formatting and normalization. Figure 3.2 shows the layout of a graphic tablet first designed and implemented by the Citibank treasury/forex operation in London. Gone was the keyboard, replaced by the tablet and a cursor.

One of the important factors during this transition to a new forex system design in the 1980s was the redistribution of power, taking it from

B	C	D	E	F	G	H	I	J	K	L	M	Erase			•	Ø	I	2	3	4
O	P	Q	R	S	T	U	V	W	X	Y	Z	S	P	A	C	E	5	6	7	8	9
Set up Short	Set up Fwd	Re-Value																	Local Re-Value		Abort Set up
	Ø	1	2	3	4	5	6	7	8	9			Clear Page No.	Print Screen	ENB Index	Fwd Posi-tion	Spot Posi-tion	Set Page No.	Ref-resh page
Set up Spot date	NUL	Ø	1 JAN	2 FEB	3 MAR	4 APR	5 MAY	6 JUN	7 JUL	8 AUG	9 SEP	OCT	NOV	DEC				Enter Date	Abort Date
		•	Ø	1	2	3	4	5	6	7	8	9	M	MM	MMM	BUY	SELL
10 M	20 M	50 M	100 M	200 M	500 M	1 MM	2 MM	3 MM	4 MM	5 MM	6 MM	7 MM	8 MM	9 MM	10 MM	20 MM	50 MM	100 MM	Enter Amt	Clear Amt
AUX	AUS	CAN	CBF	DFL	DKR	DMK	FBF	FFR	LIT	NKR	SFR	SKR	STG1	STG2	YEN			CCY	$
0	1	2	3	4	5	6	7	8	9			Apply Points	Clear Points
Show Hold Rate			Big figure −1	Big figure +1	Set up big figure	0	1	2	3	4	5	6	7	8	9	•	Enter Rate	Clear Rate

Bier Baum	Butler	Cosmo Rex	Fulton	God-sell	Har-low	Kirk-land	Martin	Mar-shall	Savage	Tullett & Riley	Wool Worth			Reut-ers	Telex	Phone	Money Trans fers	Clear Broker
AMEX	Barcly	BBI	Bergen	BCI	BCO Brazil	BK Cen-tral Brazil	BK of Tokyo	BOA	Bank-ers TST	Brink Mann	CBI	Chase	Chem	CIBL	Comm BK	Contil	Credit Suisse	Croc-ker	Deut-sch
DGKB	Dres-dner	EBCO	Euram Co.	Euram TST	Fed-res	FST BOS	FST CHIC	Harris	Hill Sam	HK & SBC	HYPO	Int West	Irving	John-son Mat-they	KOP	LBI	Lloyds	LZB	Name	Clear Name
Mar Midld	MAS	Mellon	Midld	Mitsu Bishi BK	MOR GTY	NAT WEST	Royal Bank Can-	SAMA	SBC	SEC PAC	Stan Chart	SUMI-TOMO	TUB	UBS	Wells Fargo	WM Glynn			Pay	Clear Pay
																	REC-EIVE	Clear RCV
										PART COMP	COMP	FOR A/C	AYI	Citi NA Jersey	HONY	CCIL	DIR-ECT	CITI
Ath-ens	Bah-rein	Basic	Belfast	Bergen	Berne	Bos-ton	Bou-nos Aires	Cairo	Chia-sso	Chi-cago	Cop-enha-gen	Dublin	Duss-eldorf	Edin-burgh	Frank-furt	Gen-eva	Ham-burg	Hel-sinki	Hong Kong
Johan-nes-burg	Kuala Lum-pur	Ku-wait	Lagos	Laus-anne	Lon-don	Los Ang-eles	Lug-ano	Mad-rid	Manila	Mex-ico City	Milan	Mont-real	Mos-cow	Mun-ich	New Delhi	New York	Oslo	Paris	No Deal
Riy-adh	San Fran	Singa-pore	Stock-holm	Tokyo	Toron-to	Vie-nna	Zurich							Cancel Deal		Enrich Deal	Over Ride	Not Con-firmed	Con-firmed
Going to Lunch	Back from Lunch		Page Fwd	Page Back	•	• ↑	Read TMD	Read AUX		Erase Det-ails		Print Blot-ter	Print Broker List		Print Ticket	Swap Deal	DEAL

Figure 3.2   Citibank's graphic tablet; a pioneering application in 1981. (Courtesy of Citibank, N.A.)

mainframes and putting it on the dealer's desk. Just as significant was the fact that dealers became involved in the design of workstations. More developments were to come.

A FOREX ROLE FOR WORKSTATIONS, LOCAL AREA NETWORKS, AND SERVERS

Since the invention of the transistor in 1947, the cost of using a computer to make calculations has been declining very rapidly. In terms of computing power, component costs have been dropping by about 25 percent per year on average, and the cost of storing a piece of information has been declining even faster, at about 40 percent per year. So great a decline in computer-related costs has created a burgeoning demand for equipment. It has also made it feasible to bring computer power to the work-desk level, and to do so at an *affordable price*. This is the secret behind workstations.

I have already mentioned workstations (abbreviated WS), which I define as a *networked* personal computer. One is thus able to communicate online with other WSs, file servers, gateways, and number crunchers (which I will discuss in Chapter 4).

Never underestimate the need for number crunchers in financial applications. The models that map the market into the computer require that tremendous power be available in realtime. The same is true in terms of *visualization*. It takes 300 million mathematical calculations per second to maintain a moving 3D image with detailed shading on a workstation screen. Three-dimensional images are today sought after in engineering, and they are coming in forex.

When we use a tool, we must appreciate its power and its usefulness, seeking the way that it can best be employed. The power of a workstation is usually computed using the following measurements:

1. Millions of instructions per second (MIPS)

2. Megabytes of central memory and of disk memory, at WS level

3. Picture elements (pixels) on the monitor for high resolution

4. Graphics and color capability

5. Supporting software for visualization and interactive handling

In other terms, not only should we consider the WS itself, but also—if not primarily—its software. This reference is valid all the way from operating systems and database management systems to applications packages and the high-level languages that go with them.

The power of the workstation should be greater the more demanding its job. Goldman Sachs, for instance, has defined two levels of WS design and implementation: a lower one for clerical personnel, and a higher, more potent one for managers and professionals. Also, as a matter of policy, Goldman Sachs sees to it that *all* WSs are networked. The same is true of other leading financial institutions. This is done in-house through LANs, and over long distances, it is ensured through the financial institution's wide area network (WAN) as well as through gateways to public and value-added networks.

One of the first LAN solutions established in forex was at Citibank's operations in London at the Strand. It featured two operating LANs: one for treasury and the other for foreign exchange, with a third one for backup. This was a pace-setting development.

Since 1981, when this Citibank WS/LAN system first went into operation, it has been fully redesigned four times, each time being substantially upgraded. Said a senior Citibank executive commenting on this steady upgrading process, "We have taken out of the WS and LAN already in operation all the personal productivity which we could derive. Hence, *we had to* significantly upgrade our solution." This is the name of the game in forex: personal productivity, and with it, a better *professional perception*.

In a dynamic market environment such as treasury and foreign exchange, only the best computer-based tools are good enough for our traders. The traders must be able to perceive market trends before their competitors do so. In addition, top management has to increase professional productivity in order to compensate for personnel costs.

Such policy is consistent with the fact that one very important consequence of both the Industrial Revolution and the Information Revolution has been the steady increase in the value of human labor. Between 1900 and 1930, allowing for inflation, the average annual wage of American workers rose by a factor of three to four, depending on the industry. There is more than one reason for expert labor becoming so much more expensive.

- As machines have taken over more and more of the physical work and routine calculations, humans have been able to concentrate on other tasks that lead to higher profits.

- As capital investments accelerated, productivity increased. More goods and services are produced for every hour of human labor utilized, and workers have acquired a share of this.

- Because of rising prices, commodities that require large inputs of human labor have been redesigned to benefit from automation. Over time, this has increased the skill and knowledge required to do a given job.

- Clients have become more sophisticated and more demanding, which requires a greater amount of professionalism on our part.

As the computer age enters the realm of peer-to-peer communications and open systems architectures, we are compelled to use the technology at our disposition for *value differentiation* against our competitors. This affects WSs, LANs, and servers attached to them, as I will demonstrate in the section on trading platforms later in this chapter.

Investing in enduser software and hardware is a complex job demanding insight and foresight. The WS is not just a name. A whole logical infrastructure sits beneath it. If we are not careful in equipment policy, we will be stuck with installing obsolete equipment while our competitors invest in state-of-the-art technology. We have to be at the cutting edge.

THE NEW GENERATION OF SOLUTIONS FOR THE 1990s

Once they decided to remain competitive in a fierce marketplace, the foremost financial institutions used the cutting edge of technology to design their new environment for forex trading. One of the concepts that took hold in the 1980s has been a long, hard look at the full cycle of data-handling operations and their transformation to realtime. A systems view was taken with the dealer's desk at the center. The better studies thoroughly analyzed the information sources coming into play, tried to find more competitive applications than those already available, and emphasized the role of multimedia communications from workstations to networks.

This concept began in response to requirements arising from globalization of financial markets, the ever-increasing transaction volume, and the resulting information overload. It also provided for the fact that new products were necessary to compensate for shrinking profit margins, to face the greater market volatility, and to respond to the decreasing time window for decision.

Personal computers came into play in the early 1980s, and a few years later home computers were used because the more dynamic forex traders could not afford not to take the job home with them. Big players had to keep a close eye on everyone else at the table, including the central banks. Sometimes the central banks were the allies in the forex dealers' betting, and sometimes the opponent.

In the late 1980s a new team of Japanese traders in New York working
for Fuji Bank took the train home at the end of the day to Larchmont (a
bedroom community just north of the city). By the time they got home, the
dollar had sunk in the Asian markets rather than rebounding as everyone
had expected. It usually costs about $5 for a one-way train ticket from Grand
Central Station to Larchmont, but the 35-minute ride eventually cost Fuji
$58 million.

This and other happenings convinced financial institutions of the wisdom
of thoroughly studying the full cycle of data handling in the ways shown in
Figure 3.3. This being done, they developed intervention points that permitted action, and lap-top computers played a significant role in the solution.
Software has been the arena which separates the sapling from the tree. The

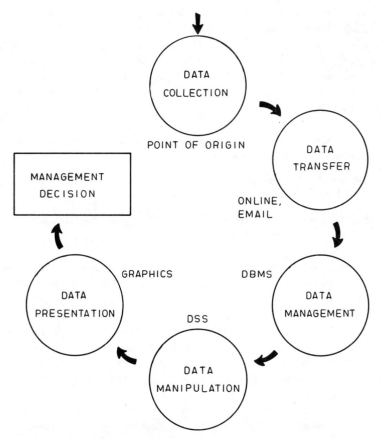

Figure 3.3   A full cycle of data handling.

foremost financial institutions know that it takes a close collaboration among several elements to create the sophisticated applications that the forex operations demand:

- The best of their systems developers

- The endusers of the solutions being projected

- The information services providers

- Independent software developers

Nothing short of the most modern and complete computing environment can provide ease of use, security, and robustness.

These developments gave birth to not only the realspace concept, but also realtime experimentation. If a reserve bank wants to disguise a move into the market, it may resort to what New York traders call guerrilla warfare. It will trade up to $50 million at once through a single bank, hoping that the market will think it is a private investor's move. It takes experimentation to find out motives. More common is the case where a central bank denies repeatedly that it plans to raise interest rates—a move that affects exchange rates—before doing exactly that.

- Forex traders today have to experiment with a number of hypotheses, and this means computer-run simulations.

- They must filter market information in realtime, so they need rule-based expert systems.

- They have to analyze and evaluate market patterns, which requires more complex models of artificial intelligence.

Forex, particularly the spot area, was one of the first corporate departments to experience the benefits of analytics. Both banks and multinational corporations have developed a series of specialized rate display and calculation screens that considerably improved the quality and timing of decision support. Analytical information available in realtime provides the forex desk with unique assistance in dealing operations. The best assistance is that performed in realtime enriched with knowledge engineering. Rates must be displayed on high-quality graphical screens, and they should be presented with color graphics.

It comes as no surprise that, since the mid- to late 1980s, the best of the financial institutions and corporate treasury departments incorporated into their forex systems expert systems capabilities. They used them not only for experimentation and consolidation purposes, but also for better quality of client service as well as for timely back-office support, integrating the front-desk operations with confirmations, settlement, accounting, and management control.

Provisions were made for steady adaptability to changes—a major deviation from the old monolithic approaches by EDP-ers. Integration of the newly developed, sophisticated software with existing applications became one of the underlying principles, and a new look was taken at what can be done with computers, communications, and artificial intelligence to improve the dealer's arbitrage capabilities.

In this sense, the 1990s now see, and will increasingly experience the following phenomena:

- Advanced dealer interfaces

- Embedded expert systems and other AI constructs

- Market simulators and optimizers

- Pattern recognition models

- Dynamic adjustment capabilities

- A full exploitation of what global communications can offer

- Emphasis on the decision line with many uses for commitment information

- Very little work in the back office, given the realtime execution

A new forex system architecture has already evolved and is being implemented by the more advanced banks. Shown in Figure 3.4, this architecture aims to support the trading organization around the world—enriched with specialized applications that are able to receive, distribute, monitor, and analyze market data in realspace. Programs are being implemented that allow realspace decision support and trade entry, giving the ability to monitor consolidated positions, and to manage risk globally via an efficient, reliable, and easily expanded system.

Multicast protocols ensure that every trader on the floor receives the fully updated, properly filtered, timestamped market data simultaneously. *Properly filtered* means that each trader receives only the data that he specifies; an expert system takes care of the screening process.

Of primary importance, of course, are realspace risk management and the control system necessary to achieve continuous operation. Methods of risk control rest on modules able to monitor all operations, check realtime

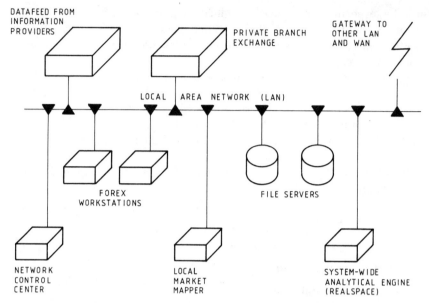

Figure 3.4   Forex system architecture of a modern bank.

limits, test exposure, validate timestamps, and identify and authenticate dealers—both our own and those of corresponding banks.

The objective is to move toward global monitoring and control; checking limits and dynamically keeping positions will be important in achieving this objective. Another major target is the exploitation of business opportunity commensurate with local and global risk.

IMPLEMENTING AN ANALYTICAL APPROACH TO PORTFOLIO MANAGEMENT

An earlier approach to dealing in currencies (and still the market norm) was to look at one currency at a time versus a reference currency. A more advanced solution is the so-called *portfolio approach*. This requires not only currency forecasts, but also expert systems capable of monitoring 10 to 20 currencies on a steady basis, including the simultaneous analysis of a few hundred potential cross-currency positions, estimation of volatilities and cross correlations, and incorporation of option strategies.

This approach calls for the development of original solutions with mathematical models not yet discussed in the literature, and supercomputers to process volumes of information at subsecond speed. Integration of these solutions into an operational package with daily updating and monitoring is a must, if a financial institution is going to have an impact in the marketplace.

Most importantly, the change is conceptual, bringing strategic planning into the picture and emphasizing a comprehensive set of management tools designed specifically for the trading room environment. By letting the forex operator manipulate *his* application parameters, we permit him to dynamically reallocate the resources at his disposition to meet the developing requirements.

The realtime integration of trading room and back-office applications, as well as the ability of traders to share realspace market data, permits the dealer to analyze market information more effectively and make better informed trading decisions.

We would better appreciate the changes taking place if we looked back a few decades and traced the evolution that has occurred. Figure 3.5 does so not only in respect to forex trading, but also in terms of information technology as a whole.

Although the majority of financial institutions probably still live with the technology of the 1970s, those that are today state-of-the-art devote much less than half of their investments to computers, communications, and software in bread-and-butter data processing (DP); most such investments are directed toward strategic issues and management control.

A strategic product is the product on which our organizations bet for their survival. In foreign operations, emphasis on strategic products becomes more necessary as currencies are traded in the forward market, where the activity of arbitrageurs ensures that forward prices reflect interest differentials rather than the currency price trends. This presents opportunities for traders with a good currency forecasting and dealing system, in which the dominant issue is one of *multidimensional evaluation*. It also points out the sense of the portfolio approach.

The multidimensional exploitation of market potential requires both clear concepts and advanced technological solutions. *Forex markets* should be exploited in a portfolio-oriented sense by a group of AI programs, each addressed to a specific marketplace and financial instrument. For instance, in one implementation along the described line, a dedicated expert system module currently in operation focuses on ECU-type transactions, emphasizing the importance of this market to the treasury organization.

Flexible, multidimensional *money exchange* should be supported, providing a multicurrency evaluation, with the ability to reflect on a reference currency as common denominator. Both go well beyond traditional trading room solutions. Trend analysis, flexibility, and multidimensionality require

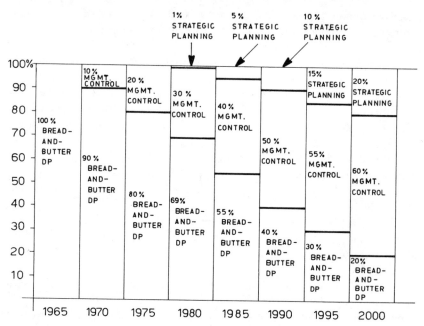

Figure 3.5   Evolution of information technology from the 1960s to the present.

consistent, easy-to-use databases and human interfaces. All applications must have the sale look and feel, enriched with a mechanism permitting traders to switch among applications faster and more effectively than they can in the typical forex system today. Besides this, trading fields such as *commodities* and *options* must be served in a worldwide sense by a group of knowledge engineering programs, each specializing in one specific issue but with all programs networked together.

Business opportunities have to be exploited through subsecond response to experimentation. For instance, in currency options caused by arbitrage between the *spot* and *forward* currency markets, there are significant divergences of option prices between banks. Advanced technological support is crucial because prices in the forward currency market are very competitive. It must be possible to switch positions quickly and efficiently, and to do so in a market that operates 24 hours a day around the globe.

Composite, multidimensional results should be supported through a synthesized picture. This can be ensured by means of another expert system module that also provides its user with the justification to back up the results of experimentation.

Such a dynamic approach to currency trading contrasts with policies followed in the past, where treasurers have tended to choose either *no cover*, which means making no forward currency hedging transactions; or *full cover*, with all exposures covered by forward transactions. The increasing volatility of currency markets has rendered such passive strategies inadequate, and it makes the portfolio approach a must.

A TRADE PLATFORM FOR CURRENCY EXPOSURE

The development of a successful trade platform to assist the dealer is not a matter of a "me too" attitude, but rather an indication of a strong commitment to leadership in the forex market. This market can be a major contributor to *our* bank's revenue, and it is growing fast.

Organizations that want to be success stories pay attention to detail. A valid solution would focus on managing *currency exposure* through the following methods:

- Forecasting currency exchange trends

- Exploiting market inefficiencies worldwide

- Being selective in forward transactions

- Steadily controlling risk

Some banks do pay attention to risk management, but they use a prefabricated package that runs on a PC as an add-on to old, nonintegrated forex applications. By contrast, profit-oriented treasuries have found out that they can greatly benefit from an integrated supercomputer implementation. In the following sections we will look into the more fertile areas for supercomputer use in forex operations.

These same profit-oriented treasuries believe that the purpose of AI enrichment is to assist dealers as well as the financial staff through supplemental information necessary to complete an evaluation. This enrichment helps to establish a plan that will ensure the maximum protection for corporate performance.

- From heuristic and algorithmic analysis of information can be derived alternative possibilities of offsetting forward currency contracts and intercompany asset exchanges.

- Simulators can lead to the optimization of decision alternatives, based on assumptions and on the logic of a currency analysis model that tracks foreign exchange fluctuations.

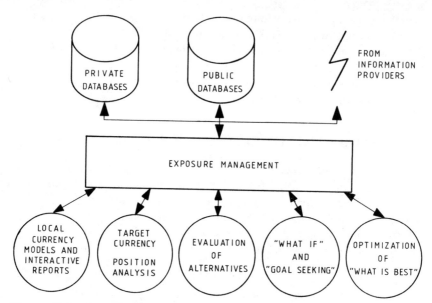

Figure 3.6   A comprehensive approach to currency exposure
management.

A comprehensive approach to currency exposure management is shown in
Figure 3.6. It emphasizes linkage to private and public databases and to dedicated modules that track local currency and a target (reference) currency,
as well as help in doing "what if" and "what is best" experimentation.

A corporate treasurer needs analytical models that can track trade sales to
and from foreign countries in the local currency. These should be integrated
with models handling suppliers' terms in suppliers' currency or in any other
currency, as well as with programs handling trade accounts receivable and
payable from and to foreign countries.

A similar method is valid for intercompany investments and commissions
(received and receivable), as well as for cost of goods sold. Income taxes
(current and deferred) should also be given due attention, with assistance
from tax-oriented expert systems.

Successful forex operations cannot be alienated from the bank's clients
just because client requirements evolve. The treasurer of a manufacturing
organization will seek multicurrency cash management and use it to track
expenses and accounts receivable and payable. He would also like presentation of inventory, either in a target currency or in many currencies in many
countries.

It would be superfluous to stress that multicurrency accrued liabilities are hard to measure; retained earnings can have different values to the corporation depending on the law of the land. The same can be said of back-to-back loans and related interest expenses. The handling of each one of these items is the subject of traditional accounting, and work in the past has typically been done one currency at a time and in a stand-alone, nonintegrated manner.

In contrast, I suggest a complex, multicurrency, fully integrated approach that is able to show in local and in target currencies the following information:

- Assets and liabilities

- Cash on hand

- Cash flow

- Comparative balance sheet evaluations by country and by currency

- Profit and loss by country and by currency using an integrated reference currency

This approach is strategic inasmuch as it provides the treasurer, and the financial institution or multinational company that executes it, with master control.

Such a well-rounded forex system will not only help to deal in currencies but will also ensure the infrastructure necessary for multinational status, including forecasts and exact estimates of exposure. Software and hardware available in the trading room, as well as human skill, must be able to handle a range of applications that interest clients: net trade and intercompany sales, operating expenses, fees, income taxes (current and deferred), foreign exchange gains and losses, and so on.

In order to calculate currency exposure, the treasurer of a multinational industrial company must know, per currency, receipts from net trade sales of finished goods, semimanufactured goods, and raw materials. The same information is needed to calculate intercompany sales and sales deductions, as well as balance sheet history, cash flow, profit and loss (P&L), and so on.

Taken together, all these pieces of information create a concept that can be assimilated into the management of a multicurrency portfolio. This portfolio may spread around the globe, and involve assets or liabilities that must be expressed in homogeneous units in order to be comparable to one another. The resulting complexity can be significant, but we have powerful tools at our disposition.

NEGLECTED ISSUES IN FOREX TECHNOLOGY

Although all financial institutions try their best to properly equip their forex rooms, they quite often miss many key issues or give them minimal attention. This is not very different from what happens in other domains, but the consequences in foreign exchange operations tend to be more pronounced.

Quite recently, two major financial institutions looked carefully at missing links in their technology, particularly at the endusers' side, and came up with very interesting results:

- Eighty percent of the work the forex operators did could not be performed with the installed technology.

- The most emphasis was placed on work that is rarely done by endusers or even considered to be rather unimportant.

Among the more important issues each of the two studies unearthed are research capabilities regarding information held in the bank's databases on customers. Their contents should have been exploited in a *database mining* process.

One of the needs that the foreign operations departments of these banks emphasized was that for document storage and online access on photonics (optical disks). They asked for optical storage of domestic and international expert finance references, documentary letters of credit, standby letters of credit to domestic as well as international customers, and so on. The need for online photonics storage is further underlined by the fact that, as statistics in the First World indicate, paperwork is still rampant. Less than 1 percent of the First World's information is stored on computers; about 4 percent is on microforms, and the other 95 percent is still on paper. The implementation of photonics primarily addresses this 95 percent of paper-stored documents. Photonics would then deal with part of the 4 percent on microfiche as well as all the information on magnetic tapes. Fully packed, some 6,000 magnetic tapes contain 1.2 terabytes. This is small game for photonics but a great improvement in terms of online service as well as in cost reduction.

Whenever we are faced with a technology gap, the process of asking critical questions can be instrumental to the identification of missing items— and it can help improve the support to be provided from the dealers' desk:

- Which value-added services do the dealers really require?

- Which of those currently supported can be improved through new technology?

- Is the current implementation enriched with the very best that technology can provide?

- Do dealers have at their command intelligent workstations filtering and analyzing realtime digital price feeds?

- Are they able to access online private and public databases without having problems with heterogeneity?

- Is the front desk connected online to the back office to automate the paperwork and cut costs?

The results of research that I conducted in the United States, England, and Japan in 1991 give generally negative answers to these questions. Advanced dealing room technology is not at all widespread. Also, many managers responsible for dealing room systems are unaware of the products available and their potential benefits.

A similar statement can be made about the analytical supports put at the forex dealers' disposition. It is not enough to roll in computerized dealing systems, giving traders fingertip access to currency trades. It is also increasingly necessary to give such set-ups *financial analytics* and, interestingly, *heuristic approaches.*

As we will see in Chapter 6, a growing range of analytical tools today allow users to critically evaluate foreign exchange performance under different economic scenarios with elaborate graphics. These tools give the user sophisticated analytical firepower, which provides the treasury department and the forex dealers with a significant competitive advantage.

For instance, one of the key problems in forex management is modeling nonlinear behavior of short-term movements of currencies, using appropriate forecasts. Work done so far along this line of reasoning documents how *inefficient* the forex markets are and which are the opportunities presented by predictive technology in forex dealing, including currency markets and cross rates.

This point being made, it is also appropriate to guard against a number of weaknesses that seem to be embedded in the use of high technology in forex. Two are foremost: unrealistic expectations and overinvestments. In terms of *unrealistic expectations,* many users of foreign exchange models, hedging tools, and futures trading programs work with expectations of gains in the vicinity of 50 percent to 100 percent annually. There certainly have been past years in which gains of significant magnitude have been made by using mathematical models, but it is unrealistic to expect such returns to continue indefinitely. There will be years when a predominance of choppy, sideways markets will result in small profits or even in losses. The period from 1988 to 1989 is a good example of such a situation. Unrealistic expectations are damaging because they cause traders to abandon a program before it has a chance to work.

The clients of financial institutions often fall into the same trap. They fail to understand that the profit potential of, say, futures trading involves leverage and high risk. They overlook the seemingly obvious fact that players should only risk the amount of funds they can afford to lose. If the amount at risk is too great for comfort, then the chances of an ill-timed account liquidation are greatly increased; this is simply counterproductive.

Another common mistake is opening a risk-oriented account *after* a strong winning period. It seems to be a natural tendency to start trading with a given model after it has done particularly well. Invariably, this results in the trader or investor (or both) being vulnerable to larger equity retracements following account initiation.

Furthermore, by second-guessing trading signals, taking some and not others, a trader can miss major market moves. It is just as bad to lose one's temper and panic during losing periods. Many dealers and investors do not have a plan for liquidating an account. Consequently, when the first significant losing period arises, they panic and liquidate it.

Use of such tactics clearly indicates that the people involved forgot that losing periods are a natural part of any winning trading system. A dealer, investor, or speculator who does not have a plan to deal with losing periods is unlikely to be around to profit during the winning periods.

This problem has much to do with psychology and very little with technology. Throwing money at the problem by buying more hardware and software will not solve it. The answer is in establishing sound policies—not in buying more equipment.

This brings up the subject of *overinvesting*. Technology provides today very cost-effective solutions, but few treasury departments, forex trading rooms, and computer installations at large take advantage of them. Instead of capitalizing on new technology, they keep throwing away money through 35-year-old tools such as mainframes and COBOL programs, and the results they get are negligible or trivial.

Investing in new technology means acquiring supercomputers, workstations, LANs, and online file servers; deductive distributed databases; intelligent networks; object-oriented approaches; and knowledge engineering. For any project, both cost and benefit should be considered, and for any project other than pure research, return-on-investment (ROI) must always be calculated.

No information technology project should start without a *sponsor* in the line departments. And it will be difficult to find a sponsor if the entry price is too high or the results too uncertain. Another forgotten issue in forex technology is the wisdom of cost justification: estimating development costs and documenting the benefit to be obtained. Another often forgotten issue is the need to establish a rapid development timetable and to stick to it. Only then can an organization obtain results.

4

Planning for Better Technology Investments

The history of foreign exchange rates is a game between governments and markets. Governors of reserve banks as well as ministers of finance typically have the opinion that both their currency and other currencies are mispriced by the markets. Therefore, at times they go to extraordinary and costly lengths to regulate exchange rates.

How do the markets decide which currency to back? Technical and fundamental reasons play a role, but above that there is *market psychology*. Nothing is as unattractive as a currency with no ready and fair market, and the more a government interferes the less the market appreciates its currency.

Negative psychology ensures that in times of trouble market makers switch away from assessing the effects of natural economic forces to watching government actions. The value of a currency becomes a guessing game about the next round of government policy, and, during the waiting period, the market becomes shallow and one-sided. With negative psychology or political unrest (or both), foreign investments stay on the sidelines until there is once again a functioning currency. This, however, does not mean that when the market psychology is not negative foreign investments would come as a matter of course, or that a country's currency will be able to hold its own in the exchanges.

During normal times, foreign exchange analysts and the forex dealers whom they consult, study at length the technical and fundamental factors characterizing each currency to calculate currency risk and country risk, and to evaluate the likelihood of extreme and one-sided market moves that may adversely affect their exposure.

Speculation abounds about possible changes in exchange rates; this information is often substantiated through simulators and expert systems running on high-performance computer equipment, from supercomputers to networked workstations. So far, technology investments have not benefited, in terms of evaluation, from procedures similar to those that traders apply in their daily job. Yet technology investments can help or handicap the treasurer's work in the financial institution or the manufacturing company.

It is one thing to have the forex traders conducting business privately, trader to trader, without realtime simulators and expert systems flashing advice. It is totally another to be able to experiment online through powerful models that amplify the trader's ability to grasp the market trends and opportunities.

The greater return on investment (ROI) in information technology no longer comes from the number of stage hands a computer can eliminate. It is instead derived from the level of innovation it gives the treasury's professionals and managers.

INVESTING IN NEW TECHNOLOGIES

In the late 1980s Citicorp, J.P. Morgan, Bankers Trust, Chase Manhattan, and Chemical Banking each made around $2.0 to $2.5 billion per year from trading foreign exchange and bonds. That represented some 20 percent of their noninterest income, versus less than 15 percent in the early 1980s.

Although profits are not the only criterion of how dynamic or how important a market may be, they do tell part of the story. The growth in the forex market has been impressive, whereas in loans a combination of fluctuating interest rates and more and tighter capital requirements made profits harder to find.

To provide better, more competitive tools to their traders, banks focus both on *supercomputers* and on analytical programs, which is the software designed to give traders an edge over their rivals. Besides helping to identify profitable arbitrages, analytical programs assist the bank in managing its trading risks better.

Citicorp has a system that can match a trader's profitability against the risk he takes. Bankers Trust extended its forex system so that it can net out the bank's position in any market in realtime. Realtime response permits the bank to hedge more efficiently.

Analytics also help banks to acquire corporate customers. In the Eurobond market, investment banks have enhanced their services to key customers by revaluing a company's interest-rate or foreign exchange swap portfolio daily, and by providing information that can lead to deals as borrowers want to take profits or adjust exposures.

Financial institutions must increasingly enhance the simple information and dealing service that they used to provide. If a bank does not know what its customers have done, it is at a disadvantage in developing profitable relationships with them, and is reduced to betting on transactions by undercutting its competitors. This means lower profits.

If a bank or treasury department does not know how the market behaves, the disadvantage is even greater. Market behavior cannot be seen by looking at one page or another of currency and commodity prices pumped in by information providers. It can only be understood through *patterns*, and this requires mapping the market into the computer.

The ability to map the market through a simulator and then exploit strengths and weaknesses by means of expert systems is the necessary condition for taking the whole currencies portfolio and turning it around. Only supercomputers can do such a job at speeds commensurate with trading requirements.

This point also applies to global risk management, including the ability to track positions, pinpoint opportunities, evaluate risks, develop hedging strategies, and do cross-market arbitrage. Investments in artificial intelligence, networks, databases, supercomputers, and workstations are in essence investments in the brains of our forex dealers, a crowd that today is significantly younger than in the past (with a mean age of 28 to 29 years) and that places greater emphasis on efficiency, productivity, and the ability to master the market.

These factors lead to higher system cost per dealer, typically at the $80,000 to $130,000 range. But this also means that for equal trade volume we need fewer dealers. Higher unit investment for fewer dealers is a better deal for the bank (and the treasury) than more dealers with less investment per person. It is a more efficient way of doing business.

If we are in the forex market, then we *must* capitalize on the fact that one of the biggest changes in the world economy since the early 1970s is that flows of money have replaced trade in goods as the force that drives exchange rates. The point has already been made that, as a result of the increasing integration of the world's financial markets, differences in national economic policies can affect interest rates worldwide as well as expectations of future interest rates.

Do we have an information technology that can track underlying changes in the major economies around the globe? Or are we just depending on prices that reflect after-the-fact reaction? If the latter characterizes our situation, then we are not positioned to take advantage of opportunities as they develop. More precisely, we are not able to capitalize on often minute changes that are calling forth huge transfers of financial assets from one country to another. Yet these transfers deplete the flow of trade revenues in their effect on the demand and supply of different currencies, hence in their effect on exchange rates.

PRIORITIZING TOOLS IN THE FOREX ROOM

The backbone of any financial institution and, therefore, of its technology, is its *network*.[1] As telecommunications technology continues to advance and because 24-hour corporate banking works worldwide, transactions move faster but are also more significant in monetary terms, sometimes making currencies even more volatile.

Investing in networks is not a matter of choice, but of survival. Says Peter Ueberroth about his experience with the Olympic Games at Los Angeles (1984),[2] "We still had more than one million tickets remaining. This was another logistical horror since the personal computers used at the individual ticket centers did not have access to the full ticket inventory and could only sell their daily ticket allotments. This meant a ticket buyer could be refused for a particular sport ticket at one center and buy twenty at another."

A similar statement about prioritizing should be made about investments in *databases*.[3] Databases should be distributed but interconnected in realspace, and they should be meticulously designed. When in Chapter 2 I discussed the common system serving the treasury, forex, and securities, I said that in just one issue, *prices*, three database sections are necessary:

1. Volume on trades and effective prices

2. Perceived prices by other institutions and information providers

3. The bank's own price estimates (corporate assets, currencies, equity, and commodity markets)

The challenge is to have these information elements available in the database for *episodic memory*–type retrieval and manipulation — that is, through ad hoc queries that are not crisp, and hence involve vagueness and uncertainty, yet permit to access a fully distributed, very large database where the information elements are stored in raw data form.

[1]See D. N. Chorafas and H. Steinmann, *Implementing Networks in Banking and Financial Services* (London: Macmillan, 1988).

[2]P. Ueberroth, *Made in America* (New York: William Morrow, 1985).

[3]See also D. N. Chorafas, *Handbook of Database Management and Relational Databases* (New York: McGraw-Hill, 1989).

Increasingly, these databases will be stored on optical disks (imaging) and feature a multiple terabyte size. Security Pacific developed a database for its forex operations that uses both imaging and expert systems. The bank also trained its forex specialists to build the access system they need themselves. Said a cognizant executive during our meeting, "The image system in forex has given significant benefits."

Banks that are concerned about their P&L in forex operations also take particular care to properly define *software* requirements for the workstations that are given to the traders.[4] This software should have the following features:

- Multimedia approaches

- Multitasking capabilities

- Multiwindowing (both under dealer control and system control)

- Realtime spreadsheets

- Expert systems

- Dynamic visualization (not just static graphics)

Among applications requirements are often found direct deal entry, exposure measurements, position tracking, and account integration. Some financial institutions believe that there is further need for speech recognition and dynamic report formats within a given interactive application.

In the context of forex operations, the term *investment* denotes a whole range of issues that must be well balanced and complementary to one another: workstations, databases, networks, supercomputers, and advanced software. Besides these investments, we must have a solid budget for *training* the forex dealers. It helps nothing to put in place an expensive system if it is not used in a learned manner.

To teach some of its more valued customers, Citibank created a simulated market environment. It costs $3,500 for each corporate customer to play the game for a week—but it can make that back in one trade. "It is a form of advertising," explains Heinz Riehl, who helped originate the game.[5]

The participants are divided into teams of two or three. Each is given 100 million fictional dinars. The monitors in each team's room become trading screens, while Citibank staffers play the roles of both brokers and reserve bankers. As *brokers*, they keep the screens filled with prices they elicit from

[4]See also D. N. Chorafas, *The Software Handbook* (Princeton, NJ: Petrocelli Books, 1984).

[5]*Business Week*, February 1, 1988.

the various participating "banks." As *reserve* bankers, they throw traders off balance by flashing news bulletins at what seems like the worst possible moment. The learning session's administrators also intervene by buying or selling currencies, to keep such currencies within trading levels known only to them. This training environment is instrumental in actually teaching people how to trade, with no risk of losing millions if learning is done live in the exchanges.

Nikko Securities took a similar approach to training its dealers in options and futures. An expert program was written to assist in the training process while data were fed live from the Chicago Board of Trade, until the Osaka Commodity Exchange was open.

Even though the training environment is not the real world, it is a microcosm that helps clarify in the minds of its players why market moves sometimes seem so strange or so exaggerated. Ultimately, fundamentals drive the market, but along the way, the traders are in charge. To survive as a trader, one has to be fearless, taking action out of *basic knowledge*, not through bravado.

Eventually, training simulators turn into trading systems. The knowledge engineers at Nikko Securities learned a great deal by observing the learning process of the dealers. Based on this knowledge, they improved the expert system, which thus changed from being a training tool to becoming a trading assistant.

A FOREX ROLE FOR SUPERCOMPUTERS

Many financial institutions are prepared to spend big bucks on computers and communications without clear-cut objectives and firmly established milestones. Not surprisingly, they suffer from the technology rather than benefiting from it because they have not yet learned that if a project is to survive and get results, it must use high technology in an imaginative manner, feature a reasonably low budget, and be very well managed. These are precisely the things that the EDP-ers cannot do because they act like the bureaucrats that they are. I learned early in my career never to assume or expect anything where bureaucrats are involved.

The trouble is that even managers who are successful in other professional fields get too timid and confused when it comes to deciding about matters involving technology. Because they do not master this particular field, otherwise intelligent business people seem to waive all their efficiency principles when they get into decisions concerning computers and communications. By doing so they miss significant opportunities, the most recent one being the use of supercomputers.

An estimated 1,000 supercomputers and minisupercomputers are now at work at tasks as diverse as doing financial analysis, examining oil deposits, and number crunching for nuclear engineering. In most of these applications, supercomputing is the enabling technology for analytics, simulation, and artificial intelligence.

Ten, or even five, years ago, we would have spoken of advanced, sophisticated applications as being appropriate for large mainframes. The trouble with mainframes is that today they are too old in design and their power is too limited even when it is augmented with vector processors. This cake simply will not bake.

An even larger amount of trouble and backwardness comes from the priesthood of the mainframes: the ossified EDP-ers. To them, modern technology is not the complex sum of developments, applications, and consequences that have taken place. It is simply what conforms to a limited, serial COBOL-oriented thinking, which itself has been petrified for the better part of two decades. Worst yet, EDP-ers have learned nothing from their mistakes. Hence, they are repeating them at an increased pace, committing significant amounts of money to events that have no return on investment. This not only spoils capital but also loses time, thereby worsening the competitive position of a financial institution.[6]

In contrast, some learned endusers such as company presidents, treasurers, and forex executives understand that supercomputers are as significant to pioneering work in finance today as calculus has been to the development of science. We have right now forex, securities, and treasury jobs that require a machine 100 times faster than the largest available mainframes, and the most advanced research projects call for 1,000 times more powerful machines.

The current estimate is that by the mid-1990s supercomputers could operate at tera-FLOPS speed, which means a trillion floating point operations per second. What will we be doing with such power? A supercomputer model of operations should involve several elements.

- One is *topology of financial markets* and their pulsation—at least for the markets in New York, London, and Tokyo, but with provisions to add more financial markets as requirements develop.

- The second is a *range of currencies* to be handled in the selected group of financial markets. We have often spoken of multicurrency models necessary to face the challenges of fluctuating exchange rates, covering a dozen hard currencies as well as the on-and-off waves of speculative movements.

[6]See also D. N. Chorafas, *Bank Profitability* (London: Butterworths, 1989).

- Last, the model requires *definition of customer profiles* based on past business experience and AI-assisted analyzers. At least *three* groups of customer profiles are needed: corporate client, institutional investor, and wealthy individual, with details on each customer being kept dynamic at all times.

These elements are necessary in the domain of currency exchange. There are also many other things we can do through supercomputers and artificial intelligence in forex and treasury applications. The following fields can be particularly enhanced through parallel processing:

1. *Market data filtering*, which as an application will be detailed in Chapter 12.

The plan should be to draw from different information providers, such as Reuters, Telerate, Quotron, and Telekurs, in many fields of operation, bringing this information together both in a pattern and profile form. Work like this is already done by investment banks on Wall Street, for instance, in forex, gold contracts, and forward rate contracts.

2. *Analytics for basket currencies and forward rate contracts.*

Forward rate contracts require a significant number of analytical tools in order to be evaluated in realtime. A few examples include this market's basket compared to that market's basket; this time range versus that time range; the British market versus the U.S., German, and Japanese markets; and so on.

The point is that traders who are on the front line need the most efficient tools technology can provide. When they do not have these tools, they are neither happy nor efficient, and they can make little or no profits for the organization that employs them.

3. *Hedging.*

To hedge a position requires correlations that go back for at least two months; some applications involve a whole year of historical data. A multiple regression analysis needs at least 50 observations. For arbitrage a minimum of two months of historical data is vital, with official readings taken every hour (Dow Jones provides hourly readings). Significant computer power is required for providing the proper information for hedging. The idea should be to normalize the available data and treat it analytically, a process that needs much computer power.

NUMBER CRUNCHING: THE CHALLENGE OF THE DECADE

Supercomputers, algorithms, and heuristics are much more crucial today than they were in the past because all major financial markets in the world have become interdependent. There is no great profit in looking at them singly, separated from one another, as most currently available computer programs do.

A financial institution as a whole, and a treasury operation in particular, takes a great risk in staying with current (and largely obsolete) software. But integrated solutions have requirements and present significant data loads. Let's see what an analytical approach may mean in terms of *number crunching*. We will do so by taking into account historical data that extends over two months (46 trading days), and by realizing that data vary on an hourly basis—24 hours per day for global trading.

By multiplying these items together, we get 1,104 information elements. But we should also account for the need to address at least five key currencies: U.S.$, £, DM, ¥, and SF—if not more; incorporation of treasury-type bonds (gilts), with at least eight per currency; and inclusion of variable exchange rates and commodities.

All this adds up to a significant data load. These last three items provide among themselves over 350 combinations, which, multiplied with 1,104 information elements, gives about 400,000 data points. We should also realize that at least ten markets change simultaneously (New York, London, Tokyo, Zurich, Frankfurt, Paris, Milan, Toronto, Singapore, and Hong Kong) and at least five financial markets trade parallel over the 24-hour time frame.

The result is a minimum of 2 million rapidly changing information elements to be number-crunched in order to get some knowledge from them.

Notice that this is only the beginning, a starting point reflected in a recent project that aims to understand market interconnectivity and interactivity. In the coming years, this application will become far more demanding because the hourly reference will no more be enough.

As Wall Street and other financial markets employ supercomputers, it will be progressively more necessary to move from the coarse one-hour interval to *minute* intervals, and then to *seconds*.

The minute level of reference will multiply by 60 the 2 million information elements to be handled in parallel, making them 120 million. And when the second becomes the interval of reference, the information elements to be handled simultaneously will total 7.2 billion—and they will have to be number-crunched at subsecond speed.

With current technology, it is simply not possible to handle the hourly limit, let alone the finer time grain. As a result, forex dealers, forex managers, and treasurers simply cannot look after the company interests. Yet this is the way the financial markets are now working and that is what the more competitive financial institutions would do.

Performance references aside, there is also the major issue of cost-effectiveness. Considering brute power alone, supercomputers (with a ratio of 1:50) are crushing the mainframes (at 1:120) in terms of costs in dollars per million instructions per second. This figure is based on number-crunching benchmarks. If the input and output chores are included, the ratio changes somewhat but still remains in the range of 1:20 to 1:40. How can anyone justify paying 20 to 40 times more for a mainframe when the alternative is so much more efficient?

Morgan Stanley did not buy the Cray computer for kicks. This is a machine that costs millions of dollars. It was purchased because Morgan Stanley's management knows that if it does not move ahead of its competition, it will fall behind—and one of the best-managed investment banks in the world cannot afford to do so. The same point is true of the two Connection Machines installed by Dow Jones, each having 32,268 processors.

It is true that, for the time being, there are not many supercomputers in the financial industry, but there is a growing lot of minisupercomputers,[7] while some investment banks and other financial institutions are buying time on supercomputer equipment. If we look at any innovation in computer use, we will see a trend in which the users start buying time on service bureaus. They want to eventually be technology leaders, and they will buy and install supercomputers on their own premises.

THE ENDUSER'S VIEW OF WORKSTATIONS AND DATABASES[8]

Assisted by high-performance computers and networking, forex traders can profit by simultaneously buying a currency that is cheaper and selling one that is more expensive. But unless a big trade can be executed instantly, the opportunity is lost.

Matching trades should therefore be one of the supporting pillars of forex system design, with the head of the foreign exchange division being the best advisor on how to proceed. Ideally, such a process should reflect the pattern

---

[7]The Connection Machine is a fine-grained parallel supercomputer of the hypercube type. Intel's iPSC-2 is a smaller one of the same architecture. A Cray is a large supercomputer having array processor architecture; Alliant and similar firms offer minisupercomputers. See also D. N. Chorafas and H. Steinmann, *Supercomputers* (New York: McGraw-Hill, 1990).

[8]This and the following sections focus on interconnection technology. The rational organization of financial databases is discussed in Chapter 6, and a later section takes as an example interactivity with a securities database.

currently followed by the trader in closing a deal, which means that the WS should support a horde of agile enduser interfaces.[9]

Leading banks understand this point very well, as documented by the fact that only *20 percent* of total microprocessor power is used for computation. The other 80 percent is absorbed by the following:

- Enduser presentation disciplines

- Consistency of visualization schemes

- Interactive graphics

- Access to heterogeneous databases

The first three items have been around for some years, but the fourth is a recent development. Its significance has become evident as the distribution of computers and databases led to their spreading across dissimilar data structures, incompatible database management systems (DBMSs), and diverse applications software and hardware platforms. This makes the sharing of information elements by applications across heterogeneous databases particularly difficult.

Failing to share results in a large number of redundancies and inconsistencies among forex applications. It also increases significantly the work the forex trader will have to do on a WS, as well as the risks taken.

Solutions that must be provided in seamless cross-database access must take into account that data is a strategic asset. It is precisely for this reason that, among leading organizations in banking, manufacturing, and distribution, interoperability across heterogeneous databases has become a major objective.

A different way of making this statement is that, though necessary, it is no longer enough to think of LANs, WSs, and the software running on them in the same way we did in the past. We also have to take care of cross-database solutions, providing for virtual homogeneity in widely distributed and heterogeneous environments.

Seamless approaches require transforming existing closed databases into open ones. A number of projects are in progress in that domain, as we will see later in the chapter. Traders need cross-database access to be able to detect developing patterns in the foreign exchange markets at any time in any place for any currency. Investment advisors and people selling financial products have similar requirements for seamless access to distributed databases in order to serve their accounts in the best way possible.

[9]See also the discussion in Chapter 8 on human windows.

One of the overriding requirements for distributed database interoperability with analytical, ad hoc queries is connected to the trend toward *customer-based systems*. There is a major transition taking place in the financial world, from accounting-based to *customer-based* solutions. In this connection, *database mining* can reveal significant *patterns;* it thus helps make the financial organization, its professionals, and its managers customer-oriented.

Database mining is the exploitation of distributed database contents through algorithms and heuristics. One area in which it has given admirable results is in ensuring that an integrative approach helps bring into perspective client-related risks, flash to attention the prevailing trend in the market, and inform traders ahead of time of developing weaknesses and risks.

Solutions to the problems posed by remote access to heterogeneous databases can be short-term or longer-term. Medium- to long-term solutions should preferably follow the evolving international standards that I will discuss in the following section.

Short-term approaches typically consist of the adoption of commodity software that is presently available and can therefore be tested. During the January to May 1991 research I conducted in America, the best programming product available for distributed database connectivity was DataLens by Lotus Development. DataLens permits Lotus 1-2-3[10] users to get data essential for analytical queries, reports, and business decisions. The user establishes a connection to the data source. 1-2-3 lists available drivers, including the database table. Then it suggests a range of names regarding the external source (or sources) for the user to choose from.

Once connected, the Lotus 1-2-3 Spreadsheet and Database module commands are used to manipulate the information elements. Table 4.1 identifies the DBMS and file management routines being supported. By making access to heterogeneous databases feasible, DataLens enhances the spreadsheet functions.

Without becoming too technical, I can state that because the distributed databases are heterogeneous, there are differences to overcome in terms of data types, character sets, and system functions. This is accomplished by means of Lotus drivers specifically designed for one supported DBMS.

In this connection, *metadata*[11] access provides an efficient manner of interconnection to heterogeneous databases. The driver itself translates between *virtual machine* and the *accessed DBMS*, addressing specifications of database calls, details of programmatic interfaces, and network definition

[10]Releases 3.0 and 4.0.

[11]Metadata are data about data, for instance, data definitions.

**Table 4.1   DBMS and File Management Routines
Supported by DataLens**

DB2	Oracle
SQL/DS	Vanguard and RBASE
Adabas	CCA Model 204
IMS	Paradox
VSAM	DBase III
Teradata	Netware SQL
Sybase SQL Server	SQL Server
RDB	SQL Base
RMS	OS/2 Extended Edition Data Manager
Ingres	DB Accelerator

of protocols. Online connectivity is integrated into the network's transport primitives,[12] and it supports an open architecture.

Currently embedded functionality permits filtering and dynamically screening of remote database contents. But DataLens services are also augmented through AI constructs, for example, the *solver* (which is also a component of other Lotus products), and *Improv* (the new generation spreadsheet for the Next computer), which includes both data and rules.

Finally, leading financial organizations are actively looking into *object-oriented* solutions to advance themselves with better methods than were available previously. There are four reasons for object orientation:

1. We have reached the limits of hierarchical, Codasyl,[13] and relational models.

2. The major new implementations are management- or professional-oriented, reaching global databases.

3. Remote database access concerns objects, not records.

4. Solutions require the semantic power of hierarchical approaches and the flexibility of relational approaches.

Each of the issues that I have discussed in this section is genuinely pressing. There is little or no return from investments in the older technologies. The challenge lies in high-tech implementation, which is where the highest ROI can be found.

---

[12] *Primitives* are the basic commands embedded into the system that make the network tick.

[13] Codasyl is a user's committee that in 1958 established COBOL, a now obsolete programming language, and 10 years later adopted General Electric's IDS database management system.

DISTRIBUTED DATABASES AND THE MIA
STANDARDIZATION EFFORT

The growing acceptance of OSI (open systems interconnection) standards is turning communications procedures among computers into a commodity. At the same time, a number of vendors have agreed on SQL-based specifications for access across relational databases (SQL stands for Standard Query Language). Vendors are also working on gateways between nonrelational databases and the SQL-based specifications, though this effort does not always meet with success.

Starting with the fundamentals, one of the problems with international standards is that they are set by committees under the auspices of the International Standards Organization (ISO), the American National Standards Institute (ANSI), and other organizations.

By necessity, committees typically reach compromises rather than create original designs, and they are more apt to describe rather than to define their adopted standard in detail. Detailed descriptions have to be done at the phase of *productizing*, and standards organizations are not renowned for that part of the job. User organizations have a better record in this connection, an example being the Manufacturing Automation Protocol (MAP) by General Motors.

User organizations can define their own standards and see to it that they become accepted de facto, provided that they themselves represent enough of a market to nudge vendors into compliance. Two major efforts in cross-database access and virtual homogeneity worth noting in this connection are Data Access Integrated Services (DAIS) and Multivendor Integration Architecture (MIA). DAIS is a project promoted by the American Electric Power Research Institute (EPRI), and its goal is to provide federated-type seamless access in an environment characterized by incompatible distributed databases. MIA has been set up by Nippon Telegraph and Telephone (NTT) in collaboration with five computer vendors.[14]

The MIA goal is much more rigorous than that of DAIS, and it handles operating systems (OS) issues as well as workstation requirements. Figure 4.1 identifies the four domains to which MIA addresses itself: communications, operating systems, database management systems (DBMS), and workstations all the way to visualization. Normalization takes place in two phases, respectively known as Version 1 and Version 2.

MIA Version 1 focuses on a *standard software platform*, emphasizing particularly the communications and OS end. DBMS and WS standards are

---

[14]The five vendors are DEC, IBM, Hitachi, Fujitsu, and NEC. See also D. N. Chorafas and H. Steinmann, *Networked Databases* (Academic Press: San Diego, 1992).

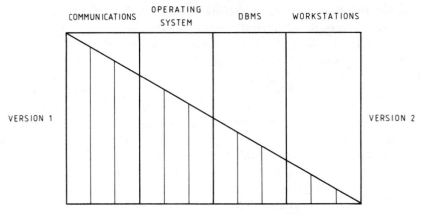

Figure 4.1   The four domains of MIA.

described here but will be defined in detail in Version 2. The currently available Version 1 definitions ensure program portability through five different OSs: MVS by IBM, VMS by DEC, the MVS-compatible by Hitachi, Fujitsu, and ACOS NEC. NTT bets on the size of its procurement of computers and software to obtain *vendor adherence* to the Multivendor Integration Architecture standard.

As NTT's Dr. Fukuya Ishino[15] suggested during our meeting in Tokyo, the Telecommunications Intelligent Network Architecture (TINA) is the basis of MIA. TINA has been proposed by the leading telcos of the First World with the following goals in mind:

- Easy portability of applications software

- Emphasis on user-friendly human-machine communications

- Simpler networking interfaces

- Seamless integration of heterogeneous databases

- Continued growth of programmer productivity

- Protection of investments in applications software

The whole development rests on the premise that it is desirable to provide the enduser with a unified, high-level view of all computers and databases.

---

[15]Dr. Ishino is director of NTT's communications and information technology laboratory at Yokohama, and intellectual father of MIA.

This will free the enduser from having to know which particular databases to access in order to get urgently needed information, or to cope with the fact that different names in different databases may actually mean the same thing, whereas the same name corresponds to different information elements in diverse data resources.

Truly utilitarian solutions reach deeply into the semantics of the information in the database. They also set the basis for intelligent networking, competently serve enduser requirements, and help in software portability among different platforms.

With this idea in mind, MIA's development centers around the definition and implementation of three common vendor interfaces:

- The *application program interface* (API) between system software and APs

- The *systems interconnection interface* (SII), which affects communications protocols

- The *human user interface* (HUI) for visualization and workstation operations

These three standard references have been worked out for all general purpose computers to be procured by NTT, from large-scale hosts to 32-bit workstations. The networking goals of MIA Versions 1 and 2 are shown in Table 4.2.

Regarding the user interface, the MIA Version 1 HUI style guide adopts the following standards:

- *Motif:* OSF/Motif style guide Revision 1.0, which is UNIX based

- *Open look:* AT&T Open Look Graphical User Interface Style Guide; Interface Style Guide Release 1.0

- *CUA:* the Common Users Access of IBM's Systems Application Architecture (described in the Advanced Design Guide, SC26-4582-0)

X-Windows is also supported in the first two of its three versions. These versions are WS based, WS with maxi linkage, and mainframe based.

According to NTT, enduser-directed interface capabilities must provide the ability to use metaphors (through windows, icons, menus) as well as keep consistent and transparent interfaces. User-friendly, homogeneous windows to heterogeneous data structures are another requirement. Just as important

Table 4.2 Networking Goals of MIA Versions 1 and 2

	Resource to Be Transferred	Data Structure
Version 1	Message	Arbitrary
	File	Record storage sequence
	Mail	Letter (envelope and text)
Version 2	Database	Meaning relationships among information elements (semantics)
	Document	Pages, chapters, figures, tables, and so on
	New computer power	Supercomputers, knowledge engineering–enriched workstation

are efficient dialogs for ad hoc queries and long transactions, and tools for direct manipulation by endusers. Protection against unexpected destruction must also be accounted for—a very important consideration for forex traders as well as treasurers.

DATA ACCESS INTEGRATED SERVICES (DAIS)

A number of financial institutions in Japan are seeking to capitalize on the MIA standards for virtual operating systems compatibility, and standards under development for heterogeneous databases accesses as this development goes under way. Their aim is to adapt this technology to the financial industry's requirements. Such adaptation is possible because the basic communication between computers and the execution of queries uses standards such as those of OSI and remote data access (RDA). However, as the system designer gets further into issues specific to the domain of application, the requirements themselves become more focused.

Concurrency, integrity, and contingency determine the way transactions are executed, but also reflect business rules. Furthermore, a unified view of all the databases assumes a rich representation of data and applications semantics.

What this point means pragmatically is that other peoples' solutions have to be studied with care. If technology transfer is to be successful, there should be an interactive transfer of information among system designers.

This process stands a good chance of succeeding as long as the basic concept behind a given project is valid—as is the case with DAIS, whose developers have the following goals:

- Implementation of an integrated architecture

- Independence of operating platforms

- Uniform access to heterogeneous databases

- Remote update capabilities

- Coexistence with local data systems, which retain their autonomy

Other DAIS goals are systems extensibility (while observing OSI compatibility), security, and the enforcement of access restrictions.

Particular attention has been paid to mapping DAIS into the ISO/OSI infrastructure. In the DAIS version of OSI's applications layer, four sublayers can be distinguished:

1. *Programmatic interfaces* are enduser-oriented, aimed at facilitating communications with the distributed heterogeneous databases.

2. *Data access primitives* address themselves to the distributed database network.

3. *Mapping* is the layer of the universal database access procedures.

4. *A link to applications services* interfaces to the presentation layer of ISO/OSI.

The link to applications services is not part of DAIS, but of the *utility communications architecture* (UCA), which has also been developed based on the six lower layers of ISO's open system interconnection.

DAIS avoids the creation of a global database schema, which became a trap for many organizations that tried it, and instead advances the *common data model* (CDM). This is a set of concepts and abstractions providing the enduser with a way of describing information elements.

In the case of DAIS, CDM employs a modeling approach to describe all available information elements in the distributed systems through static properties of their information content, operations that may be applied to the data, and particular local schema characteristics and their semantics. DAIS does *not* propose to integrate the local conceptual schemata, a wise move. As a senior executive of BBN said in the course of our meeting,

"There are customers of ours who tried the global schema approach, but none completed it yet. All of them have found many more problems than they thought they [would] encounter."

PROJECT CARNOT AND THE SQL ACCESS GROUP

The productizing of OSI and ANSI standards is done by the SQL Access Group. This is not a standards organization, but a Los Angeles–based outfit that 40 vendors participate in. Its object is to develop detailed specifications for three products:

- Applications programming interface (API)

- Remote data access (RDA)

- Formats and protocols (FAP)

SQL Access' API communicates through the network with a server process providing access to target databases. Formats And protocols (FAP) employs message-based protocols virtually transparent to the applications programs. This reflects RDA norms, also adopted by NTT's MIA, EPRI's DAIS, and MCC's Carnot.

The goal of the Carnot project of the Microelectronics and Computer Development Corporation (MCC) is interoperability across heterogeneous databases. This effort distinguishes four different layers of services for interoperability across heterogeneous databases, of which the lower two are fairly advanced.

Starting from the bottom, these layers comprise *communication services,* which provide the basic interconnection between computers based on OSI and TCP/IP, and *support services,* providing network-wide utilities such as SQL-based Remote Data Access, message handling (on X.400), directory services (on X.500), and an information repository dictionary system (IRDS) for the storage of database schemas.

The upper two layers are still in an early definition status: *transaction handling* (particularly of long transactions) and *semantic services.* Both can be of significant interest to forex and treasury implementations when they become available.

The fact that MIA, DAIS, and Carnot use the SQL Access Group output leads one to believe that they may end up with a great deal of common ground. SQL Access has also formed a cooperative agreement with X/Open. The X/Open Portability Guide has been selected because it defines existing practices, including add-ons to SQL-89, and it reflects research on implementations, with extension to dynamic SQL.[16]

Value differentiation made through the effort to create new products supports the *client-server* model in the implementation of distributed databases and provides session management for all remote connections. By and large, these extensions aim to handle dynamic SQL capabilities embedded in the newer ANSI SQL versions, and to improve error handling procedures in online implementation while implementing remote data access norms.

Developments made partially in cooperation between America and Japan promote the remote data access protocols as an emerging international standard that specifies communications disciplines to be used with distributed databases and a method for accessing the capabilities of database servers within open systems. RDA is the ISO specification that links the application (user or client) to the local or remote file server. Its operations are always invoked by the initiator (RDA user) of the connection.

RDA's formats and protocols (FAP) provide the logical bridge to the remote database. FAP specifies the request and response message formats between a user and a server. It also establishes the protocol and rules that both user and server must obey in order to *interoperate*.

An API/FAP platform is positioned in the ISO/OSI context. The applications programming interface (API) interconnects the application itself to the intermediate database execution environment. API deals with SQL syntax and semantics as well as its usage in connection to the add-on capabilities under development.

All these work in normalization, and standardization should be examined from the perspective that foreign exchange dealing consists of two major functions, proprietary trading and customer order facilitation, and that both require computers, networks, advanced software, and seamless connectivity between a sprawling range of heterogeneous equipment.

To meet the requirements for customer order facilitation and proprietary trading, it is absolutely necessary to stop reinventing the wheel. With the human resources, time, and money we can save, we should be doing truly advanced applications.

As the last three sections made quite evident, the role of databases in treasury and forex operations can hardly be overestimated—but it has been underestimated in many cases, always leading to the conclusion that their implementation was a severe mistake. I will further discuss in Chapter 5 the contribution of databases, after examining the role of online datafeeds, and most particularly of the market data filter.

---

[16]SQL-2 and SQL-3 are currently under development by ANSI and SQL Access; the first addresses transaction environments, and the second, graphics and advanced enduser services.

5
Market Data Filtering

Entropy is a thermodynamic measure of the amount of energy unavailable for useful work in a system undergoing change, as expressed by the second law of thermodynamics. Entropy is also the degree of disorder and disorganization in a system or a substance—and in this sense it is applicable in the information sciences as well as in finance.

An increase in entropy is synonymous to *lack of pattern*, or randomness, in organization; maximum entropy reflects a state of total disorder. In this sense, when we say that we use artificial intelligence to conceive and recognize patterns, what we essentially imply is that we attempt to decrease the amount of entropy in the system.

The fact that the laws of thermodynamics are applicable not only in matter and energy[1] but also in finance is most significant because it permits us to deal with an organized and fairly stable body of knowledge, as well as tools that are already available and tested. Both the first and the second laws of thermodynamics can be helpful in financial studies. The first law of thermodynamics excludes the existence of a demon who creates energy from nothing. By contrast, it also focuses on transformation, stating that degradation is irrevocable over time.

According to this law, left on its own, the entropy of a system tends to increase over time. Entropy should not be confused with *enthalpy*. Entropy reflects the change of internal energy, and enthalpy maps the rate of change of orderliness, for instance, as observed in heat release.

In computers and communications applications, and most particularly in heuristics processes, *entropy* is a measure of the information content of

---

[1] *Matter* is anything that has mass and occupies physical space. *Energy* is defined in physics as the ability to do work. Mass and energy are equivalent.

a message evaluated as to its uncertainty. *Filtering* aims to decrease the amount of entropy. To achieve this goal, filtering must be done in accordance with specific criteria that help retain only what is essential and, in the process, *classify* and *order* the available information. This is important inasmuch as market data are often voluminous; dealers can easily become snowed under information elements that are rich in content as well as valuable in making market decisions.

Filtering is not done in the abstract, but with specific goals, typically related to a financial instrument, in mind. Furthermore, it should be executed in realtime, and because market data input is often very large, timely filtering frequently requires the use of supercomputers.

ENTROPY, INFORMATION, AND COMMUNICATION

It is a matter of common experience that disorder will tend to increase if things are left to themselves. An *increase* in entropy is interpreted as the passage of a system from one probable state to another with a corresponding amount of disorganization. A *decrease* in entropy works in the reverse way: Taxonomical classification puts in order the available information elements — and this is a notion to be implemented in data filtering.

Mathematically, the ratio of the actual to the maximum entropy is known as *relative entropy*. A high ratio of relative entropy indicates redundancy in information, which must be removed through filtering to obtain a lower ratio.

Although the fundamental concept of entropy relies on statistical mechanics, the distinctions made between order and disorder and certainty and uncertainty are very helpful in finance. Such distinction is typically done by the living observer and is not inherent in the physical world. It is this observer who senses that, as entropy increases, so does disorder, and vice versa.

The concept of entropy helps in understanding the relationship between *information* and *uncertainty*. Information means freedom of choice; and freedom of choice means uncertainty. The measure of information is defined by Dr. C. E. Shannon as the *logarithm* of the choices we have available.[2]

Dr. Shannon's information and communication theory introduces the concept of *negative entropy*, its statistical measure being the same as that of information. Orderly information is therefore the negative of uncertainty; the two observing the following relation:

$$\text{Negative entropy} \rightleftarrows \text{Information}$$

[2]*A Mathematical Theory of Communication*, Bell System Technical Journal, 1948, No. 27.

However, in the sense that negative entropy leads to information, information implies the acquisition of *knowledge*. By contrast, in the sense information leads to negative entropy, information implies power of organization.

Information measures can be used to evaluate any kind of organization. A structure is based upon the interrelations among organizational units, parts, and components. Information measures can demonstrate when such interrelations exist with information decreasing as entropy progresses.

There are, however, limits to which the laws of thermodynamics can be applied. For instance, there is no principle of conservation of information, as there are principles of conservation of matter and energy. The total information can be decreased in any system without increasing it elsewhere, but it cannot be increased without decreasing it elsewhere.

This second rule is invalid in cases of knowledge transfer. Knowledge can be increased in any system without decreasing it elsewhere. In fact, whereas *knowledge is wealth*, mental (virtual) wealth contrasts to physical wealth: the more we distribute our physical wealth, the less we have of it, but the more we distribute our knowledge the more we have of it—because we gain from interaction with other knowledgeable persons.

Transmission or storage of information is associated with the temporary existence of the system in a state of lower entropy. Hence, change of entropy can be taken as a measure of the amount of information, or of the significance of information to a system that possessed it; that is, there is an effect in that system's processes and this effect is elicited by the new information.

Communication is the change of information from one state to another. Signals and messages convey information to the receiving system only if they do not duplicate information already in the receiver. Market data filtering specifically focuses on this particular aspect and on its consequences.

Market data filtering addresses multimedia channels; the filter should therefore differentiate between data (and therefore signs) and text. With *data*, a sign gets its meaning by the place in which it finds itself, whereas *text* has meaning through its content and sentence structure.

There is an erroneous tendency to confuse data with digital information.[3] Data comprise a form of message and have a message content. *Digital information* is a mode of handling and transmission. Market data filtering is typically done on digital information, and it involves both data and text.

In any system, there is a relation between input and output, and our objective is to maximize *output*—not input. Figure 5.1 demonstrates some limiting curves that have been experimentally developed regarding this input/output relationship: Although different living systems have their own

---

[3]IBM made this mistake, and so did ISO and CCITT with ISDN.

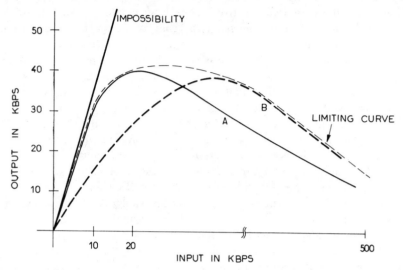

Figure 5.1   Limiting curves for input/output relationships.

characteristic curve (see Figure 5.2), the inverted "U" shape has been found to be common to all of them.

Screening the incoming input, applying thresholds, and maximizing useful output (to be presented in a comprehensive manner) is the role of the market data filter. Treasury and banking operations for which such data filtering may provide noteworthy results include, but are not limited to the following:

1. *Foreign exchange*, both for actual operations and for training of forex dealers

2. *Arbitrage* for forex, securities, and other types of transactions

3. *Portfolio swapping*, considering investment horizon, margins, and so on

4. *Securities trading*, particularly on a global basis involving information from many exchanges

5. *Underwriting*, including market evaluation of outstanding deals and investor acceptance

6. *Portfolio modeling* based on management-defined criteria

7. *Treasury operations*, in a whole range of activities including cash management

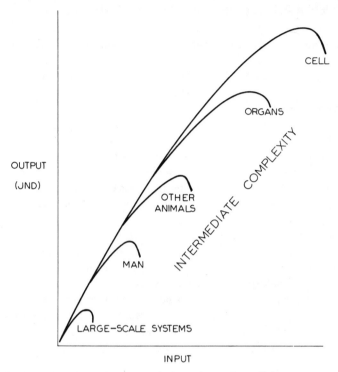

Figure 5.2   Input/output relations in various living systems.

Other possible implementation areas include credit spreading, asset and liability management, spread and gap analysis, credit scoring, budgeting, and the monitoring of financial positions. Marketing is still another example.

Complex organizations need data filtering solutions much more than the simpler ones do. As Figure 5.2 demonstrates, the input/output relation in a cell is of a totally different order than that prevailing in a large-scale system, the latter being far more limited in terms of possible saturation. This is the family of inverted "U" curves based on the research of Dr. James Grier Miller and presented in a NATO seminar given in Chania, Crete, in the summer of 1978.

I must stress that, although it helps in better decision making, data filtering is no substitute for sound judgment. It contributes in roles and responsibilities only when management knows what to expect from the use of the technology at its disposal and appreciates the assistance it can get in shaping its vision of the market and its business opportunities. Still, it is the qualified professional who should make the final decision.

AN APPLICATIONS CONCEPT OF INPUT FILTERING

The basic aim of a data filter implementation should be that of providing a fine-grained solution to the market datafeed handler currently available in most treasury operations—for instance, taking a direct feed from a wire service such as Reuters, Telerate, or Quotron and subjecting this information to screening criteria.

Because screening criteria are never static and typically change with time, the chosen solution must be easily modifiable to meet new system requirements. The data filter should accumulate this data with an adequate audit trail (timestamp, origin trace, sequence identity), and rearrange the data as per application needs. In one financial implementation, these have been defined as event sequencing, time sequencing, source sequencing, and so on.

The market data filter should work interactively, and this requires making it able to extract relevant information elements upon request. One type of request is that these match either patterns or concepts; another is the performance of analyses on the data as well as modeling.

Because the data filter will act as a gateway between information providers and the company's internal information system, the *filter elements* should *front-end* processing power. Both may, however, be executed through artificial intelligence on supercomputers, and up to a point they could work in parallel.

Design should focus on a data-driven system, particularly one that possesses true data flow characteristics. Massively parallel computers are an ideal platform for this application, as they lack both centralized control and centralized memory, leading to the possibility of writing very simple software. In such machines, instructions or other atomic units of computation are triggered only by the arrival of messages; execution can address many different information elements at the same time, with node-to-node comparisons; and synchronization of individual operations is accomplished implicitly through the exchange of messages.

Each node in the data flow graph may be seen as a logical processing element. These elements are *interconnected* explicitly through the architecture of the machine. This is also the foundation on which rests *object-oriented* programming, which through simple means solves a major problem encountered with conventional systems: the coordination between data and commands.

The idea of a front-ending market data filter fits precisely in this discussion. Its operation is reflected in Figure 5.3, an architecture that ensures interfaces to financial information providers; helps in implementing standard

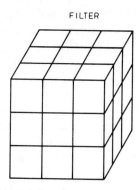

FILTER

- INTERFACES TO FINANCIAL INFORMATION
  PROVIDERS
- APPLICATION OF IE STANDARDS
- TIMESTAMPING AND OTHER HOUSEKEEPING
  CHORES
- INTEGRATOR FUNCTIONS FOR VERY FAST
  PROCESSING

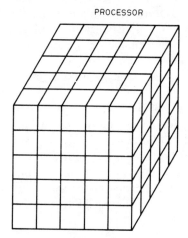

PROCESSOR

FUNCTIONS AS EXPLAINED
IN HYPERCUBE DISTRIBUTION
OF FINANCIAL CENTERS

Figure 5.3 Hypercube architecture of a front-end data filter and associated back-end processor.

information elements; makes feasible timestamping and other housekeeping chores; and acts as an integrator function for very fast processing.

Projects undertaken along this line of thinking project the associated integrator functions in three ways:

1. Front-desk support through powerful workstations interconnected to back-office functions by means of local area networks[4]

2. Data filtering as a server to a group of workstations leading to an extended database capability

3. Number-crunching functions also on parallel machines, these too working on a server basis

One example of the logical structure of the processing functions in the supercomputer server, in a hypercube application, involves currencies, corresponding banks, and financial centers. The software in this number cruncher is designed for arbitrage operations, and it supports a growing palette of analytical tools, including artificial intelligence constructs.

[4]See also D. N. Chorafas, *Local Area Network Reference* (New York: McGraw-Hill, 1989).

Pattern recognition is done at WS level specific to the job of the en-duser. Because real-life, applications-oriented pattern recognition programs require number-crunching capabilities, they must be executed at the supercomputer server. In this sense, the market data filter for incoming text and data streams must feed both the number-crunching engine and the workstations.

This duality in system design helps both in terms of integration and in speeding up the process. I emphasize, however, that the functions of the data filtering server are different from those of the number cruncher even if the latter is fed with digital, realtime market data streams from various service vendors (information providers).

The mission of the market data filter is not to process but to sort and classify incoming information streams as well as to perform the following tasks:

- Time-stamp the information elements

- Restructure them per specified profile

- Alert specific applications of event occurrence

- Move the data to be retained to the workstations and the number cruncher

- Do the same with historical databases

- Provide other utilities as they become necessary in the evolution of the environment

Figure 5.4 shows the configuration of a network that involves workstations, a number cruncher hypercube, a database server, and a data filter. Since image applications are part and parcel of this solution, fiber optics should be used for the local area network. (The installation is point to point, not FDDI, although the figure shows multitapping, which was the first implementation on coaxial cable).

Enriched with knowledge engineering, the large-capacity supercomputer solution at the market data filter front end made it wise to thoroughly reconsider and reevaluate the datafeed sources, appropriately choosing the screening criteria of interest to the professional workstation on a second-by-second basis, and the historical database at the local server and remote repository. In this specific case, it was decided that the data stream from information providers would be sensed first by the communication software, which alerts the screening program about the incoming information elements. These elements go to their assigned hypercube node to be

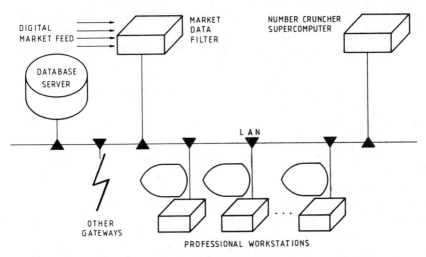

Figure 5.4   Sample LAN configuration for a treasury environment.

filtered and subsequently forwarded to the workstations or the database server or both.

Such an application significantly improves upon present-day practices, where many financial institutions receive from their information providers a steady but unsorted stream of data elements. For instance, Telerate supports some 3,000 to 4,000 pages, which include information on the financial market, politics, and other news items.

Currently, information providers also sell their clients some applications packages, but many treasurers and banks have been asking, "Is it possible to improve upon the current situation?" The answer is *yes*, through the outlined solution. Improvements on present-day solutions should capitalize on the shortcomings that have been sensed. There is, for instance, a dual problem with many user organizations. First, data from the information provider are not structured into useful information for the enduser. As a result, the enduser is snowed under a mass of data when only a few specific elements (or a pattern) to make a fast decision are needed. Second, as far as most user organizations are concerned, the operation of some sorting and rearranging of market information is fully batch. In the majority of cases, users must ask for information for themselves or their clients one day in advance. Extraction typically takes place during the night run, and the extracted data are sent (or downloaded) to the user the next day.

At a time when interactive networks and realtime responses are expected by institutional and other investors, this is evidently not a competitive system. Solutions should definitely focus on realtime response, the immediate handling of input data, and the execution of applications lists using knowledge engineering constructs—for instance, taxonomical classification.

CLASSIFICATION AND ORGANIZATION AS PREREQUISITES

Given the glut of financial market information and the diverse sources of its procurement, three main tasks constitute the organizational prerequisites to competent execution of the data filtering job. The first is *classification*; the second is *metaknowledge*; and the third, *identification*.

Taken together, classification, identification, and metaknowledge reduce entropy in the system. They affect the degree of organization by *reducing disorder*. Through classification, every information element (IE) has one and only one place in which it fits best within the overall context. Metaknowledge provides the rules through which such ordering is done. A unique identification system allows the user to give each IE a proper name, thus making them callable entities.

"Guide the people by virtue and regulate them by *li* [sense of propriety], and the people will have a sense of honor and respect," Confucius said. Confucius insisted on the rectification of names, calling a spade a spade. "If the name is not rectified, then the whole style of one's speech is not in form, and then orders cannot be carried out; if orders are not carried out, then the proper forms of worship and social intercourse cannot be restored; if the proper forms of worship and social intercourse are not restored, then legal justice in the country will fail; when legal justice fails, then the people are at a loss to know what to do and what not to do."

- An *identification code* is a composition of numbers (binary, decimal, octal, hexadecimal, or other), letters, or both, used to identify an item (or data).

- A *classification code* enables this item to express its relationship to other items of the same or a similar nature.[5]

Identification (ID) should be a short number designed for cost-effectiveness in terms of error-free data transcription and transmission. It should be unique for each IE. The classification code (CC) should be a descriptive number whose goal is to provide detail, give a sense of order, cluster together homogeneous entities, and remove ambiguity.

[5]See also D. N. Chorafas, *Handbook of Database Management* (New York: McGraw-Hill, 1989).

Years of experience in the implementation of information aggregates have demonstrated that a single number cannot perform both functions. It is a problem of specialization. The way to develop an efficient coding system is to select the most compact, complete, and methodological solution to classification and to implement it in the population of items (or data) to be stored and retrieved in mass memory media.

The concept of *metaknowledge* comes exactly at this point. With the exception of extremely simple cases, no classification scheme can be one-layered. As with *taxonomical* organization, widely used in the biological and physical sciences, we need a multilayered classification structure in which every higher-up layer is a metalayer to its lower layers.

This concept of *layers* and *metalayers* helps bring into perspective another basic tool in artificial intelligence, the concept of *inheritance*. The qualities and characteristics of the top layer (metalayer) are inherited by those layers beneath it. This avoids repeating such characteristics every time, instead focusing on the structure of a given layer and its contents.

Metaknowledge is knowledge about knowledge. The choice of a metaknowledge-based solution brings the major challenge of organizing and representing the knowledge in a prototype fashion. It permits building meta-models on top of the models, thus establishing rules that govern relationships.

Consequently, such a structured view of a project helps both in better defining the different activities and in controlling the level of effort needed. Internally, all information about a given entity is stored in a frame structure composed of slots, which come in two types: relation slots, connecting the concept to other concepts, and attribute slots, defining characteristics of the concept.

Inheritance of attribute slot values flows across arcs in the network, and knowledge engineers must focus on modeling the declarative components. The latter are primarily composed of standard production rules because the elicited expertise tends to be of the form "IF...THEN," where the "IF condition" matches slot values of frames. Such a design concept makes it feasible to extend the explanatory capability to multiple modes, in which the same knowledge is displayed in different ways for visual cross-validation of the state of the knowledge bank.

Rationalization in the internal organization of the database is synonymous to the reduction of its entropy, and therefore to the identification and classification system employed. A classification-based retrieval system is instrumental in applying the opportunities presented by rapid developments in microprocessors—now cheap enough to serve as control elements for solutions such as *logic over data*.

Furthermore, although network facilities make local document output desirable, and certainly preferable to centralized reproduction and distribution by traditional paper-based methods, unless the database is organized in a rational manner (as we will see in the following pages), the benefits will be largely diminished by higher communications costs. Hence, both cost reduction and greater efficiency, from the enduser's viewpoint, militate in favor of superior organizational approaches.

Finding a computer-based coding system that can provide the needed dependability is a difficult and challenging undertaking, particularly because there is as yet little theory able to meet identification and classification requirements. The problem with organizational work concerning information elements starts exactly at this point, and the following sections will present the solution that I have developed over 30 years of experience.

RELATIONAL AND OBJECT-ORIENTED APPROACHES

The best implementation of a classification system is a flat file, as shown in Figure 5.5a. Each of the 100 pigeonholes can be subdivided into 100 finer grid elements, and each of these into 100 more, thus giving a relational structure based on families, groups, and classes. In such a classification system, similar items can be grouped into homogeneous categories by using their similarities and the relationships developing therefrom. This is primarily a *taxonomical* approach.

Different families, groups, or classes of items (and data) have distinct classification needs. Therefore, a taxonomical organization may not end in a one-to-one correspondence between the classified items and the corresponding identification code. In this case, the solution is to use *further definientia* to reach the level of detail that can provide an unambiguous link between *classification* and *identification* for each and every item.

- To a classification code that includes family, group, class, and further definitions corresponds one and only one identification code.

- This identification code is essentially just a number in arithmetic progression. It tells nothing in terms of classification, but it can be qualified through a *suffix* and an *origin*.

In the specific case of the market data filter, the origin may be chosen as that of the information provider: Reuters, Telerate, Quotron, Telekurs, and so forth. Information from many providers overlaps, but classification focuses on content, not on origin. The *suffix*, too, is important. In the case of the market data filter, it should be allocated to the timestamp. The latter is a vital characteristic of incoming information, but it is not part of generic information.

Only generic qualities that define the nature and content of an *entity* should be considered in the classification code. When we proceed in this way, we see that the family is a *metalayer* of the group and of the class; the group is a metalayer of the class but is subordinate to the family *inheriting* its characteristics. Thus,

$$XX \quad - \quad XX \quad - \quad XX$$

Family   *Group*   *Class*

is essentially a three-layered structure with family at the top and class at the bottom, as in any taxonomy.

Taxonomy is necessary in reducing entropy. A collection of sources such as books, drawings, reports, or abstracts alone will not originate research or invent anything, but, if efficiently classified, they will save time that engineers and designers otherwise waste in seeking buried or widely scattered information. The same is true of information elements needed by traders and investors. Organization is the process by which the economies come in.

The handling of accounting data is one of the oldest computer applications. It is also one of the least structured, as client accounts, supplier records, purchased items, and inventories (to name a few) have common information elements that are structured at different times and in different ways—being, as a result, heterogenous and incompatible among themselves. But we cannot provide homogeneity without identification, and this has as a prerequisite the process of classification.

The concept and process of classification is one of the pillars on which rests artificial intelligence. Pattern recognition, for example, would be impossible without taxonomy. The same is true of filtering.

The classification matrix that we develop should include all entities we deal with, but identification pyramids should be built by family or group of families. For example, each of the following issues will require a family of its own: currencies, corresponding banks, and exchanges. Because developing a cohesive classification and identification system requires time, and because different people will work on it, it is only normal that some inconsistencies or incompatibilities may develop. For this reason, research projects on AI in Japan have introduced the process of *equilibration.*[6]

[6]See also D. N. Chorafas, *Knowledge Engineering* (New York: Van Nostrand Reinhold, 1991).

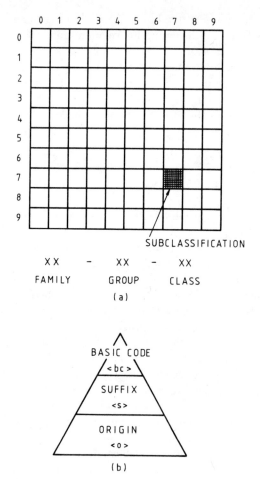

Figure 5.5   (a) Classification matrix; (b) identification pyramid.

Equilibration is essentially a test made by AI software on other AI software as well as on information elements in the database and on the classification and identification codes themselves. The object is to ensure that there are no contradictions in the system or gaps that will make it inoperable.

Testing is a major and vital phase of any system. Tests are necessary to ensure connectivity between different families, groups, and classes, but at the same time verify their isolation properties when treated independently of one another. Tests are also needed to confirm the data flow and information capture as well as to evaluate the necessary throughput for handling the upper limits of a projected data flow. In addition, testing helps ensure end-to-end link integrity and security.

The concept and practice of equilibration are so much more important within a distributed information environment, which, for efficiency reasons, is organized along *object* processing lines. Objects are callable entities that typically include both commands and information elements. Objects permit the factoring of knowledge out of applications programs, and this results in more shareable, independent entities available for referential integrity tests.

Intelligent objects have expert systems rules associated with them that automatically fire when the object is used. This provides greater capabilities regarding knowledge and data manipulation than conventional data processing approaches could ever give. An object-oriented language is one that supports an object-intense environment and its processes. Not only does it map instructions into code, but it also gives the necessary structure to the commands. An object-oriented programming style helps in developing solutions to the problem of referential integrity within a relational database.

An object-oriented approach solves many problems presented in relation to database mechanics but does not necessarily cover all dynamic issues. Other challenges have to do with global recovery from crashes in a distributed database environment as well as diversion caused by different users and their objectives. The foregoing issues are typical with DBMSs but now have to be examined once again for object orientation, including the following elements:

- Internal references in system usage caused by ad hoc requirements

- An incredibly rapid transaction and message turnaround

- Specificity to hardware (HW) and software (SW) characteristics in a nonhomogeneous environment

- Heterogeneity of problems being approached within the same applications landscape

The fourth issue has rarely been accounted for. All available programming routines, and all routines now in development, make the assumption that schematic knowledge is the same. In reality, in a distributed environment everybody's database is different. As we integrate a variety of procedures, we discover a great diversity in data structures and handling approaches leading to incompatibilities.

This has driven serious researchers to the proposition that, in order to manage distributed databases (DDBs), we have to establish a *metamodel*, looking at the DDB as if all data are in the same structure and format. Though the metamodel field is still very weak, the foremost financial institutions are expressing considerable interest in this research, to which they allocate the best of their rocket scientists.

ENHANCING THE FUNCTIONALITY OF DATA STREAMS

An expert system is the best approach to a consistent and thorough handling of filtering criteria. In fact, not just one, but a family, of expert systems will be necessary: one per set of criteria applicable to a specific workstation or group of workstations, and another group for filtering needed for the historical database.

Among other prerequisites to the implementation of a market data filter is, as I said, the timestamp. In one financial institution, timestamping works in seconds with the following algorithm: "Midnight before 1/1/2000 input date/time." Timestamping is presently being supported at the seconds level, reflecting market feed requirements. This is a good idea, but it should be extended to the one-thousandth of a second level (one Therblig is equal to 0.001 second) to meet developing needs.

Therblig timestamping will be increasingly necessary in a global marketplace, and we do have input/output devices on new-generation computers such as the hypercube, which can support processing at the level of one-thousandth of a second. This gives a bank or treasury operation a competitive advantage in a realspace operating environment in the financial markets, because proper timing is at the core of profitable financial operations.

Another prerequisite is to ensure that the online *time-price index files* are updated in realspace, with a function used to distribute time-price data pointers to the indices. For instance, a hash function can perform bit operations on the *currency* and *market* keys through the execution of logical functions.

The algorithms to be chosen should be tested for their validity, and they should provide time-price indices, permitting a fine grain of *market-currency* combinations with multifunctional keys for hash collisions.

Furthermore, to account for future implementations of the market data filter, system design should be modular and able to incorporate numerous new key values and hash collisions, as well as dynamic indexing of utilities necessary to restructure the time-price index files.

Such work can benefit from AI constructs, which permit the system to know its enduser through a *profile analyzer*, automatically actuating the indices to be used and the lists to be extracted. This will make feasible a very effective market data filter application, similar to the one that Quotron operates in its international services.

The block diagram in Figure 5.6 explains the main components of the suggested approach, which rests on a modular, expert systems–enriched solution. We must recall what Japanese bankers say: "Supercomputers are made for artificial intelligence, and AI should run on supercomputers." Examine four of the five functions in Figure 5.6:

- The interface to information providers will always be necessary, and, as technology advances, this front ending will have to be upgraded and improved through new, more effective interfacing mechanisms.

- The task of the profile analyzer is to know the enduser's wishes for information. This can be done through a simple expert system, as has already been done in many investment-type applications developed by financial institutions.

- Activated by the analyzer's results, the personalized market data filter should automatically operate on incoming data streams as well as on the database, without taking precious time of the enduser.

- The deep model should execute the logical constructs and number-crunching operations that the enduser wants, and support a palette of activities from which to choose. For instance, one currently executable feature in financial applications is a paste process, used to combine data in currency key selection requests. Other routines exploit query types and aim to uncover underlying factors in a volume of supplier-specific information elements.

Massively parallel supercomputer facilities permit a process of decomposition and the implementation of mapping strategies. This can typically involve decomposition along five axes of reference made feasible through parallel processing:

- Domain
- Control
- Object
- Layered
- Hybrid

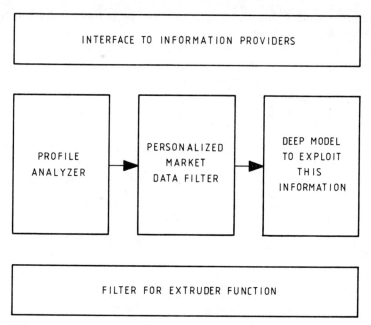

Figure 5.6   Use of profile analyzer with a market data filter.

Domain decomposition should focus on markets and currencies—as well as currencies within a market. It must include prices and timestamps. Correspondingly, *control* decomposition divides into two parts:

- *Functional* decomposition, of the query, partial query, update, or paste type
- *Hierarchical* action with query node focus, able to exploit the internal networking characteristics of parallel computer architectures

In one application along these lines, knowledge engineers have developed a state transition graph with key branches being markets and currencies. It allows listing of all markets and selection of the object market (idem for currencies). The graph also applies timestamp range and lists timestamp-price pairs.

In light of these developments, we will examine one of the domains of implementation of the classification and identification processes discussed previously. This application is particularly important in view of the fact that market data filtering involves millions of information elements, which must be handled in realtime within a realspace topology.

The identification and classification system is able to support flat files, permitting an unambiguous identification of exchanges, moneys, corresponding banks, companies, assets, and other key factors required in each application domain. Mathematical and statistical libraries do exist for the execution of the mechanical part of filtering activities.

Algorithmic and heuristic solutions should themselves be flexible and modular to face both bit streams and the fact that much data arrive from information providers in the form of pages, which contain news and prices for different market instruments. Some examples of money rates services are: foreign exchange, bank notes, eurodeposits, and precious metals. But some market commentaries are unstructured and, as such, complicate market data page selection. At the same time, users ask for various kinds of query support through ad hoc requests.

Intelligent querying capabilities are, for instance, required to obtain currency lists in realtime; to select market, date, and time ranges; to elaborate price and time lists; and so on. Each of these groups of queries has its criteria, which can be nicely structured in role-based expert systems even though the queries themselves are not crisp because of the vagueness and uncertainty they contain.

RATIONALIZING THE STRUCTURE OF DATABASES

I have often made reference to the need for a well-organized database but have not yet defined what a database is. In principle, a *database* is an organized, orderly collection of information elements designed in an application-independent manner. The *information element* (which is a data set) is the building block of the database.

An information element is any *object* that can be stored, retrieved, and generally addressed following a data handling request. Bits, bytes, records, files, real or conceptual sections of the database (subschemas), schemas, and eventually the database itself fit under this broad definition. I have mentioned the wisdom in classifying and identifying the information elements to reduce the entropy in the database.

The database itself is a corporate resource. Because it includes all files and other endogenous and exogenous information elements pertaining to the operations of the enterprise, it constitutes a storehouse of *multimedia* IEs, be it text, data, graphics, image or voice, needed for any purpose whatsoever. This aggregate must have the following attributes:

- It must be managed in a uniform way.
- It must be projected and defined in a coherent and comprehensive manner.

- The aggregate must be available for diverse applications.
- It must be accessible to all authorized users online through data communications.
- The aggregate must be able to support important housekeeping services such as recovery, security, and the like.

An information element can be a page or a string of pages (scrolls); in general, it is any format supported by real or virtual storage capabilities. A reference to an IE is totally independent of its *content* and of its *location*. It is instead dependent on the storage and retrieval (calling) facilities, and on the need to identify this information element for reasons relating to retrieval, processing, and visualization.

An encapsulated information element is one whose internal structure is accessible only to the machine. Some examples of encapsulated information elements include *pages* with virtual storage, *scrolls* as logical groupings of pages addressed as an entity, and *objects* within the increasingly popular domain of object-oriented databases.

Traditional data models are basically record oriented. Their development was motivated and influenced by primitive file systems as they existed with paper-based storage, whose structure was mapped onto punched cards and subsequently onto magnetic tapes and magnetic disks.

Developed in the 1950s and implemented in the 1980s, the concept of hierarchical database structures reflected this paper-based approach, and though obsolete it still dominates the banking industry. Hierarchical databases offer few, if any, opportunities for rationalization, but we do have a much better ground with relational and object-oriented databases.

Within a streamlined database operation, the handling of information elements can be both user visible and user transparent (following system specifications). For user-transparent solutions, the machine needs a lot of software support. Such requirements, and the organizational prerequisites behind them at the user's site, lead us to the concept of database management systems.

Database management merges the user's need for system support (and for more sophisticated data manipulation techniques) with the technological capabilities of computers available to do the job. The identification and management of the distinct entities referred to as IEs respond to the requirement of handling all functions associated with retrieving, sorting, updating, and filing data that belong to a given data structure.

Precisely because of the dilutive effects of entropy, the proper organization and structure of a database presupposes considerable preparatory work. It requires an image of what is to be done now and in the future; precise goals in terms of database integration, both in distributed and in centralized environments; pruning of all unwanted redundancies; and elimination of differences and contradictions at the IE level.

All matters regarding understandability, efficiency, and consistency must be studied and resolved. The proper programmatic interfaces must be established between the IEs and the processes (application programs) they serve. This is a different way of stating organizational prerequisites. A rational system involves both programmatic interfaces and the study of their effect on the integration of the database as well as on subsequent applications.

Management of databases requires a data dictionary, definition language, and knowledge-based rules such as the default layer. The *data dictionary* contains these elements:

- Data definitions

- A directory of the IEs

- Limits and checks

- Security commands and passwords

A *definition language* addresses itself to predicates of a certain complexity. The *default layer* is based on assumptions. A higher level is that of constraints; still higher are system definitions. The goal is to provide a much more flexible approach than that currently supported by information technology. A default should not look like a firm assertion and should be subject to the definition layer:

- An example on the definition level is a bankers' "guaranteed check"

- Constraint level: "Not valid over $1,000"

- Assumption: The issuer was in the city where the check was issued on the day of its issue

- Facts: Amount, date, signature

This four-level structure is logical. The definition language introduces an outer behavior layer, which is expressed through sets and may use possibility theory. Its expression includes methodology, heuristic rules, operators, and search procedures.

The methodology involves the notion of setting up a query by reformulation, and rules do the actual triggering. A frame is like a query. Instances can go in and out of a frame. Declarative facilities can be added as rules; typically, they are procedural.

A knowledge-based classifier is able to take two definitions and tell whether one specializes the other by analyzing the implications included in a statement. This is an important feature in multiple databases and distributed information structures. A distinction is made between handling data (facts, or episodes that change frequently) and knowledge (which tends to accumulate but changes much more slowly).

The classifier can help organize the intentional knowledge in a hierarchy. It requires the notion of inconsistency, which calls for more semantics than current logic programming languages support. As different research projects help document, the mapping of knowledge banks into computer code is one of the hardest tasks ahead, as knowledge banks become very complex and acquire thousands of rules.

But the benefits can be significant. An object-oriented environment permits polymorphism; that is, the same procedure name can mean different things, depending on the message the object receives. This is considered to be critical to financial information systems of the 1990s, where message exchange will dominate a great many operations on a 24-hour global basis.

HANDLING A RELATIONAL DATABASE
THROUGH PARALLEL COMPUTERS

For an applications example, consider the content of a *securities database*, consisting of input from stock exchanges and involving a select list of companies (say, about 1,000 stocks) that *our* investment bank is interested in following. The data comprise companies, prices, currencies, and type of share.

Data come in steadily. In the typical present-day implementation, they are processed and a shopping list is prepared according to the ongoing applications that are usually operating on serial computer equipment. Benefits to be obtained from implementing a parallel computer come from *speed of response* and better *data extraction* algorithms as well as heuristics. In some applications, algorithmic approaches may suffice. By contrast, in cross-issue searches and in cases involving uncertainty, heuristic solutions are recommended.

Consider an example where a given set of search parameters includes market code, currency code, and closing price. Programs can be written to retrieve such parameters given a shopping list of interest to the enduser (here the wisdom of using a rule-based expert system becomes apparent). Knowledge engineers can develop a *state transition* graph for this database application; one implementation utilizes the concept of select search mode.

A four-way sort is effected through a four-step process:

1. Retrieve all companies, list companies, and select company A.

2. Retrieve all markets, list markets, and select market B.

3. Retrieve all currencies, list currencies, and select currency C.

4. Retrieve all shares, list shares, and select share D.

Down its tree structure, the state transition graph permits reaching the desired level of detail, for instance, along the retrieve companies path. Retrieve markets for company A; list markets for A; select market B; retrieve shares for C and B; list shares.

The results desired by the enduser can be structured ad hoc. For instance, the query may be "Retrieve date-price history of share D, and then list date-price pairs," with many markets as well as several currencies having been considered. This is where *parallel processing* presents its most significant advantages over the serial approaches, which have thus far dominated database usage in the financial industry.

In an applications-oriented sense, a fine-grained parallel computer such as a hypercube will feature at each of its nodes resident processes communicating with the distributed database, the local server, or both; the enduser (via a dispatcher); and expert systems written to manage the selection and update of IEs.

Processes running in parallel include a query manager, update and data selection algorithms, data-combining operations, and heuristics for intelligent database access. Such processes handle timestamps and lead into agile user interfaces.

Dispatchers running in parallel (which can be clones) can effectively support multiple operations routing to and from the target workstations and user applications. They can also support multiple services and data pages handle multiple market datafeeds. Parallelism is an excellent approach to handling high transaction rates with multiple datafeed input.

In terms of logistics, a command procedure must be developed to extract data in a flexible manner as the endusers' shopping lists change. Menus should support several types of user-defined queries. One application does so by class within the company, market, currency, and share, interconnecting these classes by means of a state transition graph and handling the whole process in an enduser-oriented sense through the dispatcher.

The enduser interface programs run in step with the dispatcher, the latter being the traffic director of messages sent to and from the user interface as well as to and from the hypercube. In one recently developed applications environment on a parallel computer, four types of programs control the application:

1. The query node with the dispatcher distributes work to other processors on the hypercube.

2. The update node receives new data from the workstations or the information providers or both; it operates on the file system and runs memory-based tables on the hypercube.

3. Routines for partial data structures handle queries with incomplete keys.

4. Routines for global queries process them with complete keys to retrieve the needed tuples.

Within the context that I have just described, I can see an excellent opportunity for the implementation of fuzzy queries. On this issue, Yamaichi Securities, among other financial institutions, is very active; Yamaichi works in collaboration with the Laboratory for International Fuzzy Engineering (LIFE) at Yokohama.

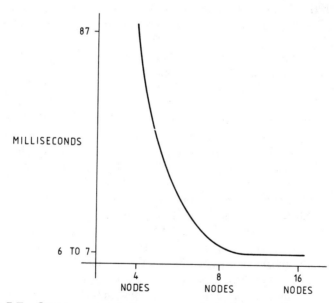

Figure 5.7   Company, market, currency, and share queries to a database using a parallel computer.

Fine-grain parallel computers have many advantages; foremost among them is the handling of ad hoc queries and their parallel execution. One of the benefits derived from the hypercube implementation is demonstrated in Figure 5.7. It compares response time in milliseconds from the operation of four, eight and sixteen nodes, and demonstrates that eight nodes is the optimum number per application; reduction in the response time levels off beyond this configuration.

6
Analytics in Forex

One of our main preoccupations when we build a network for foreign exchange operations is ensuring that trading is never interrupted. Downtime can leave existing positions badly exposed. Providing high availability is a relatively solvable problem that we approach with the mathematical tools of reliability engineering. This is just one example of putting analytical tools to work in *our* bank.

In the decade of the 1990s, mathematical analysis will play an increasingly important role in the background of fault-tolerant systems, as well as the foreground: bringing commendable results in the management of the treasury, foreign exchange, and securities.

We are now ready to capitalize on the solutions that were developed during the last decade. A number of research studies have concluded that bond and equity prices follow a Monte Carlo approach (random walks): Past price behavior does not necessarily predict coming prices, although chartists would dispute such a statement. With forex markets taken as a group, technical currency forecasters seem to perform better when they use random-walk approaches.

The development and use of analytical methods is the job of Wall Street's rocket scientists. The mathematical models they develop are necessary to simultaneously compute price trends, interest rate differentials, cross correlations, and volatilities. Realspace simulation and experimentation allows recommendation of the optimum combination of positions to yield the best return-to-risk ratio. It is not the single tool, but the systems approach, that helps in trading performance. The view must be global and involve all key currencies.

The role of the enduser should never be underestimated. He is the expert, and his specialized knowhow must be employed to develop customized currency products that can handle exposure and assist in trading. The simplest approach is to cover exposure selectively by selling the foreign currency forward against the domestic currency. A more flexible strategy permits converting exposure in one currency to another, provided that total exposure does not exceed preestablished limits. More complex are forward transactions.

Up to a point, the treasury, forex, and securities markets have become the real-world version of the movie *Rollerball:* no preestablished penalties, no time limits (other than trading proper), no substitutions—only endurance. As competition gets stiffer, the demise of marginal trading operations gets closer because there is already far too much contention in this market, hence the wisdom of sharpening up our tools.

COMPUTER-BASED MODELS AND KNOWLEDGE ENGINEERING

Computer-based models in foreign exchange dealing use *pattern recognition* techniques to identify profitable trading schemes, on the theory that price movements tend to repeat themselves over time. Surveillance applications also use pattern-matching and searching approaches, which can be more effectively executed through parallel logical operations.

Logical functions form the basis of all pattern-matching and searching algorithms as well as heuristic approaches characterizing a financial environment. What distinguishes one forex dealer from another is his or her intuitive understanding of the economy, the markets, and their financial instruments, in addition to commonly available quantitative analysis possibilities. This is the area that can be improved through artificial intelligence (AI).

Artificial intelligence shaped up during the 1980s in its implementation in the financial industry as a *concept,* but also as a set of *tools* and a *technology.* AI is enabling computers to understand and manipulate information much more directly than is possible with conventional programming approaches and techniques. As Figure 6.1 shows, AI as a concept is much bigger than the domain of supercomputers, which are objects we use to reach specific goals.

Capitalizing on these facts, the foremost financial institutions have now in operation exchange advisory systems, including such fields as the foreign currency options market. Their aim is to limit the risk associated with fluctuations in international currency without limiting profit opportunities. Expert systems provide advice for the initial development of a strategy in foreign currency option trading, and they suggest modifications following

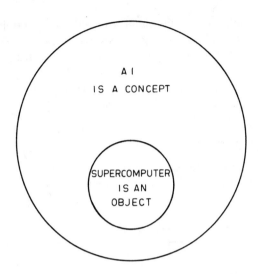

HENCE, AI IS MUCH BROADER THAN MACHINES.

Figure 6.1 Relationship between artificial intelligence and supercomputers.

price movements. Their recommendations are based on market outlook, expected prices, price volatility, and market risk profile. They also contain a "what if" capability for the evaluation of alternative market and currency conditions.

In Chapter 4, I said that the new generation of computers is made for number crunching and artificial intelligence applications. Artificial intelligence means *knowledge* readily available at trader workstations, though the background work may be done by supercomputers. The industrialization of knowledge transforms the work of professionals from opinions, which are often incongruent, to a factual and documented diagnosis and a fairly homogeneous rule set to be used in operations. AI constructs facilitate the development and testing of alternative hypotheses and assumptions as well as their weighting. They also include subjective judgments.

Not every problem can be approached through AI. Another key tool is *simulation*. Digital simulation is a working analogy of a physical system (for instance, the forex market in New York) run on a computer with software.

When analogous systems are found, the experimentation done on the *microcosm* of a simulated environment can then provide significant clues

in regard to the behavior of the *macrocosm*—the real system. Analogical
thinking has its roots in the physical sciences, but it is a process increasingly
applicable in finance. The underlying concept is shown in Figure 6.2.

- Quite often, we cannot proceed directly from the real-world problem
  to its solution because we lack the means do so.

- An alternative approach is to use abstraction, starting with the idealization of the problem that we face.

- The next step is concretization of our thoughts and their logic expression through *modeling;* this model is mapped into computer memory
  through software.

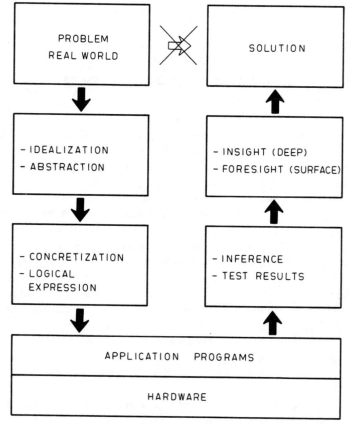

Figure 6.2   Basic structure of analogical thinking in finance.

- From workstations to supercomputers, we use the embedded power for inference to do projections and test results.

- The insight and foresight gained by means of experimentation leads us to the solution we are after.

Complex financial models using simulation and AI are integral parts of what has become known as *interactive computational finance*, which is an essential element in today's competitive arena on Wall Street and in the other major financial markets.

The interest expressed by leading financial organizations in computer-based models and AI is justified by the fact that this enhances their competitiveness and their profits. In addition, AI shells[1] ensure that more sophisticated and better integrated applications are developed faster and at less cost—applications that work more smoothly and easily than yesterday's software.

INTERACTIVE COMPUTATIONAL FINANCE

In the race to buy low and sell high, financial organizations that do not master high technology are either shut out from the start or jump in with incomplete knowledge and get burned. A good example of implementation is provided through financing: Pools can be built, reducing pricing risk, and responses can be given to a greater number of requests for price quotation within a given time frame.

There is a strong relationship between the level of support we provide our dealers and the results they get. Working online and getting subsecond responses, the foreign exchange trader benefits from the ability to construct more complex transactions and price them at a lesser risk. Through economic models he is able to solve previously intractable problems, and keep on doing so even if the complexity of the model steadily increases, because such complexity is transparent to him. Split-second experimentation provides the base for more stability of earnings.

Financial modeling is done to solve problems. A *problem* is, by definition, a matter involving uncertainty and requiring solution. For its solution, we need a line of conduct that we propose to adopt and follow. That is, practically, what interactive computational finance is doing.

The course to solution should be algorithmic. As I have already discussed, an algorithm is a predefined procedure that, step by step, leads us

---

[1]See also D. N. Chorafas, *Knowledge Engineering* (New York: Van Nostrand Reinhold, 1991).

from variable input data to the results we seek, and eventually to the solution of the problem. An algorithmic approach aims at reaching end results through a formal, well-established sequence of computational events. Not all approaches, however, need to be (or even could be) algorithmic.

With expert systems, we typically use *heuristics*, which leads us to the discovery of problem solution but without the assurance that such solution will be found. This is done by making plausible (and fallible) guesses as to the best thing to do next.

Heuristics is not synonymous with logical probabilities, but nearly so. For instance, the way Mycin (one of the better-known expert systems, designed for medical diagnosis) approaches problem solution is to assign a *certainty factor* to each of its 500 rules. This is an example quite applicable in a financial environment. It is also the way the mind of the forex trader works. The trader does the following:

- Assigns certainty factors to the mental rules he is using in dealing

- Associates weights to each class of information that he is handling, with the goal of making a decision

The whole concept of *analytics in finance* can be found in these sentences. Any approach that does not reflect the way in which the trader's mind works is invalid, and in cases it may be counterproductive.

Every financial institution has its share of invalid approaches, whether stored in the time capsule or, even worse, still in use. They have typically been developed by EDP-ers who know nothing about the forex business, and quite often they are the result of split responsibilities. Here is a similar example from a different domain: "I was told by the Mossad," said Juan Antonio Samaranch, chairman of the International Olympic Committee, "that its mistake at Munich was having two main security groups working together."[2]

Interactive computational finance can only bring value to the institution if the sophisticated software it requires is developed by the people who will employ it (the endusers) through expert systems shells. Don't ever bring EDP-ers into this process. The results will be a fiasco.

The endusers themselves should appreciate that, in terms of the development of logical constructs, a great deal of the contribution comes in the form of heuristics; that is, *nonprocedural* processes based on trial and error and often involving vagueness and uncertainty—like other fields of science do.

---

[2]Peter Ueberroth, *Made in America* (New York: William Morrow, 1985).

Speaking of physics and physicists, Dr. Werner Karl Heisenberg had this to say on the *principle of uncertainty:* "You can predict nothing with *zero tolerance.* You always have a confidence limit and a broader or narrower band of tolerance." This is true not only in physics but also in finance.

Heuristic approaches reflect *qualitative* reasoning and (sometimes) *quantitative* results. But heuristics can also imply a *classification* order necessary to achieve efficient search strategies. The building of patterns through machine intelligence is based on heuristics.

A slightly more mathematical approach suggests that, no matter what model we use, we need a fundamental theory. Heuristics uses *possibility theory,* which helps us incorporate intuitive logic embedded in a comprehensive structure, the qualitative assumptions we make, and classification tools to help in the recognition of underlying patterns.

Imaginative applications in interactive computational finance have shown that the interactions and interdependencies developed through possibilistic reasoning can be used for prediction as well as for the solution of complex problems that defy procedural approaches. This is precisely the aim we have after we develop computer-based models in a financial environment. Whether we should use algorithmic or heuristic solutions depends on the particular problem.

EXPERT SYSTEMS FOR DECISION SUPPORT[3]

A particularly dynamic area of the foreign exchange market is currency options. These options are attractive because the risk attendant on the fluctuations in international currencies is relatively limited, in relation to the profit opportunities, although consistently profitable trading in them is very difficult.

The problem confronted by the trader of foreign currency options is that, in order to develop a sound strategy, he must thoroughly analyze the market's outlook, expected price movements, price volatility, and so on. Because there are many approaches to foreign exchange options analysis, a great deal of expertise is required in managing currency exposure. To start with, *the amount of data is enormous.*

These two points help identify the framework of a decision support system (DSS) useful to this and other cases. It starts with problem identification and proceeds with data collection—to be followed by evaluation, initial

---

[3]Several of the notions underlying expert systems implementation are explained in Chapter 7.

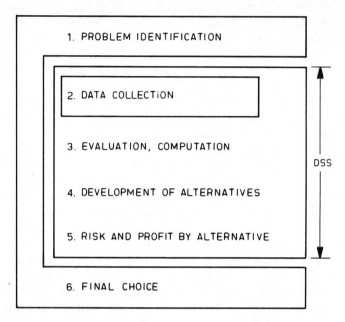

EXPERT SYSTEMS EXPAND THE SOPHISTICATION OF THE
DSS AND EXTEND THE IMPLEMENTATION PERSPECTIVE.

Figure 6.3   Decision support system has many aspects and
components.

development of alternatives, calculation of risk and profit for each alternative,
and financial choice.

Aiming to present this procedure in a comprehensive manner, Figure
6.3 follows the aforementioned steps sequentially. But in a complex environment like foreign currency options, such steps should be handled in
parallel; hence comes the need to improve upon past methods by using
parallel computational engines (supercomputers) and artificial intelligence
constructs.

In their role as decision support tools, expert systems expand the sophistication of a DSS and extend the implementation perspective. They also
change some of these applications' taxonomical characteristics, as we will
see through a specific example.

In terms of assistance to trader decisions, the logical possibilities supported by expert systems are better than the previous approaches because
they make it feasible to modify behavior according to the trader's degree of

belief in an outcome, depending on the inputs he receives and the way the output is judged after a certain pattern has been developed. For their part, supercomputers significantly reduce response time, and, as I have already explained, fast response time is at a premium. The window of opportunity is narrow, the leverage is large, and small percentage improvements in performance typically have a significant financial impact. The goal of a supercomputer-run artificial intelligence construct is therefore to seize opportunities that an expert trader might overlook or misinterpret. This is done by performing quantitative *and* qualitative analyses, evaluating a broad range of alternative strategies to identify the plan that best suits current trading goals.

To be accepted by the dealer, the solution must offer a convenient, supportive method. Both customization and ad hoc functional enhancements are necessary to meet individual trader requirements. One must account for the fact that the traders of all foreign currency options have access to the same data—the difference lies in how they interpret these data.

In terms of performance, the value differentiation lies in expertise at developing, and then exploiting, successful financial strategies. Qualitative analysis of a system offers the possibility of a much stronger interpretive approach than algorithmic procedures. *Hypothetical reasoning* enables qualitative evaluation of multiple strategies, as required by, say, foreign-currency options trading, thus creating a competitive advantage for dealers who use this method.

Such foreign exchange systems practically replicate the trader's thinking. Said the chief technology officer of a money center bank in New York, "The payoff for the forex expert system came through a clear definition of the information the trader needs and its filtering." This and other financial institutions extended the decision support functions that they had already implemented. One of them found it necessary to restructure the applications environment.

- Table 6.1 presents the organization of information elements done in the past to help in the implementation of a decision support system in forex operations.

- Table 6.2 indicates the restructuring that was necessary to develop the best IE architecture when the preceding application was enriched with expert systems.

By comparing Table 6.2 to Table 6.1, one can see that, contrary to the DSS structure, the architectural requirements of an expert system are greater because the latter is richer in reasoning capabilities.

Table 6.1 Structural Relationships for Decision Support Systems in Forex Operations

Facts	Rules	Reasoning Methods
A. Market		
Currency forex positions	Profit-loss calculator	Spot effect positions
Contract rates	Dynamic equilibrium	
Calculating chores	between forex and money markets	
	Line of credit criteria	
	Trade criteria	
B. Internal		
Profit centers		
Lines of credit		
Trading limits		
Customers/locations		

Table 6.2 The Restructured Expert System Environment in Forex Operations

Facts	Rules	Reasoning Methods
A. Technical Information		
Forex rates	Stop loss	Moving average
Deposit rates	High/low	Curvature of graphs
Volume	Capital limits	Relativity evaluation
		Support levels
B. Fundamental Information		
Inflation rate		
Interest rates		
Balance of payments		
Money supply		
Capital investments		
C. Psychological Factors		
Expectation: bullish/bearish sentiment		
Date		
Time		

During the design of this foreign operations support system, emphasis was placed on finding executable orders advising the dealer accordingly. Another focal point was eliminating manual intervention, thus avoiding errors caused by writing the wrong information. Two tangible benefits have been obtained:

1. More volume with the same number of traders, as electronic communications did away with the paper log jam, leading to automatic allocation of executed trades.

2. Better profitability through the dual effect of identifying business opportunities through pattern analysis and making the online inquiry much more user friendly.

The expert system calculates exposure in various currencies, correspondents, and exchanges at high speed. The structural approach followed in this application is shown in Figure 6.4; each level of reference is mapped into the machine in a matrix form. Figure 6.5 shows the visualization of pattern recognition in a currency matrix. The goal is to identify developing patterns in currency exchange by mapping the frequency changes taking place and the amounts involved into a reference matrix. Shades and dynamic color graphics have been used for easy visualization of cross-currency exchanges. Attention has been given to the wisdom of handling currency repurchase and reverse transactions. The system also provides liability accounting as well as compliance to corporate policy, which can be stated in four key phrases:

• Good profits

• Minimum exposure

• No speculation

• Hedging

Exposure data from all accounts is instantaneously available. Trading decisions are supported through charting, and the trader can experiment with the advice received from the expert system. A different AI module handles *advice rating*. Table 6.3 gives a glimpse at this process. The advisor consulting with this module is typically an expert trader.

Notice that the advisors are weighted on the basis of the outcome of their past guestimates. The strength of a piece of advice is weighted with this rating. In addition, a tally is kept on how often advisors agree or disagree on whether to sell, hold, or buy a currency. The use of possibility theory permits fuzzy responses (such as hold and sell).

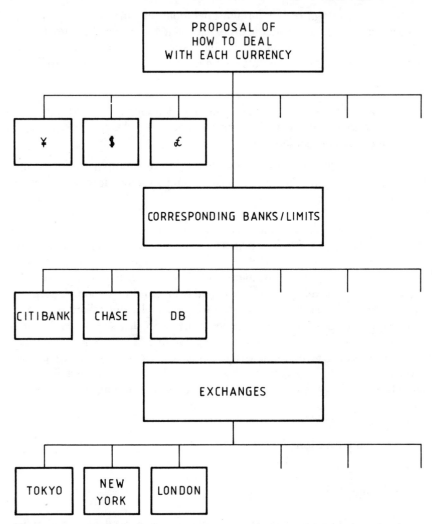

Figure 6.4   Forex expert system structure with networked, specialized modules.

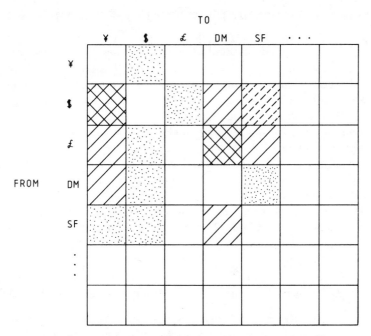

PATTERN RECOGNITION THROUGH PARALLEL PROCESSING AND MAPPING OF TRANSACTION PROCESSING

Figure 6.5 Pattern recognition in a currency matrix.

Table 6.3 Possibility for Advice Rating Regarding Currencies

Advisor	Advisor Rating[b]	Strength of Advice[a]			Weighted Advice[a]		
		Buy	Hold	Sell[c]	Buy	Hold	Sell
A	5	3	0	0	15	0	0
B	2	2	2	0	4	4	0
C	1	0	3	2	0	3	2
.							
.							
.							
a	3	0	2	3	0	4	5

[a]Weighting is done on a scale of 0 to 5.
[b]1 to 5; if 0, the advisor is dropped from the list.
[c]One of the advisors is the expert trading system.

USING PROTOTYPING TO IMPROVE PERFORMANCE

Nearly 30 years ago, digital simulation, discussed earlier, was used as working model for the abstraction and idealization of a physical system. This way, we could study it and optimize it through computers prior to building the system itself. This followed a long tradition from the 1940s, when analog simulation was done through differential analyzers and scale models.

Prototyping is also a working model, and in the context of interactive computations finance it is a model of a logical system. The prototype is the software program's specification: a dynamic, not a static, one. It is computer based, and it requires no rigid documentation like that called for by classical system analysis.

Here is a list of what I believe will be trends in financial management in the early to mid-1990s; clear-eyed financial institutions and industrial organizations should be able to use them to advantage:

1. *The use of protoypes,* as they have been implemented in engineering and are used in computer-assisted software engineering (CASE).

2. *Computer communications,* increasingly characterized by global networks emulating exchanges practiced by humans.

3. The management of *large databases* distributed throughout the operations landscape and assisted through AI.

4. Systems integration of communications networks, databases, processing routines, and enduser functions.

5. *Visualization* and *human windows* to make enduser interactivity more agile and the human-machine interface more friendly.

6. The *increasing use of expert systems,* by way of implementing machine intelligence.

The catch is that the success study and experimentation for the implementation of issues 2 to 6 itself rests on the competent application of prototypes. Prototyping is therefore not only one of the issues highlighted in professional interests in this decade—it is also a good policy.

A prototype is the ideal vehicle for the systems effort in forex operations. It permits us to experiment on a new generation of computers and communications technology as well as on applications software. It also makes feasible a quick turnaround in the development process because we are able to demonstrate that the system under study meets requirements—or, alternatively, to correct deficiencies without delay. With a good prototype we can immediately implement a basic structure:

1. Testing and better determining the users' needs

2. Evaluating the system concept behind the desired solution

3. Getting feedback from the user and making improvements in realtime

4. Continuing to manipulate the prototype until it satisfies the enduser's requirements

5. Giving the domain specialist the ability to confirm what he sees in the prototype

6. Enriching this prototype with details, evolving it toward a working system after the endusers' requirements are satisfied

Through these steps, the prototype becomes the specification for the full system. It is a living specification, not a static one like the traditional paper documents of a systems analysis.

With a good AI shell, we can prototype a small-scale expert system literally in a day. Instead of writing plans on reams of paper, we get a head start on the development process through a computer-based solution, this approach being part and parcel of the more advanced applications in computer-aided software engineering. In contrast to classical DP, prototypes supply a solution that can be delivered early in the process of software development. Experience shows that it is very useful to have at an early stage a view of the applications, and this is what a good model can offer.

CASE helps to significantly increase the knowledge engineer's (and also the analyst's or programmer's) productivity by making it feasible to bring the enduser into the picture. The software product benefits from the brains of the domain specialist, and the knowledge engineer better understands the user's needs. As a result of interactivity, it is possible to get an instantaneous response leading to immediate correction of deviations.

Computer-based, interactive approaches followed during the development process avoid time lost because of the interminable changes to which software is usually subjected; they also greatly simplify the maintenance chores. *Maintenance* consumes today up to 80 percent of human resources in the software development department of a computer organization, though well-run banks and securities houses have surgically trimmed this unelegant expense through CASE tools.

Processing, databasing, interfacing, and communications systems design must also be approached through prototypes prior to large-scale investments, for implementation reasons. Prototyping has much to do with expert systems, and expert systems with prototyping. With fourth-generation languages[4] a modeling process has been done through the primitives of a DBMS. Indeed, one of the best tools with which to map a processing routine into the computer is software that manages our data and allows us to access our databases effectively.

With knowledge engineering we prototype through fifth-generation languages: the expert systems *shells*. They are building tools that consist of *primitives*, with which we construct software in a very agile and productive manner.

Software should be made to optimize not the way machines work but *the way people think*. This is being achieved through implementation of AI. Expert systems modules already support a wide range of users through the following means:

- Interactive dialog with the database

- Multiple communications disciplines

- Easy access and manipulation of text, data, graphics, and image

- Intelligence-enriched answers to queries posed by endusers

- Logical pathways to the solution sought by the designer of financial products, the trader, and the investment advisor

After we strip off the scientific glitter it becomes apparent that prototypes (and expert systems) are simply a new and advanced programming paradigm. The human windows, logical inference, algorithms, and designs used are fairly straightforward and can be easily understood by almost every banker, and the structure of the prototype can easily be demonstrated through visualization.

However, one important thing to remember about the current state of AI technology is its intrinsic capabilities and limitations. The by now more traditional expert systems are rule based, using sets of IF...THEN...ELSE guidelines to process the required information or knowledge. The new generation of expert systems involves fuzzy sets and neural networks.

[4]See D. N. Chorafas, *Fourth and Fifth Generation Languages* (New York: McGraw-Hill, 1986).

A TECHNICAL ANALYSIS AND REASONING ASSISTANT

Embedded within an interactive computational financial environment, analytical tools and heuristic models provide useful assistance to forex dealers. Table 6.4 gives an example from a foreign operations expert system that was built as a prototype. These rules demonstrate one of the solutions that have been followed; it is not the only one. Other approaches employ these constructs:

- Design tables and decision trees

- Slots and metaslots

- Bayesian (conditional) probabilities

- Operating characteristics curves

- Fuzzy sets (particularly possibility theory)

- Neural networks, which emulate the way neurons fire in the human brain

This relatively simple example helps demonstrate how expert systems can be applied to financial problems. A foreign currency transaction is defined and solved using sets of logical inference rules. The expertise can be easily extracted from various sources, including human experts, texts, and manuals. Rules are built based on such expertise, and the decision model practically follows a logical tree:

- Currency trend is *weakening*

- Advice is *strong*

- Action is *sell*

Or, alternatively:

- Currency trend is *stable*

- Advice is *hold*

- Action is *hold all*

Table 6.4   A Simple Expert System for Currency Exchange

IF	⟨Currency weakens⟩
	AND ⟨Advice strong for selling currency⟩
THEN	⟨Sell large part⟩
IF	⟨Currency stable⟩
	AND ⟨Advice strong for holding currency⟩
THEN	⟨Hold all⟩
IF	⟨Selling currency⟩
THEN	⟨Compare selling via other currencies⟩
IF	⟨Deal with Bank A⟩
THEN	⟨Examine total limits with Bank A⟩
	AND ⟨Examine currency 1⟩
	AND ⟨Examine currency 2⟩
	AND ⟨Examine currency n⟩
IF	⟨Tests are positive⟩
THEN	⟨Make deal with Bank A⟩
ELSE	⟨Choose alternative partners⟩
IF	⟨Sell currency advice is country related⟩
THEN	⟨Examine country risk⟩
IF	⟨Country in turmoil⟩
THEN	⟨Review exposure in investments, not just currency⟩

The decision support model can also accept a quantitative expression, and, in this case, representation will be

- Advice to sell > 60 percent

It can also suggest to the foreign currency trader a course of action. For instance,

- Do exposure calls
- Do calculation

The trader may interactively call exposure information to his screen by selecting an *icon* or by drawing on his screen a simple block diagram, as in Figure 6.6a. He can also compare currencies by using both current and historical data (Figure 6.6b).

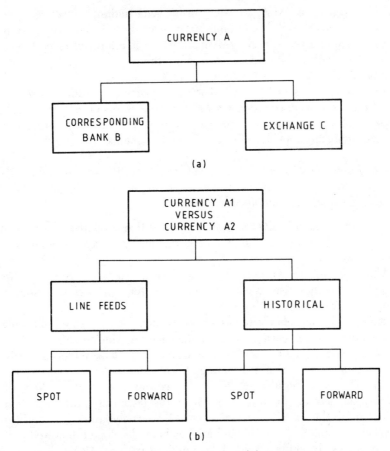

Figure 6.6   Block diagram for forex trader: (a) exposure; (b) comparison of exchange rates.

Among the advantages of an expert system in the trading domain is the fact that the interactive explanation facilities being provided are of significant aid to the dealer's daily work. Through such support the human-machine interface presents a comprehensive picture of market behavior, helping the dealer in digesting large amounts of data and evaluating courses of action, given the prevailing market conditions.

Informal approaches can also be made explicit, and this is what Manufacturers Hanover Trust has done with its technical analysis and reasoning assistant (TARA). In use since May 1988, this expert system has been built to help foreign currency traders in their decision to buy, sell, or hold market positions.

The objective of TARA is to help in financial trading, as well as to contribute to the bank's ability to innovate in forex dealing. The expert system addresses the currency trading domain, which is a form of price forecasting dealing, with the question: "Where are the prices going? Up, down, or sideways?"

TARA capitalizes on the fact that the success of a trader's forecast is based upon the accuracy of analysis and the timeliness of prediction. Large amounts of money can be lost or gained in an instant. There are the two popular approaches for determining price movements:

- *In fundamental analysis,* the goal is to predict the supply and demand for a commodity, such as currencies, based on economic forecasts, political events, and market psychology.

- *Technical analysis* is a forecasting method that capitalizes upon historical trends. It draws heavily on charting and statistical techniques.

Although fundamental and technical analyses are sometimes seen as contradictory and in other cases as complementary, neither approach has a standard formula for prediction, and both require substantial interpretation by a skilled trader. Some traders choose to pursue one strategy or another, but most use a combination of technical and fundamental analyses. This underpins MHTC's decision to use an expert system in order to read live data, model and analyze them, run a rules base, and recommend profitable trades.

Said Thomas Campfield of MHTC in his presentation at the May 1988 SMART FS meeting in New York, "Since the technical approach is better documented, the initial deployment of TARA heavily favors this methodology. The fundamental knowledge base has been developed, however, and is in the process of being tested. Like the wise trader, TARA will integrate both approaches in the future."

On the technical analysis side, the expert system charts, calculates trend lines, decides on degree of support, and reads live data, updating the chart as necessary. Based on trends and estimates, the model recommends buying, selling, or holding as appropriate and also defines the window of opportunity in trading as well as the possible profit if a deal is made within that window.

Typically, 50 windows are active but not simultaneously displayed. More are added as additional currencies are tracked. Fifteen years of historical data can be called into memory and accessed from any module running in one of these windows. A six-month intraday model for British pounds may require 300,000 data points.

Ten or more synchronized processes are either running or waiting to be run. The system is connected to a live, in-house datafeed that is active 24 hours a day. The rules of the model account for the fact that in forex trading knowledge is fuzzy, experts disagree, dealers are loaded with a large volume of live data, and the human mind cannot easily grasp a multifaceted, fast-changing situation. This also explains the technological and psychological hurdles that had to be overcome in building TARA.

- The biggest *technological* problem was that of integrating the live datafeed with the knowledge bank and doing so without losing critical response time.

- The major *psychological* issue was gaining interest among traders with widely varying styles, as well as teaching them how to use a higher-level tool to enhance their personal trading strategies.

Because experts disagree and because there are neither crisp rules nor panaceas, it is imperative to experiment. The expert system provides for experimentation, and this gives the bank a competitive advantage. As Campfield suggested, "We know a lot of our competitors. They do expert systems, and in case we remain inactive this puts us at disadvantage. We also know that even if we fail in the model, we end by understanding the trading context better."

REMOS AT BANKERS TRUST AND THE DEALER SYSTEM OF MITSUBISHI BANK

This chapter has stressed that increasing volatility in foreign exchange trading means that the trading room requires sophisticated computer support. This has been the goal of Bankers Trust's Resources Management Online System (REMOS). It provides the foreign exchange trader with a fully automated multibranch, multicurrency, and multi–profit center trading facility. REMOS has been designed to combine a streamlined data entry, online dealing results, timely credit checking, and profit and loss evaluations, and to give both dealers and trading management a full spectrum of online support capabilities.

With this idea in mind, the *spot trading* facility was designed to automate clerical activities, allowing traders to concentrate on vital professional decisions. Online operations allow an immediate update of trading positions, enabling traders to perform tasks in less time than previous processes would permit. This subsystem shows the net currency positions with the following elements:

- Position adjustments

- Spot effect calculations based on forward trading

- Average cost of establishing these positions

- Profit or loss incurred

In addition, a *forward trading* subsystem incorporates the functionality of the spot blotter while providing the ability to handle a varied selection of trade types—for instance, processing for *swaps*, *outrights*, and *options*. The construct gives the trader pertinent data on forward swaps.

As each transaction is entered, an online credit check is made. Based on established limits, credit availability is calculated and displayed. When credit problems are detected, the trader is provided with an appropriate error message; he also receives details of corrective action that may be taken.

Cash flow analysis is another subsystem. To manage the daily funds required for contract settlement, a comprehensive cash flow review is provided, showing daily *liquidity* and *gap* positions for available outstanding contracts. The positions supporting this information are maintained online as each deal is entered. They are organized within the profit center, thus permitting analyses by portfolio and at institutional level.

The overall design goal of Bankers Trust has been to enhance the trader's professional capabilities. Immediate update of all critical data structures positions the system's user in such a way that he can support an appropriate trading strategy, responding quickly to market conditions. REMOS also provides for the management of independent portfolios, each maintaining separate positions, incurred costs, and resulting profit or loss figures.

Investment, corporate, or commodity positions can be established in a management portfolio and tracked without being affected by the actions taken in the trading portfolio. This data is immediately updated with each portfolio's trades and is available online.

Expert systems functionality has been integrated into REMOS as the consequence of a large AI prototype that Bankers Trust built in the mid-1980s in the forex area. Another point to note is the front-desk-back-office integration, which resulted in a reduction of back-office personnel from 54 to 12 people.

Through AI the Mitsubishi Bank in Japan is able to keep a composite view of all deals its traders make at any point in time, calculating exposure in realtime. Its dealer system currently serves 125 traders at the home office; the next step is to integrate the overseas network into the dealer room by expanding capacity, improving worldwide security, and providing backup routing. This new dealer room implementation enhances the international status of the Mitsubishi Bank, featuring a sophisticated artificial intelligence construct that (as the Japanese financial community suggests) runs on a Cray computer—one of the largest machines available today.

A leader in the implementation of the best technology available, the Mitsubishi Bank has used since mid-1987 a system for forecasting exchange rates based on four currencies: yen, U.S. dollars, Swiss francs, and Deutsche marks. The functioning of this system rests on technical analysis. This construct calculates trend and range and has given quite accurate information over the years.

Successful organizations, such as Mitsubishi Bank, Bankers Trust, and many other financial institutions, lead in technology implementation and make steady improvements. One of the coming applications of AI in finance will be in fuzzy sets and neural networks. In America and in Japan, banks and securities houses well versed in high technology are already utilizing fuzzy set–based expert systems in their operations. Yamaichi Securities is an example.

The use of fuzzy sets and neural networks characterizes the second generation of expert systems, which goes beyond rule-based models like the example given in in Table 6.4.

- Possibility theory permits us to handle vagueness and uncertainty, which cannot be easily done through rules and frames.

- Neural networks make it feasible to attack fields that cannot be handled through other means, for instance, signature recognition.

Contrary to probability theory and Boolean logic, which rest on a binary system using 0 and 1, possibility theory works by accepting subjective judgment as well as ambiguity: Something is likely, or not so likely; maybe it will happen, but it is just as likely that it will not.

Fuzzy sets not only reflect such qualitative, subjective judgments but are also enriched with an additive theorem, which allows summing up different possibility distributions into an integrative curve. Japanese financial institutions, as well as manufacturing firms and transport companies, make the largest known investments in fuzzy engineering. In April 1990 the Ministry of International Trade endowed the Laboratory of International Fuzzy Engineering (LIFE) with $70 million to be invested over five years.

Neural technology is loosely modeled on how the brain works, using hundreds of simple processors operating in parallel and a learning software that adapts to the application. The problem with neural networks is that the technology is still in flux. In January 1990, Nynex Corporation's science and technology center received a patent for a neural network technique that enables computers to read handwriting with greater accuracy.

Such inventions have widespread applications in financial services; signature recognition is important in domains ranging from check processing to the handling of forex vouchers. The neural network application developed by Nynex can allow the computer to read the information directly from a check, a voucher, or a customer order.

Complexity problems are addressed today through neural networks. Citibank is one of the financial institutions known to be most active in neural networks, in addition to many Wall Street firms and Japanese financial institutions. One of the focal points of this research is signature recognition, a milestone in the true automation of payment documents.

Incorporated into a larger system, neural networks recognize and read documents that have been scanned into a computer and digitized. The neural network module can be supplemented through other constructs such as external knowledge sources (for instance, past investment or payment history), possibility theory, and probability theory. All this together helps define current perspectives, but also the shape of things to come.

7

Contributions from Knowledge Engineering and Simulation

As financial professionals know from experience, successful trading in money markets and capital markets is not a kid's business. Treasurers, fund managers, dealers and research departments constantly monitor many prices to detect significant events and trends.

Opportunities are constantly sought, and the exposure to risk has to be actively managed. Both risk and missed opportunities significantly affect profitability. Therefore, the scope of computer-based models as assistants is increasing. As data on prices is now being provided in machine-readable form, projections, evaluations, and complex calculations can be performed at high speed. Positions can be constantly monitored and experimentation done under different scenarios.

As with all professional and business lines, the most important asset is the knowledge used by treasurers, fund administrators, and research experts. If computers could be used to capture this knowledge, rather than merely to perform repetitive mathematical or data processing tasks, this would increase the treasurer's business scope. It will also provide him with a significant competitive advantage.

As I will demonstrate in this chapter, knowledge engineering provides the methodology, tools, and procedures to capture the knowledge of experts for use throughout a financial organization. Particularly important is the ability to analyze the markets in realtime and ongoing changes. This has to be done constantly and consistently, 24 hours a day—manual procedures can be of no assistance in this task.

But mathematical models and expert systems alone will not ensure the needed support. A whole infrastructure must be created that includes deductive distributed databases and global intelligent networks (see Chapters 11, 12, and 13).

The simulators and knowledge engineering constructs that we develop will give the best results if they work online and feed on rich databases, both private and public. I discussed in Chapter 4 what this means in terms of preparation.

Not only steady datafeed but also realtime data filtering is necessary to retain what is important out of the rapid expansion of the flow of information in an environment of increased market volatility. The treasurer has to face complex markets with more derivative instruments, tight margins, low volumes, and growing competition.

The systems that technologists provide must help solve these problems by easing the pressure on the front office and filtering datafeeds to display only information that requires attention. Such systems must respond to events more quickly and consistently than previously possible. And they should give leading experts more time to enhance their knowledge by performing all routine tasks through software.

What the preceding paragraph outlined is tantamount to increasing organizational leverage through computers. This can be done by distributing the knowledge of the treasury department's best experts throughout the organization, using knowledge engineering, and by ensuring that consistent money management and trading strategies are adopted in all markets and at every location.

Intelligent, computer-based mathematical models can give hedging advice, identify arbitrage opportunities, and constantly monitor significant events. They can help in asset allocation and portfolio management, perform financial analyses, and provide their users with effective, realtime solutions for their daily jobs.

QUANTITATIVE APPROACHES TO TREASURY OPERATIONS

The message conveyed by the introductory paragraphs is that financial and industrial supremacy in the 1990s and well into the twenty-first century will rest on the ability to master one's own actions within a fluid market. Competitiveness in such a market requires the mastery of a growing number of *financial instruments* and an embedded enabling technology that spans from production to distribution to the skillful handling of financial issues.

Quantitative approaches to treasury functions can be effectively handled through *algorithms*. An algorithm is an established procedure defining the computational process that leads from variable input data to desired information or other results. Algorithms may be deterministic or probabilistic, but in either case the solution procedure can be guaranteed to give a prescribed answer if we follow through its prescribed steps. Quantitative analysis has been introduced into macroeconomics through the Leontief model (late 1940s); was extended to microeconomics by means of operations research and linear programming (1950s); got more sophisticated with digital simulation (1960s); further advanced with decision support systems (1970s). But it really became popularized in the late 1970s and early 1980s through spreadsheets and personal computers.

Computer-based *qualitative* approaches entered the treasury functions through *heuristics*. This was a development of the 1980s, involving trial and error in problem solving. Heuristics is particularly helpful in relatively diffuse and difficult problem areas for which no deterministic solution strategies are known to exist—and this makes it one of the fundamental disciplines in AI.[1]

Natural languages supported through artificial intelligence will play an increasingly significant role in financial environments. This is also true of simultaneous machine translation; the competent management of very large databases, including the evolution of self-sustaining *idea databases;* the generalization of parallel processing (supercomputers); and intelligent networks operating as fault-tolerant systems.

New types of software such as expert systems and efficient, logic oriented programming languages can be instrumental in promoting the treasury function. A number of breakthroughs in robotics and measurement will contribute to this goal, with the most significant consequences resulting from the cultural change that places emphasis on computer literacy.

Quantitative approaches are not new in business; metrics and measurements have been basic tools in financial navigation for many years. This is a parallel to the navigation of ships going back to antiquity—though it is from the thirteenth century onward that measurements became the navigator's keynote.

- The astrolabe has been the chief instrument for reckoning positions.

- The compass and increasingly sophisticated maps for direction finding were also used.

[1]See also D. N. Chorafas, *Knowledge Engineering* (New York: Van Nostrand Reinhold, 1990).

- Trigonometry allowed calculation wind of current-induced changes in course.

- The hourglass measured time and therefore speed.

The hourglass originated in Venice, and Chinese navigators used not only the compass and sternpost rudder but also a combustion clock. They kept incense sticks burning in the ship's shrine, measuring elapsed time by the number of burned sticks. It sounds rudimentary? If so, the same can be said of a number of tools still in use in treasury operations, though they are being updated.

Every bank has a story to tell about its effort to develop better measurement and navigation tools. The financial services division of Chemical Banking, for example, selected *account reconciliation* as a business area for expert systems because the problem is well defined, it has the support of management, and a payback does exist. As a service to its clients, the bank issues a statement from the account reconciliation services (ARS) department, reflecting the status of the client's account. These reports list transactions that occurred in the demand deposit account (DDA) and enable the client to manage cash flow more effectively.

But the ARS and DDA statements differ in their reporting of balances, with discrepancies arising approximately 5 percent of the time. The task of reconciling these discrepancies is tedious and time-consuming. To manage the additional volume requires temporary staff for peak periods at the beginning of each month, with a significant amount of time spent on repetitious training.

An expert system[2] based on the knowledge of the senior reconcilers provided many benefits. It expedited the reconciliation process, reduced the number of temporary staff, and shortened the training period. The initial project goal was to build a prototype expert system that would assist the department in training inexperienced reconcilers. The first phase was knowledge acquisition.

Expert reconcilers begin their task armed with various reports, checks, deposit slips, and copies of transactions for error correction, data adjustments, and so on. They are problem solvers, adept with numbers, and they understand the relationship of numbers on a report and know what action is required.

---

[2]As I demonstrated in Chapter 6, expert systems are software constructs that experts in specific professional domains enrich with their knowledge. This new type of software gives advice and justifies the opinion that it offers its user.

Based on these premises, a prototype was built to reflect the reconcilers' knowledge. After tests of the prototype, additional rules were written to handle all reject reasons, and rules were added for the following problems:

- Needed error corrections

- Return items

- Handling of certified checks

- Combinations of these three issues

Rules were also developed to automate deletions and additions as well as to handle out-of-period items. A tutor mode was incorporated to help in using the system. Subsequently, the architecture was enhanced to allow data integration, with the mainframe account reconciliation system creating a tight coupling of information to be used by the expert system.

This AI construct is now able to reconcile the majority of account discrepancies present in Chemical Banking. For statements that cannot be automatically reconciled, it identifies specific problems and makes recommendations to the reconciler, thus improving overall productivity and quality of service. [3]

THE GROWING ROLE OF EXPERT SYSTEMS

I have given an example in which knowledge engineering was instrumental in improving service and reducing cost in banking. Similar approaches can be used with a number of other applications in the global treasury reporting and analysis function shown in Figure 7.1:

- Service monitoring for companies and banks

- Value date profiles

- Comparative return on investment (ROI), return on assets (ROA), and return on equity (ROE)

- Cash flow forecasts

- Investment risks

---

[3] For a comprehensive review of the use of expert systems in America, Japan, and Western Europe, see D. N. Chorafas and H. Steinmann, *Expert Systems in Banking* (London: Macmillan, 1991).

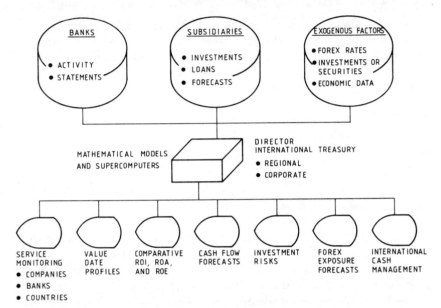

Figure 7.1 Global treasury reporting and analysis system.

- Forex exposure forecasts
- International cash management

Other treasury areas, too, can benefit from metrics and expert systems implementation, for instance, *treasury stock;* that is, a corporation's own stock that has been issued, reacquired, and not canceled in accordance with a formal procedure specified by law. There are four important elements of this definition, and compliance can be ensured through expert systems:

1. Treasury stock must be the company's own stock (holdings of the stocks of other companies are not treasury stock).

2. Such stock must have been issued.

3. It must have been reacquired by the issuing corporation, by purchase or donation.

4. It must not have been canceled.

Cancellation of stock is effected by a procedure prescribed by law: this procedure places the stock in the status of unissued, or even unauthorized, shares. This, too, can be controlled by means of AI constructs.

Expert systems can also be instrumental in evaluating a stockholder who acquires unissued stock at a discount, assuming a contingent liability for the amount of the discount. This means that, if the corporation is unable to pay its debts, the creditors may demand that stockholders who acquired unissued stock as a discount pay the corporation the amount of that discount.

The treasurer also needs metrics and expert systems for management of *intangible assets,* which are not available for the payment of debts of a going business and depreciate greatly in case of liquidation. The principal intangibles are bond or debenture discounts, brands, catalogues, contracts, copyrights, designs, formulas, franchises, goodwill, leaseholds, licenses, mailing lists, models, patents, processes, trademarks, and treasury stock (when it is, incorrectly, carried as an asset).

A similar statement about the profitable use of expert systems within the treasury can be made in connection to (1) the management of *current liabilities,* which are obligations whose liquidation is reasonably expected to require the use of existing resources properly classified as *current assets;* or (2) the creation of other current liabilities.

Current liabilities are all short-term obligations, generally due and payable within one year. They are usually incurred in the normal course of business and must be paid on fairly definite dates. A short-term bank loan may be contracted for the purchase of merchandise, the payment of salaries and wages, a premium on an insurance policy, or for accrued interest on a mortgage.

Among current liabilities are notes payable to banks, different types of trade acceptances, accounts payable, loans payable, accruals, advanced payments, reserves for taxes, reserves for contingencies against possible losses, and dividends declared but not paid. They can all be tracked through expert systems operating online.

Quite often values on the asset side shrink. Obligations never shrink, and it is not unusual for the liability side to increase when debts are discovered that apparently were casually overlooked. Omissions are human. That is why, through knowledge engineering and networked computers, we can greatly improve treasury operations.

Dividends, too, are a treasury area of responsibility that can be assisted by artificial intelligence:

- Under what conditions does a company have a legal right to declare a dividend?

- What are the exceptions?

- What are the laws of the various countries in which the stock in question is quoted?

As a matter of course, countries differ in their regulations. In general, a corporation has a right to pay a dividend if it has a surplus produced by realized profits from operations or extraneous transactions, or from premiums on the sale of par value stock. But there exist implicit as well as explicit exceptions to this rule.

An expert system knows the rules and the exceptions by country, as well as how to reconcile them. Dividends cannot legally be paid from surplus created by writing up assets to higher values, because the profit has not been realized by a sale. At the same time, the surplus need not be decreased by writing down fixed assets merely because their market value has declined.

ASSUMPTIONS UNDERLYING SIMULATIONS

A number of traditional, numerically based computer aids have not proven themselves able to support the demands upon them because they focus primarily on events in the past. By contrast, business is interested in the future. The use of forecasting models made an improvement over this method, particularly if it is integrated with

- Rich databases

- Online market datafeeds

Forecasters are simulators, and simulation is a working analogy (a similarity of properties or relationships without identity) making it feasible to proceed through analogical reasoning.

Simulation studies are powerful tools for experimentation. When we are able to construct analoguous systems, measurements and observations made on one of them can be used to predict the reaction of the others. Simulation involves the construction of a working mathematical model that presents the aforementioned similarity of properties or of relationships among components and critical variables characterizing a physical (real) system under study. In this manner, we can do the following:

- Preoperate the object under investigation without physically constructing it

- Forecast its most likely behavior and predict trends

- Decide on the direction events may take, and experiment on the optimization of characteristics

By building simulators we enable ourselves to visualize the behavior of unfamiliar systems on the basis of knowledge about how familiar systems act, and of the expected resemblance of the former to the latter.

As seen in Figure 7.2, which builds upon the concepts introduced in Chapter 6, this involves a process of *abstraction and idealization:* We move from the known physical world, which we first simplify and then describe

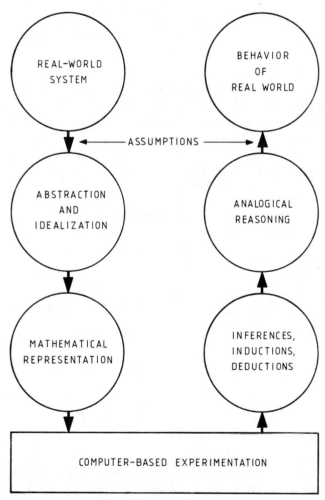

Figure 7.2   From abstraction and idealization to analogical reasoning about the behavior of the real world.

by means of mathematical equations, toward a computer-based model that can be operated at high speed under a number of assumptions.

Once the results of the experimentation have been obtained, we return to the real-life system by means of *analogical reasoning*, as suggested in the beginning of this section. There is practically no risk in building mathematical models because this work is now well under control. But when it comes to business systems, the risk is in the *assumptions* we make.

An example will help identify the type of risk taken with assumptions. In the late 1970s, right after the second oil shock, President Carter called for the "moral equivalent of war" to achieve energy independence for America. He proposed an $88 billion crash program centered on producing synthetic fuels from oil shale and coal. Set up by the government, Synthetic Fuel Corporation enticed major oil companies to launch huge shale projects: then oil prices softened and interest evaporated. Today, what remains of an effort that was supposed to produce by 1992 an estimated 2 million barrels of synthetic fuels a day is a Unical plant churning out about 6,000 barrels a day—almost three orders of magnitude less.

The forecasters and the policymakers faced a debacle. As OPEC tightened its stranglehold in the 1970s, the policymakers began to view shale resources as a key to energy independence. Andrew Gulliford [4] frames the tale as a morality play in which the villain's role is played by the world's biggest oil company, Exxon, which in 1980, shortly after buying out Atlantic Richfield's interest in the huge Colony oil shale project near Parachute, issued a white paper on shale's future. In reality, the "villains" were the assumptions that led to the forecast.

- American production of synthetic fuels could reach 600,000 barrels a day by 1990 and 8 million barrels a day by 2010, Exxon predicted.

- Reaching those goals would require investing more than $500 billion, moving more than 1 million people to western Colorado, and digging six huge strip mines, each larger than any then in existence.

The assumptions were shaky, but Exxon even proposed a number of detailed moves, for instance, diverting water from the Missouri River, some 700 miles away. To jump-start the industry, Exxon said that it would sink $5 billion into the Colony project and build a town for 25,000 workers.

Nothing like that has ever happened, and just two years later, in May 1982, Exxon dropped the project. The assumptions were wrong primarily because the political implications were not considered. The company's white-paper

---

[4] *Boomtown Blues: Colorado Oil Shale, 1885–1985* (Boulder, CO, University Press of Colorado, 1989).

projections show how astonishingly far off the course a large corporation can go in its work.

Without question, technological and environmental obstacles hinder the exploitation of shale, but these were known well before such forecasts were made, and they should have been given their due weight in the plan. The same is true of oil pricing, and most particularly of the political outcome in presidential elections.

False assumptions have a tremendous impact on treasury operations, and there is no mathematical simulator that can correct that effect. Computer-based models will process quickly and efficiently what people decide in terms of crucial factors, interrelationships, and analogies. However, the effectiveness of this procedure depends entirely on the hypotheses on which such models operate.

Simulators or no simulators, investments or trades made by the firm rest on the ability of managers and professionals who are on the front line. Viable systems start and end with valid assumptions.

AN INFRASTRUCTURE FOR FORECASTING MODELS

In the past, both simulators and knowledge-based systems were expensive to develop, difficult to understand, and cumbersome to use. Over a period of nearly two decades (the 1960s and 1970s), mathematical models were considered to be too difficult for management to understand. But since the invention of the *spreadsheet* there are inexpensive tools available with power and functionality required by many applications.

The more sophisticated tools have the ability to reason in realtime and are designed for applications where thousands of variables are monitored concurrently, for instance, financial trading. Such systems reason about events in continuously changing markets by scanning areas of interest and focusing on potential problems as well as opportunities. They incorporate not only mathematical simulators but also the knowledge of human experts that relate market behavior over time, expressed in rules that form the core of the models' reasoning power. This approach combines the discussions on expert systems on simulators. For effective man-machine communications it also incorporates a graphics-based environment (see Chapter 8 on human windows and Chapter 9 on intelligent graphics).

Applications development is done in a way that easily enables the expansion of prototypes into complete systems, providing in the process all the tools necessary for effective communication with endusers. The best-designed constructs ensure online access to live datafeeds, as well as private and public databases, take maximum advantage of existing programs, and feature an open architecture, which allows easy communication with a multitude of software supports.

Solutions built within the realm of treasury and forex operations assign a timestamp and validity interval to prices, estimate volatilities, and project market trends, thereby ensuring logical reasoning with up-to-date information and timely advice.

Such solutions help devise a suitable hedge once an important trade has been executed; constantly monitor for events such as significant volume or price changes in the market; and explore a number of alternatives simultaneously:

- Different trading strategies can therefore be followed at the same time, with the most appropriate for current market conditions being selected.

- The ability to change analysis in realtime ensures a better response to events. Prudential Securities, for example, has developed a futures technical trading program (FTTP), which provides its traders and its clients with appropriate decision support. Enriched with mathematical simulators, this program features three trading methods designed to capture the longer-term trend in the futures market.

Each FTTP trading method consists of two separate systems, of approximately equal merit if estimated on the basis of past performance.

- When both systems are in buy modes, a net long position is indicated.

- When both are in sell modes, a net short position is given.

- When the two individual systems are in disagreement, a neutral position is recommended.

According to its developers, this dual structure attempts to limit the risk on any individual trade. However, the amount of risk allowed on any trade—that is, the amount of price movement needed before a liquidation or reversal signal is received—can vary, depending on the nature of the market price action.

The model deliberately does not use intraday stops because its developers felt that such orders increase the chances of being thrown out of good positions, and are vulnerable to greater slippage upon execution.[5] But because

---

[5]Slippage is the difference between the theoretical execution price and the actual transaction price.

of the risk inherent in assumptions discussed in the preceding sections, Prudential Securities recommends that FTTP signals be used to trade only portfolios rather than single markets.

The caution is appropriate. As I mentioned earlier in the chapter, simulated performance results have certain inherent limitations. Unlike an actual performance record, such results *rest on hypotheses*[6] and are forward oriented: Because the trades have not actually been executed, the projections may have under- or overcompensated for the effect, if any, of certain market factors, such as lack of liquidity.

Simulated trading programs are also designed with the benefit of hindsight. Such programs cannot ensure that any trade will or is likely to achieve profits or losses similar to those shown by the simulator; still, the experimental evidence presented can significantly assist the trader's hand.

Three alternative scenarios are being used by Prudential Securities as traders' and portfolio managers' assistants. The first is *swing (FTTP1)*, whose two component parts are based on patterns formed by market swings.[7] To diversify the approach being taken, one component system uses daily data; the second employs weekly data. As stated previously, concurrence in results advises *buy* or *sell*. Contradiction in predictions tends to indicate *hold*.

The second scenario is *pyramid (FTTP2)*, which generates signals when market conditions appear to offer an enhanced reward-risk environment. When such a condition is identified, the established procedure suggests doubling position size. Because of this feature, to keep risk within equivalent boundaries, more funds are required to trade FTTP2 than either FTTP1 or FTTP3.

The third scenario, *dual trend (FTTP3)*, employs two completely different systems to generate likely trend-following signals. Even if this approach is characterized by flexibility, the developers correctly advise that markets in the future could prove to be substantially different from markets witnessed during the survey period (1975 to 1989). This will affect results even though the survey period and range of markets tested were broad enough to include bear, bull, and sideways movements.

Another issue that becomes significant with computer-based trading has to do with the possibility that many traders following the same guidance system could adversely affect its overall profitability. This problem has become evident with limits, and it accelerated with program trading.

---

[6]A hypothesis is a *tentative* statement made to lead to the solution of a problem, but that requires testing and verification.

[7]A market swing is the price move from a relative low to a relative high or vice versa; its definition, however, depends on the number of days in the moving window used to identify relative highs and lows.

FUZZY ENGINEERING: A NEW GENERATION OF TOOLS

A simulator constructs an idealized real-world environment or process through algorithms. An expert system usually employs heuristics. The expert's knowledge is modeled using objects, values, and rules.

- *Objects* are described in terms of attributes, characteristics, and relation to other objects.

- *Values* for attributes of objects such as a given stock, bond, or commodity can be obtained from external sources including digital feeds, databases, and simulators.

- Most *rules* have been of the "IF . . . THEN . . . ELSE" form, describing how to reason about events or how to respond under certain conditions.

These rules can be prioritized, grouped together, scanned, and used when required in the execution of a certain program. This is what swing, pyramid, and dual trend do.

The number of rules required to reason about events is a function of the application being handled as well as of the desired degree of detail. The more modules we add to reflect such detail, the larger the expert system becomes. Typically, both the simulators and the expert systems are focused. A single system does not cover *all* treasury functions: rather, several constructs are developed— more precisely, one per domain.

Figure 7.3 shows, as an example, the division of treasury functions into five major classes. Each of them can and should be subdivided into more precise domains. An expert system will address itself to each subdomain; however, some modules may have components that are of interest to more than one implementation area.

Properly planned simulators and expert systems address another issue that escapes the attention of less refined systems: The human cerebrum consists of two hemispheres, left and right.

- The left hemisphere performs *analytical* functions and is in charge of logic, language, and calculation.

- The right hemisphere processes information intuitively and addresses *conceptual* issues.

Images, music and, other sensory information are processed by the right brain, in addition to emotion, as well as functions like imagination, creation, intuition, and macroscopic decisions.

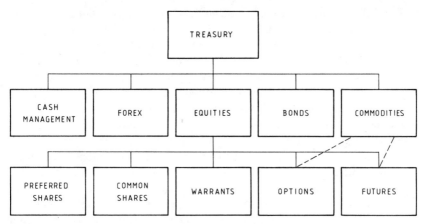

Figure 7.3 One of the leading financial institutions divides treasury function into five major classes.

Simulation treats primarily numerically oriented issues. Rule-based expert systems address logical functions. But neither can support *conceptual* capabilities, nor *imagination* and *intuition*. Long associated strictly with human response, these characteristics have been for the first time—in the very recent past—mapped into computers through *fuzzy engineering*. An example is fuzzy control functions.

The more traditional automatic control acts in accordance with well-established mathematical rules: It cannot execute intuitive control measures that are very easy for skilled people. For example, in a human-machine system, ordinary mathematics could represent the action of the left hemisphere, whereas the human operator contributes the conceptual ability that resides in the right hemisphere.

Fuzzy computer models play an intermediary role, translating language or interpreting meaning between mathematics and the conceptual contribution by human users. This intermediation is difficult, but there are already valid examples and fruitful applications of fuzzy logic.

One of the most imaginative projects to which fuzzy engineering has been applied concerns the conceptual processing necessary for *situational recognition* in a financial market environment. This has been done by:

- Analyzing the status of market conditions

- Examining prominent figures in the market

- Establishing interrelationships between prices, trade statistics, and other details

As I will demonstrate in the following section, results obtained in this area by the Laboratory of International Fuzzy Engineering (LIFE) of Yokohama, Japan enabled determination of a useful methodology. A system can be organized to reflect status of market conditions, details of situational indices for each status, each interrelationship, the information to be extracted from the news media, and representation of that information.

In a practical implementation in forex operations, a method of updating the situational model has been devised based on statistics and news data. This work is done online, accounting for the fact that rapid communication of recommendations and warnings in the trading environment is essential. Visualization has been given due attention, on the premise that information is more quickly understood when presented graphically.

As markets change, risk profiles alter, and opportunities arise, messages may not only need to be flashed on the screen, but also interpreted using fuzzy rules. At the same time, diagrams are best presented using animation.

To reason about the current state of the market and our organization's exposure, it is not only important to be able to input trades as soon as they are made, but also to reflect on changes in market sentiment immediately as they are detected. This requires computer assistance that can comprehend *qualitative* concepts, and therefore semantics, leading to the following constructs:

- *Fuzzy computer architectures,* where both fuzzy and conventional processors cooperate in multiuser and multitasking environments

- *Fuzzy software,* consisting of a language processing system capable of handling fuzzy data but also having an interface with currently existing languages

- *Fuzzy hardware,* including fuzzy chips capable of parallel processing large-scale, fairly complex fuzzy rules

Treasury and forex operations can greatly benefit from this three-level approach, but there are other applications domains that can do just as well—for instance, high-level automation that does not address itself to the usual automatic control chores, substituting physical labor, but executes complex jobs such as management or supervision requiring knowledge and the ability to make decisions.

As an example, one of the projects at LIFE is a fuzzy-neuro control system. In this project the neural network performs the functions of the left brain, and the fuzzy logic provides the integrative capabilities between neural network and human user—hence right brain tasks. The purpose of these efforts, which are quite recent, is to develop a new generation of information-processing systems whose function is analogous to human reasoning abilities. One of the important topics, for example, is image understanding. In most applications of pattern recognition, fuzzy theory is used as an alternative to probability theory, but a pattern can also be considered a source of *meaningful information*.

Taking the price pattern in the financial markets as an example, the challenge is to characterize *meaning* by fuzzy sets. This can open vast implementation horizons—from treasury and forex to any other domain of human activity that requires imagination, and not just skill.

SUPPORTING FOREX OPERATIONS THROUGH FUZZY ENGINEERING[8]

Designed and built by LIFE, FOREX is a fuzzy engineering system for predicting trends in foreign exchange. Not only does it take into account all relevant economic indicators, but it also *accepts news* found to have a substantial effect on forex markets. The FOREX construct:

- Uses qualitative information to predict exchange rate trends of yen against dollar

- Interprets and integrates information obtained from input numerical data and news, based on knowledge concerning economic mechanisms

This fuzzy system understands and manipulates political and economic conditions that surround the foreign exchange market, making predictions on future trends based on these conditions. Factors are expressed and manipulated using *possibility theory*, and predictions are made by employing the fuzzy integral.

The whole approach is characterized by a major departure from past practices, where mainly quantitative data was used for predictive purposes. This simplification downplayed the fact that factors regarding political choices and statements made by trade officials or government representatives can greatly influence exchange rates. Therefore, both policies or statements (known in Japan as *themes*) and quantitative information must be considered. Based on this premise, FOREX rests on three pillars:

---

[8]Based on the work of T. Yagyu, H. Yuize, M. Yoneda, and S. Fukami of LIFE.

1. Price indices, employment statistics, and official statements are inter-preted, and essential information is extracted.

If a consumer price index has been announced, the annual and monthly rate of increase is calculated and a determination made as to whether these are reasonable figures.

2. All possible consequences of the information input are considered, based on knowledge of economic mechanisms.

The results of these two steps are integrated, and future trends in prices are evaluated by calculating a price index. Interest rates and attitudes are considered both on a macroscopic scale and at an abstract level based on current conditions.

3. A prediction is made on market trends, based on the results obtained through qualitative and quantitative integration.

The system architecture of FOREX consists of a state recognition part, cor-responding to steps 1 and 2 as well as the integrative task (step 3). Subse-quently, a scenario evaluation generates predictions based on state recogni-tion results and macrostates represented in terms of the following elements:

- Current and future state of the market as expressed on a macroscopic and an abstract level

- The treatment of numerical data and news by a neural network

- A fuzzy engineering scenario builder

A layered approach has been chosen going from concrete input (numerical data) to more fuzzy news items, macrostates, and the scenario evaluation procedure. This is shown in Figure 7.4. Level 0 addresses itself to time-dependent numerical data—for instance, economic indicators from coun-tries such as Japan, the United States, and Germany, as well as stock prices and various interest rates. In all, there are roughly 90 items handled at this level.

The object of level 1 is to maintain results of screened and interpreted numerical data. Although items on level 1 generally correspond to those on level 0, there are more items on level 1 than on level 0, owing to the many ways of looking at the same piece of information. Some 160 items are handled at this level.

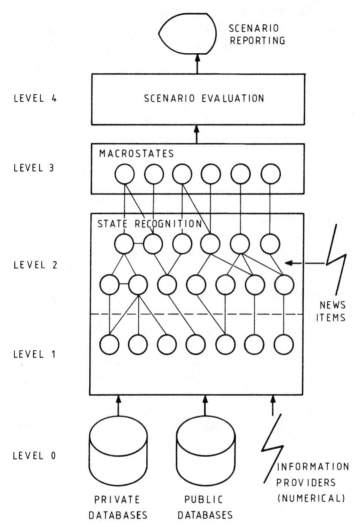

Figure 7.4   A neural network architecture for FOREX operations.

A number of issues are addressed in regard to each item when interpreting numerical data: What type information needs to be extracted? Is it possible that more than one type exists for any single datum? Which frame of reference should be used when interpreting this information? How should this frame of reference be chosen? How should evaluations based on fluctuating frames of reference be expressed?

The aim of level 2 is state recognition, including possible future trends. This is done taking into account state values on level 1, other state values on level 2, and information extracted from news input, also at level 2. Items on level 2 have been structured into a network to show relationships when states are updated. Structure reflects the fact that many state values can be determined by examining interrelationships. This level started with 120 items, but this number is expected to grow fast.

The jewel of FOREX is its handling of subjective news items. Under most current systems, news information is processed manually. By contrast, in FOREX news is first converted to conform to a normalized format before being input into the system—the value of each state variable being given by a possibility distribution over a defined range (for each corresponding state value).

The mission of level 3 is to incorporate macro-items obtained from the integration of two or more entries on level 2. Macroeconomic trends and indicators as well as metastates appear on level 3. There are 45 items at this level.

Level 4 focuses on scenario evaluation. This capitalizes on the work done at level 3, which includes items such as prices, employment trends, productivity, personal consumption, stock market trends, long-term and short-term interest rates, and the official stances of trade ministries. The last item is particularly weighted for three countries: Japan, America, and Germany.

As one might expect, the infrastructure of FOREX rests on state recognition. This is updated in terms of possible effects starting from state values that have been input. The difference between this and other solutions is that such state values are psychological qualities, not just physical quantities. The result is a solution much closer to the experts who work online in the financial market.

8
Technological Synergy

A deeper understanding of the mechanisms of communication and their place in financial organizations can contribute significantly to the exploitation of a financial market's potential. Techniques must be developed that add value to the known processes of client contact, enhancing not only the production of financial services but also their promotion and distribution.

From treasury to forex and securities, intelligent communications is the lifeblood of the financial business. It is now projected that the communications revolution of the 1990s will make the very large scale integration (VLSI) revolution look like child's play.

State-of-the-art implementation means the use of *photonics*, from imaging (optical disks) to communications (optical fibers). Value differentiation calls for the true automation of payments documents, a job which is still largely manual, and the development of human windows, making human-machine interfaces user friendly and agile.

We must look beyond today's needs to what will support our *future* competitiveness. Industrial supremacy by the end of this decade and well into the twenty-first century will rest on the ability to master both photonics and knowledge engineering because they will play a role comparable to that of VLSI devices and supercomputers today.

High-performance computation has a growing role in finance, from number-crunching data reduction to simulation and realtime processing of knowledge engineering constructs:

- Mapping financial instruments on a global basis

- Managing very large databases, on which we increasingly depend

159

- Evaluating patterns of opportunity and risk

- Providing for natural-language human-machine communication and automatic simultaneous translation

To exploit the global financial market that has been developed in treasury, forex, and securities we must *think in parallel*—hence the eventual generalization of parallel processing architectures. We must also be able to communicate around the globe without interruption, which explains the need for intelligent networks operating as fault-tolerant systems.

UNDERLYING REASONS FOR NEW DEPARTURES IN TECHNOLOGY

The coming years will see very efficient, specialist-oriented programming languages, matching a number of breakthroughs in robotics, from walking robots to artificial vision. But developing a product is one thing; employing it is another. The competent use of technological breakthroughs requires a great deal of *cultural change*—with emphasis on computer literacy and sophisticated decision support systems.

The growing technological content of financial decisions and transactions is necessary because, in both the private and the public sectors, organizations face a tougher world, a world in which they will be judged more harshly than before on their effectiveness and in which there are fewer protective hedges to shelter, particularly in finance. We could no doubt manage a client's portfolio (and our own) not through research and technology but by using our memory of past events. We should not, however, forget that portfolios stuffed with past memories soon gather dust—and so do financial transactions.

Today, competition hits harder organizations that cannot deliver—and that have to deliver through time changes in content and format. The deregulation of finance has altered the images we knew from the past, which means that financial and industrial companies that cannot *adapt* are going out of business.

Mathematical analysis is not a discipline used merely as an intellectual exercise. In finance, analytical techniques are instrumental in making searches efficient, helping to visualize rather obscure situations, and pointing to optimal solutions. Optimality will not happen by accident. It must be meticulously constructed. As every treasurer should know, success in managing the wealth with which he has been entrusted will not come as a matter of course.

Market changes oblige us to rebalance portfolios with short-, medium-, or longer-term planning horizons. When short-term planning horizons are used, this leads to tactical asset allocation (TAA), where positions are turned over within a day. In principle:

- Following the beta factor—that is, prevailing volatility—the risk of a security can be estimated from its historical price behavior, with such historical estimates forming the basis for future risk values.

- Alternatively, a mathematical model of security returns can be constructed using the statistical techniques of factor analysis and principal components analysis.

Such techniques require intimate knowledge of the ways in which and the extent to which markets are driven by dynamic forces. These techniques are typical of the new approaches to finance.

Old finance analyzed accounting rules and was rich with anecdotes. New finance is mathematically rigorous: Its theorems are proven true under well-tested conditions, and they are tested by econometric models.

Just as in science, we accept a financial theory only tentatively, until it is disproven. Theories that when proposed seemed heretical, such as the theory stating that arbitrage ensures that close financial substitutes fetch the same price, have become common in modern finance.

Some of the mathematically elaborated theories have turned into pillars of modern financial economics: The capital asset pricing model (CAPM) shows that two stocks that contribute the same amount of risk to a portfolio are, in effect, close substitutes, and they should therefore offer the same return. Quite similarly, the Black-Scholes option pricing model shows that an option on a stock—that is, the right to buy or sell for a given price at a given time—can be replicated by:

- Owning or borrowing a fraction of the stock

- Lending or borrowing money

The price of a genuine option in the options market must be equal to the price of this synthetic option, and these mathematically based findings have a significant effect on corporate finance.

But mathematical models and high-performance computers are not only used for processing purposes. Their role in *pre-processing* is just as vital. Input has to be screened in order to present only information that is vital to the treasurer, the forex professional, and the securities specialist (as discussed in Chapter 5). Through *post-processing*, the output, too, can be manipulated, structured, and visualized in the most comprehensive manner.

This can be done through intelligent charting and pattern recognition, for instance. Both are documented through practical examples in Chapter 9— but before this concept is discussed further, the concept of a human window has to be introduced.

FOCUSING ON HUMAN-MACHINE INTERFACES

The ability to provide agile human-machine interfaces, also known as human windows, has not advanced nearly as quickly as the art of processing information. This ability includes heuristic solutions for database search, which have just started being developed; presentation tools that are easy to learn and comprehensive; and the high-definition equipment on which presentation will take place.

The term *window* can be interpreted in either a narrow or a broad sense. In the narrower, a window is a rectangular section selecting a specific subarea from a presentation space. In the broader, a human window is endowed with expert systems support for simple, agile, friendly communication with the enduser.

Human windows are typically implemented on interactive screens. The clarity users can achieve on their computer monitors cannot be duplicated easily and economically on paper. High-quality printers are not interactive devices, and, per unit, they cost more than many desktop computers. In addition, there are no universal standards for printed copies; when it comes to the supported resolution, hard-copy devices are no match for video solutions.

Affordable laser printers can produce black-and-white images with resolution of about 300 pixels per inch (ppi). Options being explored include the addition of gray scales to existing 300 ppi monochrome printers and an increase in laser printer resolution from 300 pixels per inch to between 400 and 600 pixels per inch. But high resolution is not yet offered at an affordable price.

Much more can be done with interactive video displays. Although a larger display better fills the visual field, it will show no more detail if it uses the same number of pixels, which define the *resolution* of an image. Managerial and clerical workstation monitors consist of a million pixels (one megapixel) arranged in a 1,280 by 1,024 grid.

Many financial institutions comment that large screens are chosen because they provide better productivity. But better productivity by professionals also calls for the ability to display all business applications in a homogeneous manner, highlighting the position of each entity.

Charting (see also Chapter 9) has made a valuable contribution to this end. Plotting values against a time scale, a time series chart has often proved useful in identifying trends, problems, and opportunities. Another type of chart, the *radar chart*, helps communicate the strategic role of a group of controlled variables in a portfolio.

Figure 8.1 presents a radar chart from an application in auditing loan approvals. This and similar graphical presentations have been instrumental to looking at the health of the company as a whole—a dynamic graphics approach being part and parcel of the effort to provide better *visualization*.

A radar chart similar to the one in Figure 8.1 is fully applicable in the treasury and forex environments. Both Yamaichi Securities and Sanyo Securities are using it for visualization purposes. One of the goals is to achieve immediate response to market data in order to identify business opportunities.

Agile human windows with graphics support of the type discussed can also be instrumental in extending the life cycle of older applications. In

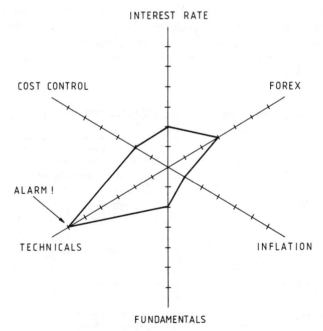

Figure 8.1   Use of radar chart in auditing loan approvals.

other words, they can serve the existing communications and computer environments, not only those newly developed. This point underlines the need for hybrid systems. We simply cannot afford to throw away current software investments, even if the programs they contain have aged. We must therefore integrate into the new systems what can be (or should be) salvaged from the old, as well as enrich the old programs with new tools.

Among the new modules to be developed, and quite certainly enriched with AI, are search and retrieval models for intelligent queries. As Table 8.1 explains, there has been a significant evolution in databases and the way we exploit them.

- The crisp database design and crisp query implementation characterized the DP/MIS environments of the 1970s, as well as decision support and information centers of the 1980s.

- By contrast, implementations done during the decade of the 1990s will increasingly feature databases and queries that are *vague* in terms of content, include soft information elements (resulting from simulations and projections), and call for searches that involve *uncertainty*.

In an *ad hoc* environment, where fuzzy queries will become commonplace, simplicity will be one of the key factors to successful implementation, and with it the ability to choose priorities. Developers should definitely account for the fact that the AI project to be chosen will have high visibility, and the projects themselves will have significant potential only if scope and domain are properly defined.

Table 8.1   Evolution of Human-Information Communication

Query	Database
Crisp[a]	Crisp and precise
↓	
Crisp	Crisp but imprecise (unknown, partial)
↓	
Crisp	Vague or stochastic
↓	
Vague	Precise
↓	
Vague	Vague

[a] *Crisp* means true or false—no shades of grey and no fuzzy concept.

Agility in developing human-machine communications is a relatively new requirement, never before available in computing. Practically all operations are memory-to-memory with the ability to actuate immediate operands, conditionalize, and multiply addressing nodes—prerequisites to workable solutions. Because the applications are new, lack of appropriate knowledge will inevitably lead to failure.

A nodal distribution of information elements managed through local processors and memory and flexibly rearranged as the program demands will permit efficient handling of problems involving uncertainty. This is precisely the solution required by nondeterministic problems, which accurately reflect real-life situations in the currency markets.

Distributed intelligence, a distributed memory system with pattern-matching capabilities and polyvalent search capabilities are required. Not surprisingly, these are features supported by computer technology of the new generation, which explains the interest in its implementation in forex operations.

OBTAINING BETTER RESULTS THROUGH PROTOTYPES

The concept of a *user-driven* rather than technology-driven design should be the cornerstone to all our efforts. By improving the analyst's and programmer's productivity an astonishing 500 percent to 1,000 percent, fourth- and fifth-generation languages make it feasible to map through *prototyping* the work we are doing, whether for visualization or for processing purposes.

A prototype is not a theoretical system. It is a working model that can be implemented on the machine for the environment for which it has been conceived. But it should be specific to the job, not a generality.

One of the major requirements is making the prototype specifications executable. That is why the basic philosophy of the specification language will be influencing prototyping procedures and eventually results. However, prototypes can tolerate incomplete functions and suboptimal times, no implementation details need be considered at prototyping level, and no primitive functions are required to be designed and coded in traditional programming languages. In contrast, prototype specifications must be easy to read and understand as well as to extend, modify, and reformat.

A windowing presentation is shown in Figure 8.2a. It can help the trader in determining which prospective deal is overpriced, priced right, or underpriced. Such presentation formats are not new, but they have often been based on guesswork. However, consider the following:

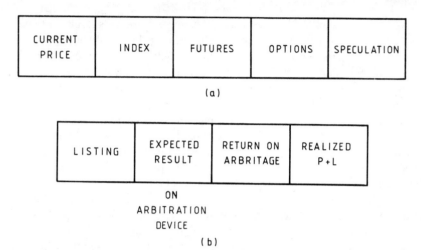

(a)

(b)

Figure 8.2 (a) Prototype of a windowing presentation; (b) format for arbitrage after prototyping.

- What the system designer thinks may not be exactly the same as what the dealer wants to see.
- Prototyping permits the dealer's wish rather than the designer's to prevail.

The dealer may, for example, want more information, or the same information presented in a different manner. Some dealers prefer graphical presentation with tables only on request, for clarification purposes or to give a quantitative input.

A prototype significantly helps in adjusting the presentation format and contents to the individual trader's wishes. As an example, Figure 8.2b shows the structure of an arbitrage screen after the dealer tinkered with the prototype to make it fit the way he wanted to receive the information. In other words, prototyping gives the enduser the feeling that he can rise to a position where he might really push through his own innovative approaches. Treasurers, forex traders, and other users fed with output screens incompatible with their needs are getting restless. Prototyping relieves such tensions.

Two of the primary reasons for the difficulty in successfully developing and evaluating new technological solutions are:

- The gap between what the enduser wants and what the analyst thinks the enduser wants or needs
- The fact that it takes a long time to develop a system through traditional approaches

Quite often in financial implementations, evaluations are complex because many system parameters may change dynamically. Prototyping methods can be applied to preevaluations, investigating design alternatives, performance, and reliability characteristics; the developer can also apply qualitative and quantitative measures to a certain construct.

Through prototyping, technology can be implemented in a modular (reusable) form in a computer-based environment. But a prototyping tool should be flexible and organized in a modular fashion to provide truly enhanced experimentation capability.

In a complex system project, for example, the user should be able to specify system configurations such as the number of nodes, network topology, number and location of processes and resources, and the interactions taking place between these processes and resources. Any technological system can be modeled as a set of clients and servers; each server provides a service to the clients of the system, and the client can request a service by sending a request message to the corresponding resource.

A consultation is the dialog between the system and the client, which results in some conclusion. The client is seeking the system's advice, recommendations, or direction for a particular problem. The system provides conclusions based on the knowledge in its rules and in the information in the distributed database associated with the consultation.

The client may be a treasurer seeking an analytical response to his query, or a salesperson taking new orders over the phone and requring the status of inventories or a project's advancement. Or, the client may be a bank officer creating a savings plan for a customer, or a personnel officer screening résumés.

A client is simply any individual in any field who uses the system for advice. Typically, the enduser is unaware of the content or structure of the knowledge bank, of the way databases are distributed, or of how workstations are networked. What concerns him is the proper presentation and accuracy of the end result. Therefore, whether the system is simple or complex, an integral part of the design should be the support of graphical enduser interfaces from the specification of requirements to experimentation on trading options, execution proper, and control over the execution of transactions.

A decision support system must be user friendly, online, and interactive; otherwise, the money spent on it is for naught. The point is that prototyping helps attain these goals, provided that we know how to exploit it as a useful tool.

PROVIDING FOR POLYVALENCE IN EXPERIMENTATION

Polyvalence in experimentation should capitalize on the fact that, even if large amounts of information are needed for processing and simulations, supercomputers make the necessary computer power available. Parallel processing has broken the barriers that in the past caused massive data problems.

Armed with knowledge of algorithms and heuristics, and with the appropriate computer power, a financial institution has at its disposal the means for factual decisions. Typically, a simulator may involve about 2,000 variables and 100 to 200 time periods.

New technology should be chosen over the old, not only because the dimensions of this problem can be impressive but also because the ability to investigate alternatives is essential. The interaction between elements of the balance sheet may change and must be steadily redefined. Assumptions regarding monetary policy, inflation, interest rates, and GNP forecasts must be experimented with and changed interactively.

Another basic requirement is that the system be easily updated with actual results for quick turnaround of alternative comparisons and evaluation of the confidence level in the existing forecast, or a revised one. All of these objectives must be accomplished in an environment in which management, technical specialists, and the expert system builders can communicate easily and directly.

One of the reasons why I have emphasized the analytical and the experimental approaches is that *profitability* is determined by how well we manage *risk* and *opportunities*. Typically, it is not lack of information that is a problem in financial management, but rather the efficient access to and meaningful study of that information.

Hence, in well-managed financial institutions and treasury departments, specialized tools and databases have been developed to perform a variety of analytical chores as new needs arise. Specialization should not bring fragmentation to internal analysis and planning processes; with proper linking it ensures reconciliation of reports and the ability to get critical information to decision makers through one agile interface that can integrate multiple systems.

The more advanced thinkers in treasury departments already work with these ideas in mind. One approach is to develop portfolio management *profiles*, and an arbitrage profile. Preparatory work starts with the construction of a database of historical performance of the balance sheet, financial income, and expense, as well as general costs, all by country of operations. The assembled information elements are organized to eliminate discontinuities of accounting classifications, product definitions, and booking errors and corrections.

The next step is to identify the significant items in the balance sheet that are expected to have unique statistical behavior. Using moving average, stepwise multiple linear regression, fuzzy sets, and other techniques, financial institutions and treasury departments can develop individual prediction algorithms and heuristics for each of these items.

After accounting for exchange rate fluctuations, models calculate mean balances as well as develop and validate financial income and expense information. They also include routines for forecasting personnel cost, fixed asset acquisition, and so on, integrating these elements and cross-checking historical results.

Some of the models currently in operation are still static, but they still present management with a verifiable historical system that can be enriched with financial forecasts and detailed documentation. For instance, *duration analysis* helps in obtaining a measure of *interest rate risk*. It is a relatively recent tool in asset and liability management, enhancing gap analysis by providing a current market value measure and taking future income into account.

By considering the timing and present values of all expected cash flows, duration analysis measures the sensitivity of balance sheet and income statement items to fluctuations in the interest rate: It shows the interest rate elasticity of the market values of assets and liabilities, thereby bringing to attention the extent to which a bank's net interest margin will change in an altered interest rate environment.

Such results are derived by expanding on the data and forecast assumptions used to look at gap. Experimenters measure the following:

- Interest rate exposure of the book value of net interest income

- Market value of equity

- Results according to different currency scenarios

- Market value of other balance sheet target accounts

Duration analysis also aids in determining an asset and liability mix capable of moving a given risk exposure to a more controllable level. Through simulation, profitability scenarios can be built using the current interest exposure, which is determined by gap evaluation and other measures.

Simulation can also be used to test the effectiveness of selected hedging strategies, as well as to examine correlated interest rate risk—for instance, loan prepayments or default risk that is not measured by either gap or duration approaches.

One of the most productive and most interesting areas of development associated with this work is the ability to elaborate a base of behavioral knowledge, thus producing alternate scenarios about the future as well as information regarding decisions or alternatives as the future unfolds. This requires heuristics, algorithms, and a database of exogenous variables for both history and forecasts.

Typically, information elements should include currencies, exchange rates, interest rates, savings rates, change in gross national product and gross domestic product, demographic data, and so on. The model should begin with the most obvious relationships, developing historical correlations to aid in future predictions, and then should use this knowledge to influence statistical prediction.

One of the necessary contributions is the development of a presentation technique that is easily understood and quickly leads to action. Such a dynamic system can help improve the quality of professional decisions because it reflects on accumulated experiences and permits investigation based on alternative assumptions.

RATE-SENSITIVE OPERATIONS

Although the term *arbitrage* is most often used in connection with trading activities, multinational and multidimensional business operations ensure that the underlying processes are applicable to spread management, gap evaluation, and duration analysis. Approaches to such activities can be either aggressive for profit-making reasons, or largely defensive for hedging.

For instance, high-performance institutions steadily watch the rate-sensitive portion of the balance sheet—which means practically all funding activities. These institutions usually begin with an analysis of the gap (dollar volume difference) between rate-sensitive assets and liabilities for a specified time. A bank's net interest margin performance is ultimately a function of volume, rate, and timing effects. Gap measurement helps analyze the volume component, and it is also the best starting point for evaluating exposure to interest rate changes. The challenge is to ingeniously blend the developing mathematical instruments with the financial products to which they address themselves, as well as the theory behind these products. For instance, *caps* and *collars* can be effectively used for optimization purposes.

- An interest rate *cap* is analytically the same as a strip of *put options*[1] with a uniform strike price represented by the cap rate.

---

[1]Chapter 10 contains more information on put and call options; see also D. N. Chorafas and H. Steinmann, "High Technology at UBS," Union Bank of Switzerland, Zurich, 1988, for an applications example on caps and collars.

- An interest rate *floor* is analytically equivalent to writing (shorting) a strip of *call options* with a uniform strike price represented by the floor rate.

- An interest rate *collar* corresponds to a combination of an interest rate cap with an interest rate floor, which in turn is equivalent to a series of bear spreads (long put and short call).

The value of a cap, collar, or floor program can be computed as the algebraic sum of its underlying option components. Because the component options are independent of each other, their values are additive. Here independence means that the exercise of one option in the strip does not have any implication for the exercise of the others.

For a practical example on interest rate caps, say that company ABC has taken out a $50 million bank loan for five years with an interest rate that is reset quarterly at 25 basis points over the current three-month LIBOR. The treasurer is concerned that the interest rate may rise and would like to obtain protection from rate rises over the next two years.

The plan behind this rate-sensitive operation is to limit its maximum rate to 9.0 percent for each reset period. How much does the company have to pay for this cap right to the bank? The answer requires the appropriate computation. Cap specifications and pricing factors include the following:

- *Underlying index:* 3-month LIBOR

- *Strike level:* 9.0 percent

- *Amount:* $50 million

- *Frequency:* quarterly

- Interest rate *volatility*

- *Cap rate* relating to current yield curves

Sensitivity analysis involves studying the change in cap price (premium) in relation to changes in other factors. Figure 8.3 presents three graphs emphasizing sensitivity to strike rate, term, and volatility. The price is computed as the sum of its underlying option components during the five-year period. The exercise of one option in the strip does not have any implications for the exercise of the others.

Caps and collars have a built-in advantage over *swaps* in a positive yield curve environment, and swaps lock in a high interest rate immediately. Operationally, however, a swap position can be synthesized by making a collar very narrow.

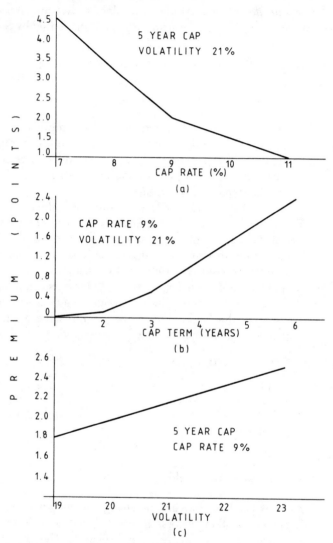

Figure 8.3 Option sensitivity analysis: sensitivity to (a) strike rate, (b) term, and (c) volatility.

Experimentation should focus on alternatives. After accounting for hedging costs, the effective interest rate cap level is always higher than the nominal cap as specified in a rate agreement. Caps and collars work best when the borrower believes that interest rates will decline but wants to insure against an adverse rate movement.

An analytical treatment is most valuable for both tax and accounting purposes. Typically, the up-front fee paid (received) is amortized over the life of the transaction, and any payments received (paid) under the cap-collar agreement are recognized on an accrual basis. If directly connected to a loan, the amount accrued is netted against interest expense; otherwise, it is recognized as other income (expense).

Caps and collars can be combined with gap measurement. The model must incorporate not only *maturity* or *repricing* information of asset and liability instruments presently on the books, but also projections for future time periods. This calls for both dynamic and static gap references but also for a range of other information elements to be used in experimentation.

Net interest margin is affected not only by past, current, and prospective rate changes for instruments already on the books, but also by rate changes for assets and liabilities that will be added in the future such as loans to be taken that are subject to caps and collars. Alert bank management measures both existing and projected gaps, and does so frequently to provide the basic information for a matching strategy, which can be instrumental in controlling risk.

FUNDING LOANS THROUGH ALTERNATIVE MEDIA

From a lending institution's viewpoint, sub-prime loans ought to be funded with overnight funds, whereas long-term assets (over one year) would be better funded through long-term liabilities such as demand deposits and certificates of deposit (CDs). A *deposit* made to the bank is regarded by the bank as money borrowed from a customer against interest from one day to five years, with either fixed or changeable terms.

A *certificate of deposit* is a negotiable paper issed by a bank. In a certificate of deposit *split*, the original face amount of the CD is split in several certificates with the same total amount. This presents a basis for experimentation and optimization.

To provide themselves with better funding options for matching purposes, alert treasury management and high-performance financial institutions are:

- Using more sophisticated techniques for analyzing and segmenting their market activity

- Experimenting on loans and their funding through alternative media

- Developing methods to effectively design, tailor, and price new financial products

Part of this approach is instituting asset funding strategies (including off–balance sheet options) such as the creation and sale of *bankers acceptances* for customer financing, and guarantees on government-backed mortgages such as Ginnie Maes. Bankers acceptances are marketable obligations of a bank arising from the financing of commercial transactions.

Generally, an acceptance is a time draft drawn on a bank by an importer or exporter to pay for specific merchandise. When the bank *accepts* the draft, it becomes obligated to pay the amount of the draft at its maturity. This should not be confused with *commercial paper*, which is unsecured promissory notes issued by corporations on a discount basis that have an original maturity of six months or less.

With the variety of instruments that have become available, computer-based asset-liability management models are genuinely indispensable for planning purposes. Static and dynamic gap analysis represented through interactive reports and reflecting interest rate risk exposure, for example, can lead to more focused decisions. Models make it feasible to include variations that are relatively unanticipated and uncontrollable because of rate or volume changes and deliberate mismatches, including those by individual business units within the bank.

Another example where experimentation can be quite profitable is *rollover schedules*. They show the complex interplay of asset or liability run-offs and run-ons, including the following:

- Maturity distributions of run-offs and new volumes

- Interest rates on maturing balances

- Rates available for reinvestment of assets or repurchase of liabilities (or both)

- Possible rate differentials between maturing rates and new rates

Computer-based net interest margin analysis reports assess the impact of variances on net interest margin. They offer input to management for developing appropriate contingency plans, and can be easily tapped through visualization.

A *performance profile* helps illustrate how the effective interest cost of a borrower varies with changes in the market interest rate. It should incorporate hedging costs into the analysis, and it can be used to compare the effectiveness of various hedging instruments. A performance profile with comparison of alternative hedges is shown in Figure 8.4.

Matched-funding–balance sheet reporting allows users to analyze the balance sheet in terms of assumptions about how certain liabilities are being

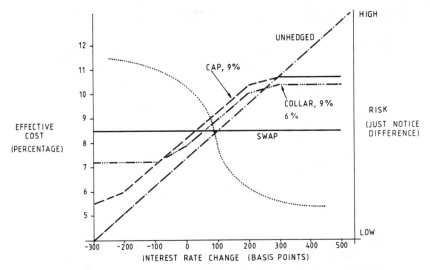

Figure 8.4   Performance profile: comparison of alternate hedges.

used to fund specified assets as well as their respective costs, yields, and spreads. Interactive reporting should reflect the way in which the bank actually and explicitly tries to fund assets, and discover ways of evaluating mismatches that have developed.

Other interactively accessible mathematical models should evaluate liquidity risk in such a way as to include off–balance sheet factors and changes in liquidity at various future times and to present cash flow analyses and loan commitment dynamics because the latter affect future loan volumes and liquidity within the asset-liability planning system.

Based on heuristic and algorithmic models that are processed by super-computers, the management of a financial institution (and of the treasury function) provides itself with a means to do swap analysis as well as help in arbitrage; finds assistance in tax planning; and searches for linkages with noninterest income and expense information. Financial futures hedging and experimentation on various complex factors is essential, as uncontrollable variables can invalidate even the soundest planning projections.

Computer-based experimentation can pinpoint failures and, from there, lead to renegotiation of loans in a down market or disintermediation effects on interest-sensitive liabilities. Such analysis typically takes into account reverse requirements and uncollected deposits in producing balance sheet projections. It considers volatility, interest rate trends and the balance management that wishes to keep between assets and liabilities.

EXPERT SYSTEMS FOR AUDITING FOREX OPERATIONS

In financial services, well-timed audits are crucial. Auditable operations deal with elements of risk, which must be measured and ranked by relative importance. Auditors, whose responsibilities include advising management on how well business is controlled, are assigned to typically report on the highest-risk activities.

Within this context, the need for auditing foreign exchange transactions is undeniable. Accuracy is of growing importance, owing to the increasing volume and volatility of the foreign exchange markets. But recognizing and identifying *patterns* of irregular transactions presents a difficult problem, because trades comprising an irregular pattern often occur in large numbers that extend over considerable periods of time. Besides, any individual trade may not appear to be irregular at all.

In order to identify irregularities it is necessary to take a group of trades and analyze them along many factors to create a pattern that flushes out abnormalities, which can cost a bank large amounts of money. The challenge is to identify these patterns, keeping track of thousands of minute details— something that human controllers have trouble doing unassisted.

Just because classical DP is of no help in this case, many financial institutions persist in using basically manual auditing procedures, even if the latter involves time-consuming approaches in recording all trades. Typically, computer printouts consolidate three months of transactions with such largely manual audits done quarterly, but not as effectively.

To remedy this situation, Chemical Banking turned to expert systems. The decision to proceed with the development of the *foreign exchange auditing assistant* (FXAA) was made after management analyzed the constraints that would affect the project's implementation. These included the following:

- The need to significantly automate existing auditing operations

- Dynamic approaches applied to online evaluation of transaction data

- Provisions for a friendly human interface, along the lines examined earlier in this chapter

Visualization was the chosen alternative, though FXAA offers the user a choice of two modes: an on-screen interactive process or hard copy. The visualized version displays each day's foreign exchange transactions, which are analytically evaluated, each on its own merits; elaborated in order to flush out possible patterns; and plotted against average and closing prices computed online by the system. Off-market trades are clearly indicated.

The user selects individual transactions and displays details of them on the lower portion of the screen. These details include an automatically generated explanation of why the transaction was considered off-market—whether it was a retail trade, part of a swap, or a passthrough.

This approach permits auditors to search for and identify off-market activity patterns, selectively adding suspect transactions to a list of other data that are saved for later examination. The expert system also analyzes and interprets trade information and recommends items for further research.

After FXAA was deployed at a pilot stage, it was tested during a live audit, comparing results by human auditors to the expert system's output. In addition, automated audit results were tested against historical data by contrasting previous manual audits to FXAA-generated audits. Measurement criteria included the following:

- Sample sizes

- Pattern identification

- Accuracy of results

- Productivity improvement

- User acceptance

These tests indicated that not only did FXAA meet the objective of increasing audit coverage, but also expanded the scope of the audit by a factor of 30. Moreover, the system investigated and reported on patterns that human auditors had previously been unable to detect.

In its auditing practice, FXAA quickly identifies potentially irregular transactions and separates them from acceptable ones—that is, those that meet the auditing criteria. Its operation permits the human auditors to focus on the tougher cases instead of searching the raw data for transactions to audit.

At the same time, management control of the audit process was strengthened as the analytical process itself became automated. FXAA has also increased the frequency of auditing. It generates monthly exception reports, which provide invaluable guidance to the auditors, helping them decide when the next formal audit will take place.

This is an excellent example of an expert system that helps *control risk*. It performs the following functions:

- It captures the expertise of the people who monitor the correctness of foreign exchange transactions, from dollars to each of the other major currencies of the world.

- It assists the human auditors in performing their work, porting their attention to possible irregularities.

- FXAA extends Chemical Banking's surveillance of transactions from spot checking to more complete scrutiny, thereby sharpening the auditing process.

Another implementation of expert systems for auditing can be found at The Equitable Insurance Company. Its internal audit department is professionally staffed to cover most of the important elements of the business over a three-year period. However, some elements need to be audited sooner or more frequently than others.

One of the challenges management faces is that these higher-risk operations must be sampled faster, despite the fact that the available internal auditing resources are spread among several hundred auditable operations. If the auditors underestimate a unit's current nonaudit risk position, potentially serious risk control, compliance, or financial issues may go unreported to management. Heuristic solutions were chosen because traditional algorithmic techniques had proven unsatisfactory. The projected system's general design was defined, and a reasonable payback has been reached. Because of the quickly shifting risk factors and the subjective nature of variables involved in determining priority ranking, consistent and complete assessments of risk demand a uniform but dynamic decision-making process. This explains the need to formalize methods and to develop a better, more consistent automated system that can perform the following tasks:

1. Uniformly apply the risk assessment methodology

2. Quickly and accurately identify the units for high-priority audits

3. Automatically generate the documentation for audit ranking and scheduling priorities

It was dissatisfaction with the results of traditional software approaches that brought The Equitable to expert systems in auditing and risk management. A study conducted by its technology research and development group concluded that the assessment process was *logical* rather than *computational* in nature. This application has all the attributes of good knowledge engineering.

9
From Charting
to Pattern Recognition

Chartism is not a new business. Its basic principle is that a graph such as a time series—for instance, a share's price—is not merely a random drawing but gives insight into the psychology of investors trading in the market by reflecting the ups and downs in prices as a function of time.

Chartists believe that conclusions about future price movements can be drawn from price patterns alone, without necessarily making research into the fundamentals of the economy or the financial and business prospects of a particular company. Nonchartists do not subscribe to this argument, but neither can refute that the intelligent analysis of charts provides a good basis for forecasting.

One of the patterns often used with charts is the *support level.* It is observed that, over a period of weeks or months, the price of a particular share may repeatedly rebound upward whenever it drops to a certain price level. From this it is deduced that there is a body of investors who are prepared to buy at that support level.

Through the study of a chart, the prediction can be made that, for instance, *If* price rebounds start becoming successively weaker, *Then* there is a danger of the share breaching the support level and falling considerably before fresh support arrives on the scene. This works in two ways: There is an *upper* support level that is usually difficult to break, and a *lower* support level of the type mentioned in the preceding example.

The concept of *trend* leads to another pattern and is fundamental to technical analysis. Predictions can be assisted by identifying the current trend, which also can give early warning of a change in the direction prices

179

are moving. Market prices do not generally move in straight lines, but rather in a series of wavelike movements with peaks and troughs. The underlying trend can be upward, downward, or sideways, thus forming a pattern that can tell a great deal about the psychology of the market and of the dealers.

Experienced market operators look for patterns. However, with the exception of simple, visible trends, finding these patterns requires a massive number of calculations, access to public databases, and a set of rules to help define a pattern by induction, eventually leading to expert interpretation of results. This is precisely how an artificial intelligence construct operates. In AI, *pattern recognition* refers to the ability of a human-devised system to recognize and *classify* patterns. Such a construct typically accepts fits, trends, and correlations as input and finds an associated output that itself is a pattern.

By contrast, *pattern reconstruction* refers to the ability of a system to reconstruct an incomplete pattern. Starting with such an incomplete pattern, an AI construct can insert missing information by retrieving the best complete pattern associated with the input, through the use of templates, for instance.

Second-generation expert systems, such as neural networks, can be trained to identify and complete partial schemata. They can also distinguish incomplete and fuzzy trading patterns, restructuring them by using information from a distributed database and a market data stream steadily received from information providers.

CONTRIBUTIONS FROM COGNITIVE SCIENCE

Whether formal or informal, knowledge is always based on the contemplation of something in accordance with a principle. In a scientific sense, this process becomes formalized into a *method*—that is, an established procedure whereby data flowing within a problem area, such as foreign exchange rates, is related to a principle that helps to explain or at least to represent such data in a comprehensive form.

As I said in the introduction to this chapter, this is practically what we do when we arrange stock prices in a time series. As Figure 9.1 demonstrates, the way we draw the time series reflects the method that we use for a representation, aiming at a comprehensive picture and adding an interpretation of trends and changes that must be watched, as they may reveal a pattern and its underlying psychographic characteristics.

Perception and the subsequent cognition are the fundamental steps in receiving a stimulus and interpreting it, and in gaining insight on possible orientation. Some animals have a terrific sense of orientation:

Figure 9.1 Price graph for London gold.

- Bees orient themselves towards their hive, they distinguish time, and they have the capability to discriminate among different flowers.

- Elks and goats eat different types of grass, but both avoid poisonous mushrooms.

- Humans, monkeys, and dolphins have developed social constructs that, to a significant extent, are based on patterns.

Patterns in the mind create coherence by recognizing schemes and developing frames of reference, leading to concept. The identification and recognition of patterns is guided by *metapatterns*, just as metaknowledge guides taxonomy and classification.

Intuition and memory often depend on pattern, and so do our actions. Said Judith Polgar, "It was a home variant. . . . I caught a view of the board and the mate pattern was familiar."[1]

How many patterns do we have in our mind? We do not really have even an approximate answer to this question, but a wild guess is 2,000 to 50,000, the lower figure corresponding to the number of Chinese ideograms. Not

[1]Judith Polgar won a women's chess tournament at age 13 in 1988 in 17 moves after sacrificing the queen and a knight.

only are we unsure about the number of patterns that exist in the human mind, but neither do we know whether these are prewired, programmed in a framelike manner, inherited, or ad hoc.

Some cognitive psychologists believe that pattern development may be a realtime acquisition process, but no one really knows how these patterns become fixed in the mind or for how long. All we know is that the process varies from person to person, and that training makes the recognition of patterns both easier and more effective.

Cognitive psychologists also believe that patterns can be both an asset and a liability for a person. This is deduced from the fact that patterns are the origin of animal behavior, and that fixed patterns have often led to fixations, ossification, and retrogression. We must therefore be very careful with the patterns we develop, store, retrieve, and manage.

Managing a pattern-oriented process is no easy task, since we do not really know how distributed and how dynamic these patterns are, or what truly makes them dynamic. But we do know of their contributions. In *vision,* a pattern depicts motion, gets more comprehensive through color, and allows perception of detail such as edge detection. In *memorization,* a pattern makes it possible to remember faces, initials, names, and special abilities of certain clients or professions.

Familiar patterns are easier to explain and comprehend. But sometimes familiarity may lead to misconception because something goes wrong in the recognition of a given pattern and its association with known schemes in terms of analogical reasoning. It is therefore often wise to base decisions on a dual approach that rests not only on pattern presentation but also on some key analytical factors against which to gauge the feedback. This should be done in a way that is familiar to the user; he can thus associate visualization and analytics fairly easily.

THINKING IN TERMS OF PATTERNS

There are reasons to believe that the animal brain was developed *by* and *for* patterns—from their conception to their interpretation and administration. The dynamics of looking around a pattern for interpretative reasons is a pattern in itself.

- Is there a core of pattern methods?
- If so, where does it lie?
- What might these pattern methods be?
- What are their advantages and their limitations?

These are very practical questions, to be asked in a variety of cases where we need not only to understand market information *better* and *faster* but also to exploit the resources we have available. This statement is based on an extensive research project conducted from January to May 1991 in the United States, England, and Japan, involving a total of 70 leading organizations.

Each of the financial institutions in this study considers its database *a corporate resource*. The majority believed that the current exploitation of databases is not commensurate with *investments* made in them and with *potential benefits*. The most forward-looking banks have engaged in a process of *database mining* to gain advantage of the wealth of information in their databases.

Database mining is the exploitation of financial databases through algorithms and heuristics; it can reveal *patterns* in the following categories of information:

- Customer preferences for financial services

- Evolving market trends

- Customer profitability and costs

- Risks in customer-oriented operations

This pattern recognition is both the result of and the impetus behind the recent reorganization taking place in the financial industry toward *customer-based* solutions, which contrasts with the accounting-oriented approaches that prevailed in the past.

Competent customer handling, timely response to changing market trends, and early recognitions of new product potential require pattern recognition capabilities. This is closely related to the logical classification work discussed in Chapter 5.

Our ability to recognize patterns seems to be largely confined to a *scalar* view, but the full power of patterns shows itself in a multidimensional *vector* space within an expanding universe. The transition from a scalar to a vector space is still an elusive subject, difficult to discuss because it is difficult to define.

But we do have some theories in other areas of pattern treatment. Within a well-understood line of reasoning, the pattern of the domain expert is based on the following:

- *Syndromes*, that is, events, items, and concepts that run together

- *Symptoms*, the observable phenomena associated with case descriptions

- *Standards,* which permit application of professional metrics
- *Processing algorithms* such as clustering, taxonomy, and analysis, as well as heuristics

All these contribute to a professional person's emerging pattern in regard to a given event or situation. His or her self-developed methodology includes values, viewpoints, contextual meaning, groupings, restructuring modifications, and hypermedia solutions.

To effectively work with patterns, we have to *reason by analogy.* There are structural and symbol-oriented analogues, as well as constellations of events we treat through analogical reasoning. In fact, there is a hierarchy of analogues, for instance, in vision. Figure 9.2 presents an example of metalayers.

Cognitive scientists usually discriminate among different levels of vision:

- Low-level vision involves edge detection and similar elementary operations, focusing on linear metrics.

- A slightly higher level allows one to proceed with cognition of objects.

- The next higher level is morphological analysis: building higher-complexity patterns from lower ones, and analyzing and composing visual information.

Prototyping (discussed in Chapter 8) also works through analogical reasoning. It is an application of our inclination to proceed through pattern structuring and pattern recognition. The building of models is, in fact, synonymous with the development of analogies, representations by words, situational logic, and mathematical expressions.

Hypermedia approaches are also an effort to effectively explore the power of pattern recognition and object-oriented systems. A hypermedia solution has information stored in a network of nodes interconnected by links, with the whole creating a pattern:

- The nodes contain different information structures such as text, data, graphs, images, voice, or other objects.

- The links represent relationships between the nodes, thus contributing to system structure.

Such structure can be subsequently used as a navigational aid or browser. It underpins a query language and is also a visualization tool. The navigational characteristics allow the user to browse through the hypermedia space by presenting him with a pattern.

HIGH LEVEL	RECOGNITION OF A PATTERN OF A WHOLE PICTURE
UPPER MEDIUM LEVEL	ATTEMPT TO IDENTIFY COMPLETE IMAGES OF SUBROUTINES
MEDIUM LEVEL	MORPHOLOGICAL ANALYSIS
LOWER MEDIUM LEVEL	STRUCTURAL ANALOGY
LOW LEVEL	LOOKING FOR EDGES AND DISTINCT SIGNS

Figure 9.2 Levels of vision and the contribution of analogical reasoning.

Machine learning mechanisms, too, are pattern oriented; more precisely, they are based 90 percent on pattern and 10 percent on reason. And as Dr. Tibor Vamos has commented, a similar mix exists in humans: "Thinking is what we do when the pattern recognition fails."

USING FUZZY LOGIC FOR PATTERN RECOGNITION[2]

Today most of the work done on pattern recognition deals with objects that are considered to have some standard pattern. But the size and shape of natural objects (such as plants and animals) vary tremendously and are not standardized. The same can be said of a number of patterns resulting from movements in the financial market.

---

[2] It is not the goal of this text to discuss fuzzy logic. For a discussion of the theoretical background, the reader may wish to refer to D. N. Chorafas, *Knowledge Engineering* (New York: Van Nostrand Reinhold, 1990).

Because pattern recognition in the financial markets is a new branch of science and experience with it is still limited, we are well advised to learn from other tools and methods after adapting them in finance. Dr. T. Terano, S. Masui, S. Kono, and K. Yamamoto have studied pattern recognition associated with crops that have different sizes and shapes.[3]

Dr. Terano and his colleagues represented the cropped features by means of natural language and processed their patterns with fuzzy logic. This approach rests on search trees, and the researchers maintain that once the hierarchical structure of feature items (in a search tree) is known, irregular shapes can be efficiently recognized.

By analogy to financial exchange rate or stock price movements, the recognition of crops makes an interesting study. Like time series of price changes, pattern recognition through fuzzy engineering capitalizes on the fact that no two patterns of size, shape, location, and direction are the same. However, two problems must be solved:

1. Finding a characteristic unique to a crop (or price level)

2. Representing this characteristic in a form suitable for machine cognition

Professor Terano and his co-researchers applied principal component analysis (PCA) to the first issue, and fuzzy set theory to the second. In the study of this problem in cognition, they used natural language as the mediator of information, conveniently representing the characters qualitatively and making it feasible to process the information through fuzzy logic.

As a first step, the local properties of the contour of a crop were detected and classified into three categories: straight, curve, and angle. Then, the general character of the contour was calculated from the sequences of the local properties. Here, too, the researchers used fuzzy set theory. During this work, the physical attributes of crops (size, shape, and so on) were kept qualitatively in frame-type knowledge representation.

To recognize an unknown crop, the researchers utilized a hierarchical structure of attributes. This was composed by examining human behaviors through PCA—a process that is easily applicable in the study of financial price movements. To detect the contour of a crop and its specific character, a two-dimensional shape of the crop was projected by camera. This contour was refined using a digital filter and an extension-constriction approach before processing the information for cognition purposes.

---

[3]This information was obtained from a personal meeting with Dr. Terano at Hosei University, Kajino-cho, Konganei, Tokyo, Japan.

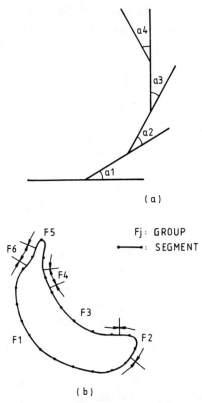

Figure 9.3   Pattern classification: (a) angle between two segments; (b) grouping of segments.

The whole contour was *divided* into several sections where the local character was almost the same. It was then *classified* into three categories: straight line, curved line (convex or concave), and angle (acute or obtuse).

In order to proceed with classification, the researchers choose several points on the contour at regular intervals, calculating all the angles a_i between two neighboring segments, as shown in Figure 9.3a. These two segments are put together in a group (section) F_j if the value of

$$| g(a_i) - g(a_{i-1}) |$$

is less than 10 degrees. For the purpose of evaluating the similarity of segments, $g(a_i)$ is defined as follows:

$$g(a_i) = \begin{cases} 5 & \text{for } a_i < 5 \text{ degrees} \\ a_i & \text{for } 5 \leq a_i \leq 35 \text{ degrees} \\ 35 & \text{for } 35 \leq a_i \text{ degrees} \end{cases}$$

Figure 9.3 gives an example of sectioning. Each section has been characterized *qualitatively*, allocating a fuzzy member F to a section whose peak corresponds to the mean value of a_i and the length of the base is equal to two times the maximum deviation of a_i.

Table 9.1 shows the degree of matching in each section of Figure 9.3b. The plus and minus signs in this table represent *convexity* and *concavity*, respectively.

Comparing F with the fuzzy expressions of straight-line B1, curve B2, and angle B3 (as shown in Figure 9.4), Dr. Terano obtained the local characters of each section. The degree of matching $N(A \mid B)$ is the necessity function of "A, given B."[4]

In examining the general character of a contour, the researchers observed that other factors can also be obtained from the study of an area, length, width, aspect ratio, number of angles, and other observable characteristics. The consideration of these factors, together with the sequence of local characteristics shown in Table 9.1, permitted them to define the shape of an object to a significant extent.

The lesson to be learned from the study conducted by Dr. Terano and his co-researchers is that patterns that so far seem to have defied dual qualitative and quantitative expression are amenable to perception and cognition through machine intelligence. This finding is of significant impact in terms of recognizing patterns in financial markets.

Table 9.1   Local Character of Contour

Group	Group Length	Straight	Curve	Angle
F_1	9	0	0.71	0
F_2	2	0	0	1.0
F_3	4	0	−0.79	0
F_4	1	0.43	0.02	0
F_5	3	0	0	0.78
F_6	1	0	−0.55	0

[4]Because this is not a book on fuzzy sets, explaining $N(A \mid B)$ is not appropriate at this point. See Dubois and Prade, *Theories des Possibilités* (Paris: Masson, 1988) and D. N. Chorafas, *Statistical Processes and Reliability Engineering* (Princeton, NJ: Van Nostrand, 1960).

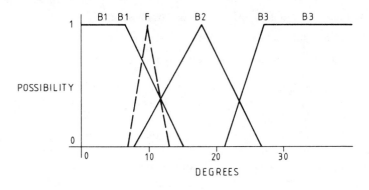

F: CHARACTER OF SEGMENT
B1: STRAIGHT LINE
B2: CURVED LINE
B3: ANGLED LINE

Figure 9.4   Identification of a segment through fuzzy engineering.

ANALOGICAL REASONING AND FUZZY ENGINEERING

As mentioned earlier in the chapter, in order to effectively work with patterns we have to reason by analogy. I have also discussed a hierarchy of analogues, which can be presented in the form of metalayers (with an example given in Figure 9.2) and stated that the best way to proceed is through prototyping—which itself is an analogue of the real world. Prototypes can be *physical* or *logical*.

• Physical prototypes are scale models like those used to study water dams and to perform wind tunnel tests.

• Logical prototypes are mathematical programs run on computers, that is, digital simulators.

When we deal with physical models, we often find it convenient to calculate the similarity of a contour through some geometrical figure, and to do so directly. If our prototype is conceptual, then the fuzzy matching technique can be used. For example, in the agricultural pattern recognition project, Terano et al. expressed a circle a priori using the following characteristics:

• The aspect ratio is almost 1.

• Percentage of curved section is about 100.

- Number of angles is either zero or larger than six.
- Percentage of convexity[5] is almost 100.
- Percentage of concavity[6] is about zero.

Subsequently, a section was described through the fuzzy sets in Figure 9.4, and a circle has been represented by the degrees of matching with fuzzy sets shown in Figure 9.5.

Other geometrical figures such as squares, triangles, bars, and ellipses can be defined in a similar manner. In all these cases, the pattern recognition of a given object is performed by comparing the local characteristics and other defined factors with those of standard geometrical figures.

Borrowed from *linear programming*, the minimax method can be successfully applied to such calculations. Table 9.2 presents the degree of matching of an angle between two segments of a banana shape (as it has been shown in Figure 9.3), with some standard figures that share similarities.

To establish a search tree structure and associated knowledge representation, Dr. Terano and his co-workers capitalized on the fact that there are many attributes by which the shape of crops can be characterized—for instance, size, shape, surface, hardness, color. Only size and shape are used in the present example, and, in any case, size and shape are the major items for the recognition of a pattern, as well as the most applicable in studying financial trends.

To make the process of pattern recognition effective, the critical items have been arranged hierarchically. Because the judgment of similarity of shape is a complex problem, the researchers studied the human sense through PCA, with a sample of people asked to evaluate the similarity of two silhouettes of crops. After that, the researchers made a similarity matrix regarding all candidate objects.

The researchers also calculated the loading factors from a similarity matrix. By interpreting these factors they identified the meaning of principal components:

- The first corresponds to the *aspect ratio*.
- The second represents the *angularity*.
- The third is *roundness*.
- The fourth is *convexity*.

---

[5] *Convexity* is the quality of being convex, being a surface that curves outward like a spere.

[6] *Concavity* reflects a concave condition, hollow and curved like a section of the inside of a sphere.

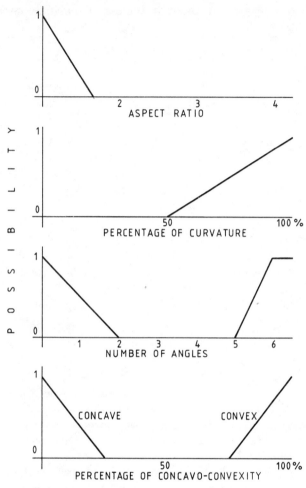

Figure 9.5   Fuzzy characteristics.

The contribution factors of other components were found to be so small that they could be neglected, but to improve accuracy the researchers adopted *unevenness* as a fifth factor. From the overall result they decided the order of sub-items composing a search tree.

During the successive phases of this research, the characteristics of each crop were collected in a knowledge bank, with the properties linguistically described in frames. Table 9.3 presents an example of this knowledge related to the shape of a banana.

Table 9.2 Matching of Banana with Standard Figures (Percentage Similarity)

	Factors				
Standard Figure	Aspect Ratio	Roundness	Angularity	Concavo-Convexity	Possible Final Judgment
Bar	0.65				0.65
Circle	0	0.50	0.50	0	0
Ellipse	0	0.50	1.00	0	0
Triangle	0.50	0.01	0.33	0	0
Quadrangle	0.50	0.14	0	0	0
Bow		1.00		0.78	0.78

Notice that this fairly detailed example on methodology is directly applicable in finance. Its sequential, orderly steps help demonstrate how:

- Analogical reasoning helps in defining the components of a cognition problem.

- Fuzzy engineering presents the mathematical tools needed for representation reasons.

When the contours of a given object or shape have been identified, the knowledge bank of the expert system is examined according to the established search tree. In the case of the Hosei University research, crops were divided into two classes at each branch point of the tree, according to the degrees of matching. The threshold was chosen at 0.3.

This technique is applicable to many other fields where the recognition of entities of nonstandard shapes is required. As the previous example and similar projects help demonstrate, the foundation of a process of pattern recognition regarding nonstandard shapes should be *taxonomical*, with *fuzzy set theory* making a significant contribution.

This is the best approach to follow in the analysis of complex patterns in the financial markets, though better known techniques in chart analysis may well be used with simpler charts based on time series, as we will see in the next section.

Generally, in the case of pattern search through taxonomical analysis we take a reference case as input, creating classification rules and testing new cases to these rules. This requires both classification skills and rule induction; Quinlan's system provides the latter.

Table 9.3 Knowledge about the Shape of a Banana

Size:	*Middle*
	Area: middle
	Length: middle
Macro-shape:	*Bar and Bow*
	Aspect Ratio: big
	Angularity: two angles
	Roundness: about 80%
	Concave: about 30%
	Convex: about 70%
Unevenness:	*Smooth*

Quinlan's Inferno is a system that deals with numerically quantified rules, using upper and lower probabilities to derive inference patterns. Quinlan's system works by taking database contents (values) and turning them into a decision tree (set of rules) along the conceptual lines of symptoms to diagnosis, which translates to market features predicting market movement. It essentially attempts to figure out which attributes are best in terms of attribute-outcome pairs. It does so by creating a matrix, or tree-and-leaves structure, sorting attributes all the way to outcome. It then backs up to rate the attributes.

The result of this approach is an efficient decision tree, applicable to the example of the Hosei University research project, and to similar cases with financial patterns. As a classification system, Quinlan's also has weighting factors, with each selected path defined as a weight and a rule.

In America, BBN and Thinking Machines, among other organizations, are working with this approach for the exploitation of different databases associated with real life projects, and they seem to have obtained good results. Quinlan's approach fits halfway between a purely rule-based construct and the more sophisticated memory-based reasoning (MBR).[7]

Because the financial markets are dynamic, we need solutions that permit understanding of patterns in realtime as well as prediction of possible patterns. This would make it feasible to obtain documented decisions immediately, allowing a company to gain a competitive edge over those who take longer to find these solutions.

---

[7]For a definition of MBR, see D. N. Chorafas and H. Steinmann, *Supercomputers* (New York: McGraw-Hill, 1990).

Without a doubt, every method has possibilities as well as limitations. Unlike the case of production rules in AI, for example, Quinlan's system cannot explain or justify the outcome. In addition, to work efficiently with it, one must precalculate values. Its advantage is that it is *dynamic* over time, whereas rules are rather *static*.

One of the aspects of this last point is that it would be feasible to use past data in order to *train* the system, as well as to validate it. As we have known since the inception of simulation in the 1960s, if the model can "predict the past," it can probably predict the future.

AN IMPROVED APPROACH TO GRAPH ANALYSIS

Analogical reasoning, pattern recognition, fuzzy sets, Quinlan's system, and memory-based reasoning are examples of methodologies designed to fit the new perspectives in interactive computational finance. Their use is even more advisable as massively parallel computers free us from the power constraints that we have experienced with AI-enriched applications when we proceeded with more complex deep modeling systems. This, however, does not mean that we ought to abandon simpler techniques.

One of the approaches favored in financial forecasting is *chart analysis*. The rules of traditional chartism are relatively simple and, up to a point, correspond with the principles followed in examining quality control charts:

- An uptrend is defined as a straight line connecting the low points of a series of ascending troughs.

- A downtrend is a straight line connecting a series of descending peaks.

- Three successive drops may establish a buy trend.[8]

Two drops call for a more risky projection. In other words, a tentative trend line can be drawn between two points, but to establish validity, a third point is required.

---

[8]This happens in a manner closely resembling an $\bar{x}$ chart in statistical quality control, where three successive points in the same direction indicate that the process is getting out of control. See D. N. Chorafas, *Statistical Process and Reliability Engineering*, New York and Princeton, D. Van Nostrand, 1960.

Once the trend has been established, technical analysts will predict that the trend will or will not continue, and trading decisions can be made to buy and sell. Sometimes, however, after a trend has been established, it will be broken, and this is a further trading indication to take into account.

Many securities houses have developed computer programs to search historical data for tentative and established uptrends, downtrends, and support and resistance levels, and to make trading decisions based on various criteria or initial results. Patterns are identified in graphical form and are produced by computer programs.

To competently perform graphical analysis, we need databases, online feed and computer models. Minisupercomputers are the best machines to use to obtain realtime response and therefore a competitive edge—but the level of machine power depends on the sophistication we seek. Different versions of chart analysis can be made:

• The simpler version will typically be used to build human expertise in terms of graphics analysis—an area where personal computer support is plentiful.

• The more complex version will be used for trading decisions and it should work not only online but also in realspace.

Chartist applications are of two classes. One is based on human knowledge and benefits from available knowledge, and eventually self-fulfillment. But such predictions are not quantified and sometimes their accuracy is suspect. Nobody exactly knows how far or how sure one person's predictive capability can go.

The other class of chartist applications is based on historical pattern analysis, exploiting rich databases. It quantifies predictions and certainties and handles multiple data, but it also needs continuous monitoring and mathematical models (which, however, do not always need to be as complex as those mentioned earlier in this chapter). This class is more difficult to handle than the other, and it calls for appropriate methodology.

A human chartist typically works with time series spanning over a few years: an example is the fluctuation in the price of silver, shown in Figure 9.6. Expert systems can be written to replicate human results and assist in uncovering events the human chartist missed, thus providing a transition between purely human and computer-based reasoning.

Through knowledge acquisition, the expert system will reflect the chartist's knowledge. Once written, it will increase the speed of processing and the extent of coverage, allowing the chartist to concentrate on problems connected to interpretation. Key issues relative to this approach are as follows:

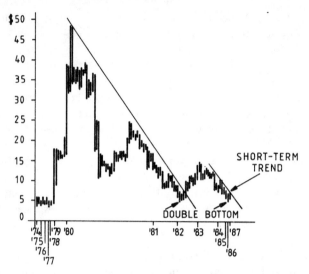

Figure 9.6   Graph of silver prices, illustrating typical procedures of a human chartist (prices from COMEX in New York).

1. Matching human perceptions in terms of congruent patterns

2. Providing historical data analysis through access to databases

3. Ensuring an agile visualization that is appealing to endusers

The first issue should be taken care of by a pattern analysis model that allows the chartist to investigate data combinations for recurrent patterns fairly accurately. Such a model should include identifiers for patterns that are already known and also create a workbench, as discussed earlier in this chapter.

APPLYING THESE CONCEPTS TO FOREX OPERATIONS

Many treasurers, traders, investors, and businesspeople are ill equipped to deal with the complex task of accurate currency forecasting. They lack the tools needed to provide an objective view of leading indicators and to highlight changing trends before they happen.

Nobody can claim to have the full range of time-tested tools for all the major markets and currency exchange requirements. But many organizations have developed significant assistant expert systems as well as intelligent graphics and pattern recognizers.[9] Those who did so are in the lead.

Such assistant tools should be shaped to respond to the requirement of the major foreign exchange functions already discussed. The following two sections provide a recap.

Customer Order Facilitation

Clients usually communicate by telephone to enter orders and obtain quotations. For the most part, the trader gets his quotations from other dealers and buys or sells for the customer without taking risk or committing the bank's capital to the transaction. He just charges a fee.

However, in the case of some large transactions, the bank may use its own capital. This means that its dealers would have to take the side of the investor, opening a long currency position to accommodate a customer who wishes to sell or buy currencies.

Having filled the customer's order, the dealer would normally trade to eliminate the position or at least to neutralize risk. Today this is called a *long transaction*, since the two trading events are related. Long transactions are excellent candidates for intelligent graphics and pattern recognition applications.

Proprietary Trading

Forex dealers often trade in currency markets for profit, using their company's own capital. Some proprietary trading is cash futures arbitrage, which aims to exploit temporary mispricing opportunities. Here, too, early pattern recognition is of great importance.

This is particularly true for other nodes of proprietary trading, where the dealer and his company aggressively take positions in currencies. In doing so, they hope to correctly guess the direction of exchange rate movements.

Proprietary trading has been a source of profits for the money center banks only when they have proper human capital and high technology to capitalize on the windows of opportunity immediately as they open. Otherwise, traders are condemned to take positions nobody else wants.

As we have already seen, systems designed properly for dealer assistance will involve a combination of pattern perceptors, mathematical analyzers,

---

[9]See also D. N. Chorafas and H. Steinmann, *Expert Systems in Banking* (London: Macmillan, and New York: New York University Press, 1991).

statistical evaluators, and heuristic approaches. The last are needed to investigate non-algorithmic issues and to reduce processing time.

Much of the technology that has been developed so far along this line of reference is based on earlier, simpler tools. By contrast, more sophisticated approaches investigate the causality of the market. For instance, once the chartist's expert system has been written, it can provide well-documented recommendations; it can also be used to help define the applicable level of accuracy: If 100 percent accuracy is wanted, then only 100 percent accurate trends will be produced. But if a flexible model has been built, then the enduser can request a level of accuracy of his choice, receive responses corresponding to this level, and make up his mind by screening the results.

One application in this area focuses on a recommendation list computed on closing prices: 200 stocks are followed, and about 10 percent are recommended each day as the trend becomes clearer, whether for buy, sell, or hold positions.

Results can be presented in tabular or graphic form. Table 9.4 shows daily recommendations of technical analysis, as the program identifies successive troughs and peaks. The minimum accuracy level embedded in this particular application is 50 percent; the effective level of accuracy of the data on the table is 61.37 percent.

The recommendation given by the system in the present example is *sell short*, and it is based on the following downtrend peaks:

- Peak of 141.0 on April 12

- Peak of 145.0 on March 7

- Peak of 146.0 on February 16

The magnitude of the downtrend is -0.125418 per day with a standard deviation of 4.849, which represents 38.66 percent of the mean.

Another expert system module evaluates the outlook for interest rates; a third estimates dividends within the next time horizon; a fourth evaluates risk. All these factors affect tradability and price.

One of the AI constructs applies itself to decisions regarding *switching*: one module works on short-term perspectives, and another on the longer term. The system itself is fairly simple, but the number of securities it follows makes the outcome calculation intensive. Such an outcome is based on rules and interpretations, but also specialists' expertise.

The model evaluates support and resistance. If a trend is moving sideways, then certain values become support and resistance levels. The rationale for this approach is this: If a price falls to the support level, then a significant

Table 9.4 Daily Recommendations of Technical Analysis

Stock Price of Company LMN

Level of accuracy: 61.37 percent
Recommendation: sell short

Breakeven prices for next 10 days

Days	Price
1	140.874
2	140.749
3	140.623
4	140.498
5	140.372
6	140.247
7	140.122
8	139.996
9	139.871
10	139.745

Expert System advises: IF price rises above that shown for each day, downtrend is broken; THEN buy.

number of investors will believe it to be good value and will start buying, thus pushing the price up. When the price reaches the resistance level, the opposite happens.

A trading strategy that successfully identifies these two levels, buying at the support level and selling just prior to the resistance level, seems to be well positioned to make profits. Nevertheless, as noted in the beginning of this section, a problem with any automated search for trends is to find the appropriate level of accuracy. It is, therefore, advisable to determine tolerance levels that reflect on performance.

10
New Tools Need
a New Culture

No two dealing rooms are the same, yet there seems to be a rather natural taxonomy of trader functions, depending on a network of dealing instruments, corresponding banks, and customer contacts. There is also the fact that the market is open practically twenty-four hours per day, although, throughout the day the trading center rotates from New York to Tokyo and then to London.

The taxonomy of major trading functions classifies them into *sales traders*, *market makers*, *customer facilitators*, *proprietary traders* (see also Chapter 8) and *derivative dealers* and *sales traders*. All need powerful tools at their disposal, as well as a new culture that will enable the forex professionals to get the best out of the new tools at the dealers' disposition.

Sales traders are the interface between the customer and the dealing room. A sales trader is assigned a small group of clients, and he is responsible for their accounts. As points of contact, salespeople relay information and quotations from other traders to the customers and look after the proper execution of client's orders—but also, most importantly, client handling.

Each of the market makers typically operates in one or more currencies. Large dealing rooms typically have specialist dealers in each major currency. Some of them concentrate in a group of related currencies, and others in important cross-exchange rates. Most take positions during a trading session but avoid carrying overnight risk exposure.

I discussed customer facilitators in Chapter 8. Proprietary traders employ the bank's, or generally corporate treasury's, capital to actively trade for profit. Unlike the market maker, the proprietary dealer may be authorized to maintain risk positions in one or more currencies.

Another species in the dealing room is the derivative traders. Their function is to trade futures, options, swaps, and synthetic instruments, working in unison with other specialist traders as well as the salespeople.

The customer calls the sales trader to buy or sell a certain currency. The latter obtains a bid-ask quote from a market maker, who may consult a proprietary trader known to be interested in taking a position in the currency. The bid-ask quotation relayed to the client is known as a *three-second price*. It must be accepted or declined immediately; if the client accepts, the trade is done.

All this takes place online. Realtime systems, and intimate knowledge of the mechanics and dynamics of foreign exchange trading are very important. The practical aspects of dealing in the spot, forward, futures, and options markets have to be supported through basic research and systems solutions and require significant knowledge.

Rocket scientists and *quantitative strategists* in foreign exchange operations are a new breed. The role of the former is to provide analytical tools, simulators, and heuristics. The latter input tactical advice to traders and to important customers of the firm. These are specific domains where high-technology tools can make a significant contribution—for instance, fuzzy engineering and neural networks.

THE MOVE TO NEURAL NETWORKS

The subject of neural networks attracted wide scientific interest in the 1950s, though both Dr. Alan Turing in the 1930s and Dr. John von Neumann in the 1940s had brought up the *connectionist* issue. The whole field of *artificial intelligence* got its name from the fact that, in the decade of the 1950s, a great deal of research focused on brain emulation through human-devised neural structures.

The foundation of neural network technology rests on two beliefs:

1. There is no reason why intelligence should reside only in a shell of bone. It can just as well be in a shell of metal or plastic.

2. Over billions of years of evolution, nature has developed a sophisticated neural system; we can learn from it and emulate it.

The first issue is philosophical. The second can be seen as the outcome of many years of research in the areas of pattern recognition, experimental psychology, brain function, and neural science. The motivation for such activity is, of course, to understand how brain cells and their interconnections are able to perform exceedingly complex calculations despite being much slower than the electronic switching devices we have available today.

The understanding of brain function can open the way to many processes and point out possible implementations ranging from military applications to telecommunications, manufacturing control, and banking. So far, neural network technology has demonstrated itself to be useful in the following areas:

- Automatic signature recognition

- Realtime performance in pattern recognition

- Robust associative recall on cue

- Ability to learn in realtime and to remember

- Control of multiple-constraint environments

- Classification and taxonomy studies

The Defense Advanced Research Projects Agency (DARPA) has a $33 million program to develop neural networks for antisubmarine warfare (ASW) and other complex tasks. Many defense contractors see success in combining the data pouring in from a variety of sensors through a connectionist model. Rockwell eventually expects to see a global *fusion center* that electronically maps the whole ASW battlefield.

DARPA has also asked aircraft companies to look into automation of a submarine's attack center based on the same principles. Neural networks are also used to counter the stealth bomber's invisibility to radar. According to DARPA, this experimental form of artificial intelligence can track aircraft otherwise hidden from more traditional means of detection.

In Japan, both the Advanced Telecommunications Research Institute (a national laboratory) and Nippon Electric (NEC) are actively working on implementing neural networks in the telecommunications field. Utilizing its internally developed dynamic neural network (DNN), NEC has created a speaker-independent, discrete speech recognition system. This DNN is a three-layer connectionist model that combines a sparsely connected neural network with a learning method, including back error propagation and traditional dynamic programming techniques.

In America, Citibank is using neural networks in advanced projects such as image recognition, the detection and identification of patterns, and signature recognition. Among other projects, a connectionist model reads handwritten characters of dollar amounts, an application focusing on the automation of check handling.

Another connectionist project promoted by Citibank is software for associative memory. The goal is to merge database applications and AI in what is called *database mining*, which essentially means enhancing the ability to recognize patterns that exist in the database.

In January 1990, Nynex announced a neural network that is able to do signature recognition. For pattern recognition applications, a California bank incorporates a connectionist board on the personal computer of some of its professionals.

In England, National Westminster Bank uses neural networks for image processing. The bank's goal is to automate the handling of payments documents, which, to a large measure, are still paper-bound all over the world—a very costly item to the financial industry because of the manual labor they involve.

Together with a Japanese bank that uses its computer equipment, Hitachi is developing a neural computer for portfolio selection. Nikko Securities has built a perceptron for investment analysis.[1] A number of Japanese financial institutions are very active in both neural networks and fuzzy engineering.

Both in America and in Japan, the two countries that have done the most research on neural networks, other applications include risk evaluation, mortgage underwriting, and delinquency risk assessment. Nestor Inc. is working on a mortgage origination underwriter system through neural networks. The model filters the general population of potential property owners using a set of guidelines, some of which are well defined.

Another connectionist model is dedicated to mortgage insurance underwriting, capitalizing on technology to counter the fact that mortgage insurance applicants are by nature a higher-risk group. At the same time, second-order underwriting performed by mortgage insurers is bound to be more difficult and prone to ambiguity—hence the wisdom of high-technology assistance.

Still another neural model is a delinquency processor. The portfolio held by a mortgage insurer contains insured risks that will become delinquent over time. This population is (hopefully) small, but is the primary source of losses for a mortgage insurer. The connectionist approach focuses on delinquency risk assessment for better loan performance.

Technically speaking, as American Express was to underline in the course of our meeting in New York, neural network concepts and applications are tied to parallel architectures. To use a parallel architecture to its full advantage, *we must think in parallel*.

---

[1]See also D. N. Chorafas and H. Steinmann, *Expert Systems in Banking* (London: Macmillan, 1990).

As connectionist models become available, they do real-life work, some of the most successful being exemplified by classification and pattern-type problems. A number of claims about neural networks are overblown, but there is a level of applications that holds real promise; the current interest is largely fed through the results obtained thus far.

A NEURAL NETWORK IMPLEMENTATION BY FUJITSU

During our meeting in April 1991 in Tokyo, Fujitsu presented an imaginative application of neural networks for stock market prediction. It is one of the best models of its type, and it is operational. This makes it a good example the treasury and forex landscape.

The neural network's user interface permits the broker to access knowledge-enriched information and prompts him to take action. This interface mimics on a single screen the environment of the market domain in which the enduser works, providing advice the way an assistant would do.

The Fujitsu neural network was first implemented at Nikko Securities but is now available to other investment banks. The model is based on Tokyo Stock Exchange (TSE) data and involves six key factors affecting the prediction process:

- Stock vector curve

- Turnover

- Interest rate

- Forex rate

- The Dow Jones average

- TSE learning curve

These six factors can be nicely presented in a *radar chart*, as shown in Figure 10.1. There is enough information available to feed this chart with a comprehensive description of market movements. In a real-life implementation, time of the day is the radar chart's seventh dimension.

Stock market prediction through neural networks differentiates itself in terms of value from more traditional approaches to market forecasting. The latter are based on technical indices, the stock index rate, financial news, and social and economic conditions, which are typically considered postmortem.

The new approach, with second-generation expert systems, is more powerful, as it reflects on the ability to learn about stock market movements,

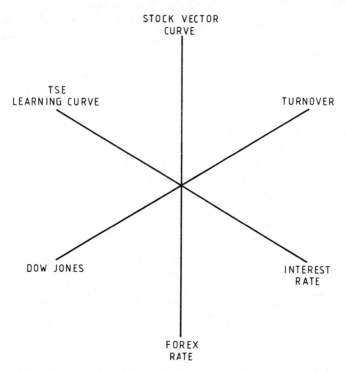

Figure 10.1   A radar chart presentation of key factors integrated in the neural network.

particularly on the way minute changes influence buying and selling. The Fujitsu neural network also provides the possibility for after-the-fact evaluations.

For the most part, the architecture of the Fujitsu stock market neural network is not meant to duplicate the operation of the human brain but rather to receive inspiration from market trends as they happen in realtime at the Tokyo Stock Exchange. These are characterized by the following constructs:

- Large numbers of very simple movements being mapped into the neural net

- Weighted connections between the elements, with the weights on the connections encoding knowledge

- A highly parallel, distributed control structure

- Emphasis on automatically learning internal representations

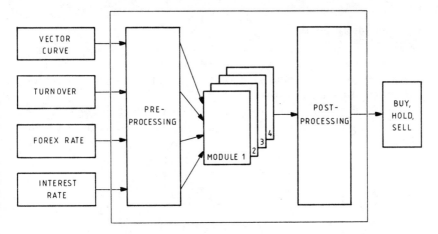

EACH MODULE HAS A THREE-LAYER NEURAL NETWORK.

Figure 10.2   Neural network for the prediction of stock value.

The question is not simply whether there are conditional statements and connections. The central issue is the character of the knowledge encoded into the neural net. Rule-based systems have traditionally been constructed from collection of empirical associations that link symptoms. This is being done better through connectionism.

As shown in Figure 10.2, Fujitsu's stock market neural net uses an architecture divided into five parts: input, preprocessing, processing proper, post processing, and output of buy or sell timing. The inputs are as follows:

1. Vector curve reflecting stock price deviation

2. Turnover at TSE

3. Forex rate: yen versus dollar

4. Interest rate for CDs, (certificates of deposit): yen only

The computation of the vector curve reflecting deviation of the stock price can be seen as a customer-oriented procedure that helps in personalization. Handling of these four inputs through the preprocessor leads to the preconditions for a buy or sell recommendation to be taken in connection to four different time ranges:

• Module 1: 6 months
• Module 2: 12 months

- Module 3: 18 months
- Module 4: 24 months

Essentially, preprocessing computes the derivative of the absolute value of each time series, one per equity. By contrast, postprocessing computes the integral of the timing alternatives.

Postprocessing leads to the recommendation to buy, hold, or sell. The developers have found that thinking about computation in terms of a brain

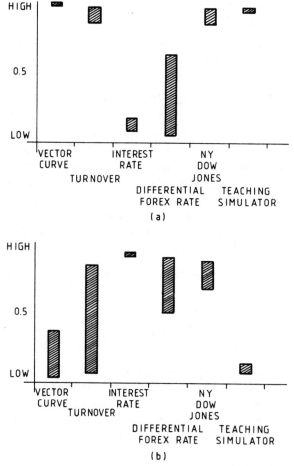

Figure 10.3 A neural network's perception of (a) bull and (b) bear markets.

metaphor rather than a digital computer metaphor leads to insight into the nature of market behavior.

This fact can be better appreciated if we recall that computers are capable of storing vast quantities of information and manipulating volumes of data in nanoseconds. They can perform extensive arithmetic calculations without errors. Humans cannot approach these processing capabilities.

At the same time however, humans routinely perform simple tasks such as commonsense reasoning. Working under constraints suggested by the brain may make traditional computation more difficult, but also leads to solutions numerical calculation cannot tackle.

By emulating the stock trader's brain, the Fujitsu neural network can perform complex logical tasks, such as interpreting a pattern or understanding a price sequence. This is shown in a practical sense in Figure 10.3, which reflects the neural net's perception of bull and bear markets.

Unlike conventional computing, the brain metaphor contains a huge number of processing elements that act in parallel. This works on the dominant hypothesis that, in our search for solutions, we look for massively parallel algorithms that require no more than, say, 100 processing steps. But the metaphor's logical inference is so great that it means a *new departure* and plenty of opportunity.

THE NEED FOR HYBRID SOLUTIONS

Whether with simpler charting approaches or with more complex ones, from pattern recognition to fuzzy engineering and neural networks, the two basic ingredients to a successful solution are *mathematics* (algorithms and heuristics) and *databases*. The latter must be rich and multifaceted, which means that significant work has to be done integrating the new approaches with the old—more generally known as data processing, or DP—where large databases can be found.

When in the late 1970s decision support systems (DSSs) came into public view and became popular because of their spreadsheet software, the need for easily accessible databases gave birth to information centers, which acted as storehouses of managerial type information, enriched through transactional databases during night runs. This is no longer an acceptable approach; it is also unnecessary if our DP chores have been converted to realtime processing as they should be.

Updating through night runs is not an acceptable practice because, among other reasons, managers and professionals wish to have wider access than what the preselected files of the infocenter typically permit. Furthermore, in dynamic markets such as forex, securities, and treasury, nothing short of realspace is acceptable.

Still, because the corporate databases are enriched through transactional processing, solutions have to be found that integrate old data processing and the new decision-oriented solutions. This is the reason for developing and implementing *hybrid systems*, which should perform the following functions:

1. Work in realtime, accessing large databases

2. Integrate new high-definition graphics applications and pattern recognition processes

3. Serve both the existing managerial applications and the new AI-based structures

All three functions have their challenges. We must not only build the new application but also interlink the AI models with the distributed databases our organization has built over the years and equip them with graphics.

Connecting the graphics interface with the reasoning mechanism is one of the keys to an easy-to-use expert system. A good graphic interface is important, all the way from communicating with experts for knowledge acquisition to the presentation and visualization chores that concern the enduser.

The challenge starts with the fact that the skillful use of system shells requires support for describing and controlling the reasoning process graphically. Although there are some first-class expert system shells for writing AI constructs, practically all of them have deficiencies in graphics facilities. A separate graphics package must therefore be chosen and interfaced to the shell.

Connecting the expert systems and graphics applications packages with databases also has its challenges. Quite often, the classical corporate databases are incompatible among themselves in data structures, organization, methodology, and database management systems (DBMS). In many cases, they operate batch (a very bad practice) and, therefore, during the working hours contain obsolete information which is of little or no use to the trader.

Both homogeneity in database design and realtime updating, are at a premium, if the sophisticated models that we build for our treasury, forex, and securities operations are to be used properly. Because today's databases, which have been typically developed over long years of computer practice, are not renowned for being homogeneous, we have to use one of three methods for their integration, going from the more feasible to the more abstract.

1. Federated databases

This approach leaves the databases as they are (heterogeneous); there is no global schema—only a data dictionary handling schemata. Such a solution is good for intelligent query systems, but not for transactional approaches.

2. Schema translation

This method calls for a virtual model of operations, which is too complex in real-life implementations. It requires establishing a universal schema as well as the conversion of non-normalized schemata.

3. Interoperability approach

This rests on the development of very powerful language that can handle distributed object management. It also requires encapsulation and standard interfaces.

The point is that there is no easy way out. Another shortcoming is the mainframe culture that still dominates the data processing departments of many financial organizations. No matter what their name or number is, mainframes are a completely ossified approach to information handling, dating back to the 1950s, or in some cases to the 1960s.

In terms of power, mainframes have been overtaken by workstations; yet we have AI and graphics application that cannot be effectively handled through mainframes or workstations because of the huge power requirements they pose. The answer is supercomputers.

It cannot be repeated too often: Endusers at the treasury department, in forex operations, or in securities trading need graphics support and heuristics to help them discover trends and patterns in the market in relation to a wide range of factors:

- The financial state of a company

- Market evolution in general and in specific sectors

- Current national and international financial political developments

- Sociological, demographic, and psychographic influences, even seasonal and climatic factors

Analyses along these lines of reference have to take into account many influential factors, making use of the wealth of financial and economic indicators that are available. This adds to the complexity of problem solution, requiring the use of the best available technology without abandoning past applications—hence the need for hybrid systems.

CAPITALIZING ON THE AVAILABLE VISUALIZATION TOOLS

A wide range of currently available statistical and mathematical techniques may be employed in producing a set of indicators that must be tied together in some way, though large amounts of time and effort are required to process the mass of data available. Just the same, the solution we are after must rely on the availability of specific information, which sometimes must be number-crunched at subsecond speed.

Parallel processing of the newly developed generation of financial applications has been a concern of the foremost banks and other institutions over the past few years. An outgrowth of this trend is the need to thoroughly understand the execution behavior of a parallel application. Computer graphics, for example, enter *twice* in this connection: first, for enduser support in charting and pattern representation; and second, as an effective aid to the programming mission.

The primary objective in the second item is to provide a graphical tool to aid programmers in debugging the synchronization aspects of an application, ensuring good performance and helping to better understand the execution behavior of a parallel application. The tools we use should be able to post-analyze program execution and accept information dynamically as the program is executed.

Some graphical analysis tools that are currently being developed are based on trace history files that record the multiprocessing state and synchronization changes that occurred in an application. Vendors should also provide with their wares multiprocessing libraries for trace file logging that support dynamic analysis routines.

As these facts help document, dynamic graphics are fast becoming a cornerstone in advanced computer implementation, whether in applications visible to the enduser at his workstation, or in program development activities which to a great extent are the province of computer specialists. The computer system's utilities library should include routines that make feasible the following tasks:

1. Reading data from a raw graph into the system, converting it into an internal representation format that can be easily manipulated.

2. Detecting characteristic features such as trends, spikes, and head and shoulders when there is a query about such events regarding a particular graph.

3. Selecting sections of graphs for closer analysis and demonstrations, as well as expert interaction to "zoom in," or detail, part of the graph.

4. Smoothing the graph, particularly when different granularities are detected with the graph, also reducing the effects of noise.

5. Having built-in intelligence to identify longer-term and shorter-term trends in the available data flow or stored information.

6. Providing a documented graph analysis approach that can respond to fuzzy queries, such as, "Tell me all you can about this graph."

An expert system should search the graph for all the special features that it knows about, and also make useful generalizations such as a summary of the graph or the contribution provided by a few basic primitives. Another function concerns the way that we map our qualitative language for describing graphs onto the actual numerical data for that graph. Such mapping must be flexible, allowing adjustments to be made online as if interacting with a human expert.

The graphics model should also have a first-class explanation facility. Every change that is suggested should be justified, including warnings issued whenever an operation is acceptable but when some further investigation may be called for.

In terms of visualization strategy at the enduser site, care should be exercised in combining the pattern representation with a linguistic interpretation of the pattern, as a basis for logical reasoning. We must account for the fact that in cases the same pattern can have different meanings for different persons in different situations at different times.

This particular challenge did not exist with earlier data processing approaches, which typically presented their output in a static graphical form. With dynamic graphics, discriminating features can be found either within the pattern or beyond it in a very volatile context, which is a rather frequent and interesting case.

Finally, when we discuss hybrid systems, we should keep in mind that the concept is completely portable toward the future as new technologies develop and have to be successfully integrated with current schemes. For instance,

- Neural networks computation is especially useful in the development of learning mechanisms assisting the trader's decisions.

- Fuzzy logic[2] can produce better accuracy and higher quality than the level obtainable through deterministic algorithms.

- Current technology provides instrumental assistance in formalizing human reasoning, making it better focused on financial events with short life cycles.

- Through new technology, comparison of patterns can be effected in a more flexible, faster, parallel way than currently available graphics tools permit.

Over the coming years, neural networks and fuzzy engineering may significantly influence our concepts of visualization, as the basic heuristics of matching the contents of the neural cells can be adjustable—for instance, to reflect the number of dimensions and choice of presentation parameters.

In this sense, combined with more conventional computers and databases, neural networks and fuzzy engineering artifacts may promote our goals of research and analysis. They will permit us to deal with uncertainties as well as compress the implementation time, thus obtaining faster payoff. This will be done more successfully if we ensure continuity with the work being done today.

TRANSITION TO THE USE OF HUMAN WINDOWS

When they were first developed, introductory projects aimed to help in agile and user-friendly man-machine interfaces (MMIs). Since then, research emphasis and goals have undergone some fundamental changes. The main reason for these changes can be ascribed to the fact that graphics technology has found widespread implementation domains.

With the growing number of forward-looking applications, specialists noticed the possibility of using the positive results of visualization in decision support, enriching results with fuzzy information processing. Professor Terano of the Laboratory for International Fuzzy Engineering (LIFE) pointed out during our April 1991 meeting in Japan that the following criteria help define a user-friendly solution:

- Serving under human operators with competence, enriching the capacity and knowledge necessary for recognition, decision, and action.

[2]See D. N. Chorafas, *New Information Technologies: A Practitioner's Guide* (New York: Van Nostrand Reinhold, 1992); and "Software That Can Dethrone Computer Tyranny," *Business Week*, April 6, 1992, pp. 70, 71.

- Decreasing the burden on professionals and managers through natural language understanding, common sense, and image understanding.

- Increasing the ability of human operators to formulate thoughts, providing for better decisions through appropriate interfaces.

- Increasingly operating at the human level, having the ability to recognize intention, as well as to adapt and learn.

No one needs this sort of service more than the professionals working in forex operations. The pace of their work and the complexity of the trades they handle makes it more than ever mandatory to improve the relationship between humans and machines by increasing user friendliness.

Borrowing an example from manufacturing, one user-friendly system based on fuzzy technology is a robot that receives instructions by natural language and adjusts its actions according to the meaning of the expressions intended by the user.

In many fields, communication with natural language is problematic because the same expression may have a variety of meanings resulting from the vagueness of natural language itself, differences among speakers, and the diversity of the situations where instructions are given. In forex, however, this is less a problem because the field has standard expressions that can be used quite effectively.

To further enlarge the domain of human-machine understanding, and therefore cooperation, researchers use advanced technology, such as fuzzy engineering constructs, to help the computer to correctly understand its user under all possible conditions. Among the subjects researched in connection to this concept are methods of representing and employing knowledge with vagueness in it and ways of systematically managing knowledge, transferring information between each type of knowledge represented.

New avenues are opened by purposely moving away from computer solutions dependent on simple yes-or-no (binary) logic, which is vastly different from the information processing methods inherent in human thinking. Because evaluations based on common sense and flexible judgment are considered difficult to achieve with traditional computer approaches, fuzzy theory has emerged as a suitable approach to represent uncertainty contained in the meaning of each word.

Fuzzy artificial intelligence is expected to play an important role in forex operations. It will lead to establishment of an intimate relationship between people and computers. The foremost financial organizations today study the implementation of fuzzy theory, seeking to efficiently use it to strengthen ties between systems and their users. These activities are instrumental to achieving the following goals:

- Promoting the advent of a highly sophisticated system as an adjunct to human intelligence

- Respecting the subjectivity and personality of each professional person

- Striving to create assistant technology in its true sense

Advanced projects in human-machine interfaces currently focus on, in addition to the aforementioned areas, investigation and definition of the communication language to be used, affecting the method of input to the system as well as making the output easily comprehensive.

FROM THE DYNAMICS OF KNOWLEDGE REPRESENTATION TO WORKSTATION MECHANICS

Good solutions can be neither restricted in scope nor partial in their coverage. In its quest to significantly improve the knowledge representation to be used within automated systems, LIFE was led to the all-important investigation of the way of reasoning. This led to the clarification of capabilities an AI construct must possess through its internal functions.

At this laboratory, the main direction of research and specific tools to be used were decided after scientists realized that vagueness should at least be handled in connection with knowledge representation and the method of reasoning.

With this goal in mind, the types of vagueness in natural language have been examined and general guidelines for the communication process determined. The same has been done for the level of control messages to be used as an output.

The basic methods and capabilities required for knowledge representation and reasoning are always fundamental. They should be chosen to contribute to the continuing ability of a machine to do the following:

- Apply its accumulated experience to present situations

- Learn through analogical reasoning by retrieving adequate past examples

- Revising its rules in conformance to the situation when it performs reasoning tasks

At LIFE, emphasis is placed on the machine's ability to recognize analogous conditions and to use more than one experience at one time. In addition, studies are made to enrich human-devised systems with learning capabilities. Both learning features and reasoning by analogy are necessary ingredients to forex solutions in general and to the competent construction of human windows in particular.

The high-technology-based methodological infrastructure that I discussed in the preceding section is an enabling mechanism that enriches an electronic trading system. It allows traders not only to *view* but also to effectively *participate in* a competitive market, profiting from machine intelligence.

There are, of course, other criteria that should characterize system design. For instance, trade execution speed must be measured in milliseconds, with a reaction time closely approximating that associated with the auction market itself. And trade execution procedures must be normalized for all time zones.

While still observing subsecond response time requirements, a system must present necessary information on the screen in the form of objects, colors, icons, and text.

- The visualization of trends and color differentiation enhances a dealer's decision style and speed of response.

- The recreation of the competitive forex environment provides an incentive to trade, maintaining the liquidity that is critical to the market.

- The system helps ensure market transparency, which is often an important component of a competitive marketplace.

In terms of presentation, much can be learned from other applications in securities and commodities trading. On the commodities screens of the Chicago Board of Trade, for example, red circles represent members who are offering to sell, and blue squares members who are bidding to buy.[3] Presentation is thus done through member-offering icons, and member-bidding icons, which are easily distinguishable. Each icon lists the member's acronym and the quantity available. The bids and offers on the screen must be at the market, or the icons will not be presented.

For flexibility reasons, member icons appear in random locations in all trading arenas. For instance, a trader's icon may appear in the center of broker A's trading domain and in the left corner of broker B's trading reference.

In this solution, the price displays of other contract months that are not listed in the trading arenas appear at the bottom of the screen. There

---

[3]This example is taken from the CBOT's Aurora, which, because of policy decisions, has not been released.

is room on the screen to display up to 10 contract month price lists, allowing participants to view current bids and offers and quantities for each. Participants can also join the current bid and offer.

Although the mechanics of visualization differ from one solution to the other, it is rewarding to learn from the best examples available. There is always room for improvement over current practices as well as for the personalization of a given approach. But learning from the foremost implementations is indispensable, in order to move ahead in business.

CHALLENGES OF CONSTRAINED SYSTEMS

The ability to graphically represent patterns and analytical trends can be perfected if operations are not random, but constrained within boundaries. An example is the use of *icons*, which are, to a point, standardized.

Icons provide an easy-to-understand interface for problem solving, a reason why computer graphics is so popular. The design of simple, easy-to-understand graphics is a task for the cognitive sciences, aiming to produce schemata that help in conveying messages as well as in feature detection.

Like finding analogies, establishing valid semantics is a challenging task. In a complex environment, constrained semantical systems operate better than random ones because the amount of information needed for discrimination becomes better controllable. Constrained systems can also learn faster, and know many meanings and usages.

In principle, generalization should take place at the most elementary level possible, on parts of figures rather than the whole. This is the role of icons. It is also feasible to use constraints in the first layers and random connections in deeper layers, doing so without loss of efficiency.

Such an approach will characteristically be taken by systems that make use of parallel information processing, with different patterns or templates simultaneously applied to an input. Different combinations of features can identify each specific template pattern. Its units, known as *demons*, are quasi-independent operators arranged in levels. Demons are typically supervisory processes.

Like perceptrons, such models can be simple or complex, according to their number of levels. As network programs, they are interesting both as attempts to simulate neural networks and as examples of machine intelligence. One approach to pattern recognition in a constrained environment is computer programs capable of *learning* to recognize trends, shapes, and patterns. A simple perceptron network has at least three layers:

1. *Sensory units,* which transduce the input signals

2. *Association units,* which are decision points where transmissions through the network are regulated

3. *Response units,* which emit signals as an output

Perceptrons may be made more complex by adding layers of units to this simple schema of three levels. More complex networks have been studied in pattern recognition and discrimination experiments:

• In pattern-recognition experiments, in-outs can be presented in all possible positions.

• In discrimination experiments, the machine is trained on one set of patterns and then tested on another set.

Because perceptrons are intended to simulate neural processes, they can be improved by addition of various constraints. A system of connections that improves generalization over similar patterned inputs is one example of an approach that can aid performance. A constraint may also be a set of property detection configurations such as the edge and corner detectors examined earlier in this chapter. Such constraints can be combined to discriminate on patterns; however, too many constraints of this sort make the perceptron less efficient.

Encapsulation of information is a constraint in the storage, retrieval, and processing area that permits more efficient design of a distributed information system. An *object* is a callable entity that may include data and commands, or data alone, and it is typically encapsulated. Precisely because they are part of a constrained mechanism, objects are the building blocks of a larger system. Programming languages can be viewed as a set of objects, and they are generally dealt with using, of course, object-oriented approaches.

A constrained approach to objects can be taken in terms of all the possible operations to be applied to them, including the properties they have, and messages they send. Some role types may be defined for an object class without eliminating the possibility of establishing new roles or the corresponding new behaviors of the objects.

We can use roles for describing object behavior, further applying constraints. For instance, a set of operations and properties associated with an object can be partitioned according to the different roles played by the object. We can draw transition graphs for role transitions and define incoming and outcoming messages for each instantiated role at each state. Similar considerations can apply to commands defined by the designer of a specific application, although some rules might be valid for more than one application. Such rules are *primitives*—that is, native commands with a base role.

Message passing is a mechanism for informing users, for instance, of possible inconsistencies or problem areas within, say, the software base. *Shared access* allows users to see the current state of an object even as it is being modified by another user.

For visualization purposes, we need procedures for estimating the similarity between a query specification and a particular object. Just as helpful is a component, within the software base, that identifies where a particular symbol is defined and where it is referenced.

Sophisticated software systems have complex requirements and need a rich set of features for their construction and operation. Role rules and global rules make it feasible to describe properties of concurrent behaviors of an object in different roles, providing both constraints and synchronization when needed.

Such role rules may cover a wide variety of systems and functions, each rule being the finer programmatic interface needed to define or actuate a certain constraint. For instance, after having identified the patterns they seek, intelligent networks may present resistance to noisy input.

A knowledge engineering module of a larger system, such as a network, must be able to effectively handle noisy, fuzzy, or incomplete information. When a network is presented with incomplete or contradictory information, the AI constructs in memory choose the best match to screen the input.

Expertise in pattern handling leads to the notion of *adaptability*. Intelligent modules are able to self-organize and learn. Such structures do not need to be programmed like algorithmic software; they can be trained through the repeated presentation of examples. With neural networks, for instance, learning can continue while the network is being used in a given application.

Another issue we must examine is *fault tolerance*. More specifically, we wish to ensure that the destruction or removal of processing elements from a network will not cause the network to fail. In this regard, a basic design premise is that, as information in the network is distributed, small pieces of it could be lost without seriously affecting performance.

In conclusion, icons, perceptrons, encapsulated objects, neural networks, and intelligent modules have in common the notion of constrained elements. Although the specific constraints applied to each of these classes, or entities within a class, may be different, the approach taken through this wide spectrum shares to a significant extent a common methodology that will eventually lead to a general theory of hybrid systems.

11
The Role of Networks in Globalization

Like many other fields of human endeavor, banking has become more complex because of the emphasis now placed on product development and marketing. This has led to the introduction of sophisticated machinery that is essential to new product planning, but it has also promoted an increasing sense of cost-consciousness. An overriding requirement has therefore developed for the steady refinement of financial techniques.

Greater attention to detail calls for a sustained effort in *bank engineering*—which, in turn, means both new tools, such as expert systems, and steady communications streams provided by networks. To support the developing perspectives in the design, production, and delivery of financial services, networks become more and more global—and increasingly complex at a higher level of reliability and better quality assurance. This is what *network intelligence* is all about.

Economic forces more powerful than any bank have set in motion a process of *globalization*, and this has brought about significant *renovation* in terms of financial instruments that can be launched. Survival can no longer be achieved by doing more of what we have done in the past.

The top management of foremost banks increasingly appreciate that to keep leadership, they must reevaluate their practices, and subject these practices to change and steady adjustment. The alternative to this process is decline, but the renovation, and globalization of our mainstream activities is no easy, matter-of-course development. It necessitates a different banking culture from what traditional business already possesses. It also calls for investments in new architectures—a key point being networks.

REQUIREMENTS FOR 24-HOUR TRADING

Money is the blood that runs through the economy, carrying food to the brains of people, companies, and nations. Who controls the flow of money—not only deposits, but also transactions—controls the bloodstream of the gross national product. As a result, the controlling organization is able to reap significant benefits.

Ensuring a stream of favorable financial moves is particularly important at a time when the broader process of economic and financial globalization is rendering national borders obsolete as accounting units. It is even more fundamental as financial instruments are thrown in the market with their risks and long-term consequences poorly understood.

We know that traders in the four corners of the globe meet through global networks, but we do not necessarily appreciate

- Where the *risk* is actually being taken

- Where the *profit* really is being made

- Who is the *ultimate buyer* of the financial product

What we more or less understand is that the *capital advantage* remains the competitive edge of the future if and when it is enriched through *marketing* approaches. A *global economy* is dominated by financial institutions that can do the following:

- Develop and deliver new services

- Successfully penetrate each individual market

- Capitalize on the particular financial opportunities each market presents

Many issues underline the need for globality, which, to be served in the best possible manner, requires sophisticated network structures. Among these reasons we distinguish expanding business opportunity, a greater potential for profitability, gains that can be obtained through broadened securities trading and foreign exchange, and growing diversification (and therefore spreading of risk).

Designed and implemented for 24-hour trading, networks can help not only in the execution but also in the control of settlements. To be a competitive weapon, they must match market growth perspectives—also a necessary condition for account control.

The knowledgeable reader will appreciate that the reasons just enumerated extend beyond the time-honored concept of a bank as financial intermediary. Such references rest on the notion that, in the 1990s, *knowledge* and *information* will very much be a *vital commodity*, and will be shared through networks.

Boards of directors and general managers are hiring consultants to overhaul their financial institutions' network strategies. New network designs cover services that go well beyond deposit taking and lending, focusing on treasury, forex, and securities. They also provide the services necessary for flexible financing solutions throughout the First World.

Major commercial and investment banks are moving today along three axes of reference in building the grand design of their system architecture in order to enhance and strengthen their operations. As Figure 11.1 suggests, these are as follows:

1. *The myriaprocessor[1] structure*, which integrates workstations (WSs), maxis, minis, mainframes (MFs), and supercomputers (SCs)

2. *Multimedia terabyte memories*, which operate online and include both hard disks (HDs) and optical disks (ODs)

3. *Multimedia megastream and gigastream channels*, from local area networks (LANs) and building automation (BA) to metropolitan area networks (MANs) and wide area network (WANs)

These networks link the bank to its clients and to its own branches. The better-organized operations focus on the new methods of financial intermediation and provide competent support for the strategies top management has chosen, both at home and abroad.

Contrary to policies pursued at home, for example, some multinational financial institutions have chosen to finance themselves from the capital markets instead of creating or buying a branch network. The only parts that take deposits from customers are insurance and fund-management businesses. To distribute products, these banks use a mixture of retailers, direct marketing, and other banks with which they are networked.

The financial groups have good reasons to steer clear of big branch networks. They reckon that any bank that has invested heavily in brick and mortar has to sell as much as possible to cover high fixed costs. But they say that bank clerks cannot master the 200 or more products sold through the average outlet, and that force-feeding customers with everything from

[1]From the Greek word *myria*, which means 10,000.

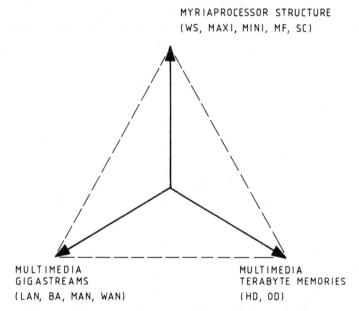

MYRIAPROCESSOR STRUCTURE
(WS, MAXI, MINI, MF, SC)

MULTIMEDIA   MULTIMEDIA
GIGASTREAMS   TERABYTE MEMORIES
(LAN, BA, MAN, WAN)   (HD, OD)

Figure 11.1   Grand design of a systems architecture.

mortgages to credit cards can often do more harm than good, especially if the result is a rash of bad debts.

Based on the foregoing strategy, instead of a monolith, the banks are a slim federation of distinct businesses, each free to chart its own strategy, to develop its own products and computer systems, and to forge its own alliances—but all of them are interconnected through an intelligent network that permits them to operate 24 hours per day.

The more the center of gravity of financial transactions swings from equity to debt, as it happens today in America and throughout the First World, the more crucial become the answers to strategic questions. And this is where the workstation should be located: at the strategic level.

Because of the emergence of 24-hour trading and the associated settlement procedures, financial institutions do not even have a choice of operating less than around-the-clock. The fast-developing 24-hour worldwide money market is forcing corporate treasurers and money managers to reassess existing relationships. Sophisticated customers want to trade *any currency* or *security* on *any exchange, any place* in the world at *any time* of the day.

To help his clients, the trader must *access* and *analyze activities* through his online workstation. He must be able to immediately reach all major money markets, execute buy or sell orders, and move funds from market to market and currency to currency.

We simply cannot afford to depend on the concepts and the tools we have used during the last 15 years, even if they have served us well. The risk is too great that financial profits will be elusive and the market will be harvested by banks that are able to keep state-of-the-art capabilities that emphasize the role of networks in globalization.

Karl von Clausewitz[2] remarked, "Every lost battle is a factor of disintegration. If we fall behind in the innovation race, we will be confronted with lost battles." The winners will be those financial institutions that know how to blend marketing wizardry with technological developments. Two of the pillars of success are flexibility and self-confidence.

Today's global prosperity hinges, as never before, on a delicate set of balances, confidences, interdependencies, and mutual understandings. Although these values are traditional, what sets them apart from past practices is the globalization of the world's financial markets, which requires that they are viewed from a *multicultural* perspective, the observance of which has a great deal to do with communications.

The leading banks and securities houses have properly understood this issue. As Robert Studer, president of the Union Bank of Switzerland, remarked, "The modern bank, like the major trading city, can . . . successfully compete if it

- Is a *key node* in the global electronic trading networks

- Makes it *easy and cost-effective* for multinational clients to do business

- Provides the means for *linking* with their communications networks internationally

- *Spreads* fixed costs over a large range of activities worldwide

- Adapts policies to *changing conditions*." [3]

Every one of these five points provides a fertile domain for intelligent network applications and development of innovative products. Having the right people in a global setting is not only a matter of distributing them geographically. Appropriate solutions come from being able to support them through networked services.

---

[2] Prussian general (1780–1831) who is often credited as the father of modern military strategy and the theory underpinning it.

[3] In his foreword to D. N. Chorafas and H. Steinmann, *Intelligent Networks* (Los Angeles: CRC Press/Times-Mirror, 1990).

THE IMPACT ON STRATEGY AND STRUCTURE

One of the subjects that commanded the attention of organization and management experts through the post–World War II years is the relative merit of decentralization versus centralization. For each solution, the pro and con arguments revolve around the advantages and disadvantages of flexibility and efficiency on one hand, and the possible loss of control caused by centrifugal forces on the other.

Decentralization gives quick reactions. Whereas the organizational chart of most banks looks like a huge pyramid with customers at the bottom and senior management at the top, that of a truly decentralized financial institution is different:

- It has fewer managerial layers.

- It is designed to emphasize that important decisions relating to products and prices should be made by those nearest the customer, not by head-office mandarins.

By letting subsidiaries operate as discrete units, a bank can easily judge the profitability of products. It also reduces or eliminates the infighting at other banks that accompanies the division of shared costs and revenues among different fiefdoms.

Technology helps subdue the ever-present centrifugal forces by using instantaneous communications and access mechanisms that networks make feasible. This helps promote management control while it sustains the required global effort. Intelligent networks aid the financial organization in obtaining and sustaining a truly international presence.

Precisely along this line of thinking it can be demonstrated that the main reason that we have to build and maintain global networks is the need to sustain and grow a *community intelligence*. This is written with a dual perspective:

- *Internal* to the financial organization, creating a multidimensional web able to link the network of branches among themselves and with headquarters as well as with the exchanges

- *External* toward clients and corresponding banks, handling multimedia communications and being able to promote the sale of financial products as well as cut down the costs of these products' delivery to the clients

Let's face it. The financial markets of the 1990s are buyers' markers, and the banks equipped to deal with them will be the winners.

To deal most effectively with a buyers' market we need a sharp, forward-looking strategy. This is the first ingredient. The second is the competent use of technology, which requires a grand design. As Figure 11.2 demonstrates, the latter is composed of three overriding architectural layers:

1. System

2. Network

3. Applications

In addition, a multitude of detailed designs are incorporated. The choice of applications will be based on options and priorities that must be well integrated, coherent, and comprehensive.

Throughout the First World, the buyers' market increasingly demands custom banking services. If we offer them, exactly what they comprise depends on who the customer is and how much money he has to invest or

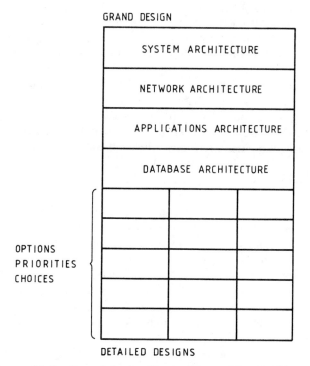

Figure 11.2 Grand design illustrating architectural layers.

trade, but it does *not* depend on *where* the customer is, because wherever he may be, he can be reached through networks.

Precisely because of networks, computers, and agile software (such as expert systems) in today's increasingly competitive marketplace, private bankers are able to be flexible. On another front, the use of intelligent networks and knowledge engineering in payments traffic comes none too soon; it can be beneficial at three levels:

1. Exceptional (large) payments

2. Spontaneous payments

3. Regular payments

Exceptional payments are typically beyond the $3 million level. *Spontaneous payments* cover all nonregular personal payments—the *one-time* type made, for example, at retailers.

Regular payments are made on a steady basis to meet a range of commitments, such as mortgage repayments and utilities. It is projected that in the early 1990s in Britain, there will be between 1.6 and 1.8 billion noncash payments in this category, of which around 60 percent will be made electronically.

Regarding exceptional payments, in London today less than 1 percent of orders going through the British clearinghouse CHAPS represents 95 percent of the total value of the orders. Another real-life example is that every night in New York, the clearinghouse of dollar-denominated international financial payments (CHIPS) handles 750,000 orders on average and 1,200,000 orders at maximum. With the average value of each transaction being $3.2 million, this represents $2.3 trillion on average and $3.84 trillion at maximum.

In order to judge how large these financial trading numbers are and what their impact might be, we have to keep in mind that the GNP of the United States is $5.3 trillion—which speaks volumes of the importance of financial exchanges and of the risks being taken.

With this tremendous amount of money involved in trading, new networks aim to develop into *electronic trading systems*, giving dealers and investors around the world 24-hour access to international financial markets. This is not a technical, but a policy, reaction to the increasingly international nature of investing.

Leading financial organizations comment that globalization has made a dramatic entrance into the forex and securities markets. But also they emphasize that the technological infrastructure able to support the necessary network characteristics is one thing, but the policies necessary to sustain a steady flow is another. Alert organizations also emphasize that, particularly in the workings of global information exchange, top management has to encourage the flow of *bad news*. If it does not do so, then bad situations will get worse. It is how quickly we can get the bad news and react to it that counts the most in separating competent management from the less competent.

Beyond information as such, corrective action requires *exceptional intelligence* with the ability to ask tough questions. The capable management of a financial institution calls for the maintenance of very high performance standards, commitment to keep on guard continually, and the ability to shed criticism.

The skilled use of global networks can also be instrumental in *time management*. Organizations that waste their time and their managers' and professionals' time do not survive in the long term. The consequences for financial organizations that waste their clients' time are self-evident.

We have to organize to combat the most dangerous of human weaknesses: *wasting time*. A professional person, like a computer systems expert, has nothing to sell but his time. It takes energy and self-discipline to do so. Self-discipline is necessary to monitor one's own intake and output and, therefore, one's productivity. This, too, is a domain where the use of networks affects strategy.

THE NETWORK AS A LONG-TERM GOAL

Sun Tzu, a great Chinese strategist whose writings have become the bible of senior executives, once said, "Order and disorder depend on the organization; courage and cowardice on the circumstances—but force and weakness come from character." A network cannot stand without appropriate organization; it has to support all circumstances—not a priori, but as they develop—and must be designed and managed by people of character.

The channels served by the network should be protected with appropriate security measures. Throughout the year, confidential financial information will represent a significant part of the load. Competitors should not know *when* and *where* we are going to sharpen our marketing edge. If they do not know where we are going to be the strongest, they will have to prepare themselves in many sectors, thus spreading themselves and their resources too thinly. We will then be able to carry on the business in the domains where we choose to concentrate.

Contrary to military implementations, the originality of financial networks lies in our ability to constantly tune them to the changing market drives.

But there are also common elements characterizing military and financial networks, such as the ability *to continue to deliver* the service they are designed to deliver. Confidentiality is still a paramount consideration.

In an example of such adaptability, private banking must practice total investment management in accordance with the client's wishes. This might mean total asset protection for an elderly person or aggressive growth for a risk-tolerant corporate executive. The whole concept of private banking is having a view on portfolio management, in equities, bonds, and cash, and choosing the best loan, the best deposit rate, and the best bank transfer. A private banker should be able to answer just about any question a client has about his money, but to do so he must access marketplaces and databases through networks.

Portfolio management is an increasingly *global effort*. For people and companies with an international life-style and assets around the world, we need a truly global approach. We have to be able to offer a worldwide service, being flexible in the products we offer, and global in the way we deliver them.

Portfolio management operations undertaken to satisfy a realtime request or query by a treasurer, institutional investor, or high net worth individual constitute what is known as a *long transaction*. This is typically a complex transaction that involves many subtransactions addressed to different, often incompatible, databases.

Sweden's Skandinaviska Enskilda Banken is one financial institution that has programmed long transactions for portfolio management in response to the demands of its sophisticated clients. As revealed in a working meeting in Stockholm in February 1992, Enskilda found through this experience that long transactions require 1,000 database accesses each—versus about 10 accesses needed for the simpler, more traditional transaction. The difference is one or two orders of magnitude.

Liberalization of financial regulations within the First World has encouraged a new era of growth and competition—an era, hence, of much more complex activities than those to which we have been accustomed. But here again, contrary to the military, the action of the financial industry is not one of swift actions by surprise, but of preparing the conditions for delivering surprises over the years, not just over a month. Therefore, one of the nonquantifiable advantages is patience in executing a well-conceived plan.

Clear-eyed financial organizations do appreciate this point and plan their investments accordingly. In my 1989 research among banks and securities houses throughout the United States, Japan, England, Ireland, and Germany, the leading institutions commented that, during the last few years,

- Their budget for telecommunications has been growing very fast, supporting megabit-per-second (MBPS) channels.

- Their budget for computers has slowed down—not because they economize on millions of instructions per second (MIPS), but because the cost per MIPS has dropped so dramatically.

These financial institutions were forecasting that, in the 1993 to 1995 time frame, network expenses will exceed those in data processing. One of the reasons is the greater contributions networks make to personal productivity and to competitiveness—and therefore to the bottom line.

During meetings with senior executives in these financial institutions, cognizant bankers have emphasized the prerequisites for establishing a systems architecture:

1. A *clearly defined* strategic plan, to be *served* by the technological plan to be elaborated

2. A thorough inventory of what is presently available, including knowledge, software, hardware, and documentation

3. Goals to be reached in markets, products, and services, as well as definition of what is needed to attain these goals

4. Architectural *definitions* (the grand design), including *concepts* and *choices* among alternatives

No financial institution, even the richest, can be all things to all people or face all circumstances. Investments have to be *focused* in order to be successful. As I had the opportunity to point out, the Industrial Bank of Japan estimates that 60 to 70 percent of capital will be spent on labor-saving projects or development and support of new products. This should be our guideline for all future investments in technology, and networks are a prime example because their steady functional evolution is a long-term goal.

EFFORTS TO ENHANCE RELATIONSHIP BANKING

During the 1980s, the emphasis has slowly but surely shifted from data management to time management. What professionals and executives want primarily to do with their workstations is not to compute but to communicate. Setting goals is the longer-term version of keeping track of our time.

But we cannot develop appropriate plans if our goals are fuzzy, or if our communications channels are clogged or nonexistent.

The new functionality in the banking industry—particularly in treasury, forex, and securities—shows that we must change concepts and methods. With the *old* concept, 98 percent of a computer system's integrative support was at the data structure level and 2 percent was at the query level. With the *new* concept which was developed out of necessity, 60 percent of the needed functionality is at the *intelligent query* level and 40 percent at the data management and data structure level. This 60 percent will steadily increase until it reaches 90 to 98 percent of total systems functionality, with particular emphasis on artificial intelligence supports that can fulfill ad hoc query requirements by managers and professionals.

These managers and professionals will be increasingly using the resources at their disposition to perform the following tasks:

• Project into future developments

• Experiment with alternative market opportunities

• Test different trading hypotheses before committing themselves to a specific strategy

Projecting ourselves into successful situations is one of the most powerful means of achieving goals. This is done through *vision*, seeing ourselves in specific problem-solving situations and being able to evaluate the path towards a solution. This is as true of financial products as of other lines of activity—including the development of networks to carry and sell these products.

The esprit de corps, the global network of branch offices, and the technological network interconnecting them are different phases of a long-term goal. This goal can be promoted or inhibited by policies that have to do with innovation, marketing strategies, and technology.

Japanese financial institutions in America, for instance, are not averse to cutting margins close to the bone to establish *business relationships*. In the view of their U.S. counterparts, this is a weakness, but the Japanese see it as *future strength:* "Patience," they say, "is rewarded in the end with profits."

Nomura Securities has an innovation department steadily working on new products that are focused on serving useful business goals. One of its projects deals with swaps technology so secretive that it is off-limits to visitors. Nomura's innovation operations benefit from artificial intelligence–driven global equity projects and trading programs capitalizing on large distributed databases. In this and in similar endeavors, the key questions have become "What is your competitive advantage?" and "How can we exploit our coming opportunities?"

A financial company finds the most difficulties if it lacks the spirit of innovation, has little or no flexibility, and cannot count on high technology to enhance relationship building. Such institutions see their placement power waning, and it becomes a vicious cycle.

Time and again during research in Tokyo, Japanese bankers emphasized that sheer stubbornness has destroyed a lot more bottom lines than large, not-so-wise investments or market shifts have ever done. The *spirit of innovation* is a basic cultural issue, not a financial one.

Any problem that can be solved with a budgetary allocation is not really a problem—it is an expense. *If* this expense bears fruit in the sense of measurable profits, *then* it is an investment. Today, the best investments are those that ingeniously combine technology and marketing skills.

In Nomura Securities, for instance, technology and marketing are married in more than one way to meet the expectation that, by the early 1990s, it will feature one million retail customers. These customers will be using personal computers connected to databases through Nomura's trading network.

This is but one example of innovation in the financial services industry, which is the world's most strategic sector of the twenty-first century. Japanese institutions have begun to develop the global infrastructure necessary to match the domestic strength of their economy. A host of new products is now emerging:

1. *Samurai bonds:* yen-denominated and issued in Japan

2. *Shogun bonds:* foreign currency–denominated bonds issued by foreign borrowers in Japan

3. *Sushi bonds:* foreign currency issued in Japan by local institutions for Japanese portfolios

4. *Stocks of the week:* handpicked by the big four Japanese stockbrokers based on investment themes

5. *Ambulance stocks:* touted to rescue important clients who have lost money on brokerage house recommendations

Much longer than these five items, the total list includes commercial paper, yen-denominated banker's acceptances, swaps, and corporate bonds with separable equity warrants attached to them. There are also mortgage-backed securities and an assortment of fixed-income products.

The steady flow of financial services, new as well as revamped old, is supported through high technology. A steady information flow—plus proper training—keeps the trader from making significant deals involving financial commitments on the spur of the moment. The most certain recipe for disaster is decision making based on emotions and misinformation.

One of the differences between Japanese and other financial institutions is that, in the former, policy specifies the following requirements (and the networks make it feasible to carry these out):

- Never make a major financial commitment with vanilla ice cream as the only option. Provide a range of flavors to choose from.

- Realspace information gives the option of saying no, as well as awareness of being constantly measured by competitors.

- Because the most powerful tools in any negotiation are knowledge and information, not emotion or instinct, traders working in realspace are able to do computer-assisted research, focusing on their homework.

- Before traders decide on a deal, they can experiment on the proposition itself and pass over some business if it may be disastrous.

Realspace information makes it feasible for traders to shift tactics during negotiations, probe weaknesses in the other party's defenses, and wear down opponents. Assisted by realspace and artificial intelligence, Japanese financial institutions are becoming experts in these strategic moves.

By mastering the information a global network provides to them, traders stand a good chance to improve in whatever they try to negotiate, by bringing the other party to appreciate that "the deal works to its advantage." This is the true sense of *relationship building* in the banking industry.

A FINANCIAL ARCHITECTURE FOR THE 1990s

In trying to envision the financial world of the 1990s we must be careful not to set things in the context of the world as it has been, but to think instead of the world *as it may be in the future*. Whether the issue is political, sociological, or technological, the financial themes in the background must be examined from the coming perspective.

Many leading banks today think and speak of the twenty-first century as the *Pacific century*. The reason is growth. Several East Asian countries, not only Japan, have been at the top of the world's economic charts—and they contrast greatly with other parts of the globe, such as Central and South America and Africa, which are in rapid decline.

As a result of these trends, major financial institutions are getting ready to face the developing challenges in the Pacific Rim, and, by doing so, they are draining human capital from other industrial sectors. My research in Tokyo in 1989 and 1991 brought to my attention the fact that MITI, among other government agencies, now focuses attention on combating the negative image associated with highly paid white-collar workers such as foreign exchange dealers justifying their pay on the terms of the work they do.

According to Japan's Labor Ministry, the average monthly salary for employees at financial companies is about 18 percent higher than that of qualified manufacturing workers, and customary twice-a-year bonuses are nearly double. How this relate to the requirements for skills and expertise in the decade of the 1990s?

Japanese financial institutions say they need the mathematical skills of engineers and other scientists to help develop new products. Daiwa Securities, for instance, suggests, "It has become impossible to design new financial products without mathematical ability, and this is particularly true with the introduction of futures and options trading."

This new supply and demand equation has its consequences. The Japanese government's Science and Technology Agency says that in 1989 only 35 graduates from the technology department of Tokyo University chose jobs with manufacturing companies, compared with 165 in 1988 and 222 in 1985. In 1988, 75 graduates from the same departments joined banks, insurance companies, and brokerage firms, compared with 16 five years earlier.

Johsen Takahashi, an economist with Mitsubishi Research Institute, adds that it has become unfashionable to do the "dirty and hard" work associated with manufacturing. In the past decade, "the idea that the era of manufacturing goods is over has infiltrated into people's minds," and this now has visible results.

On the other hand, Eiji Suzuki, president of the Japan Federation of Employers Associations and chairman of Mitsubishi Chemical Industries comments that this kind of thinking "could cause a decline in Japan's international manufacturing competitiveness in the near future." A similar comment has been made by American manufacturing industry leaders and university presidents.

Although the new balance in the allocation of available brainpower works to the detriment of the manufacturing industries, the American and the Japanese financial industries will profit from the switch of rocket scientists into banking, and will vastly improve their competitive position in the process. The foremost financial institutions not only hire the best brains that are available, but also, through high technology, make available to the traders important market information from the floors of every major exchange. The two processes are related: To attract the best graduates, a company must employ high technology.

Strategic plans, market experimentation, and high technology help create a win-win situation, if we use our resources competently. Having an idea of how other firms are positioning themselves in a market can sometimes make or break a program trade, say traders familiar with such strategies.

The transfer of knowledge and information in a global sense is a mission given to the bank's network.

- Knowing that a large firm is selling a basket of stocks for an institutional client might indicate that it is not the best time to make a program trade between index options and the underlying stocks.

- When top dealers begin to move major positions, their effect can be exaggerated by groups of speculators who try to follow the leading firm's trading footsteps. Timely communication about such an occurrence is of utmost importance.

Realspace solutions will be increasingly needed from financial analysis to trading and execution. David Band, chief executive of Barclays de Zoete Wedd (BZW), says that a dealer with a dominant share in Britain's most internationally traded shares lacks vital market information if he does not have extensive operations in New York and Tokyo.[4] Short of such networking capability, the financial institution risks losing millions in ill-judged positions.

It is not the plurality of the positions being followed but their *globality* that matters the most. About two-thirds of all British equity business, for example, takes place in the 140-odd most liquid *alpha stocks*,[5] and most of that in the 30 or so biggest. Naturally, these stocks are by far the most heavily researched, but this is not necessarily done in a global sense, which causes misreading of sentiments of American and Japanese investors.

Precisely because of lack of globality in economic and financial research, the quality of much research in many institutions is getting worse. Most investment houses say that they are dealing with this problem by hiring

---

[4] *The Economist*, October 14, 1989.

[5] The London Stock Exchange traditionally distinguished between alpha, beta, gamma, and delta stocks. Alpha stocks are those corresponding to the biggest firms and typically are the most liquid. In America, they would have been qualified for listing at the New York Stock Exchange; the beta roughly correspond to American Stock Exchange listings; and the gamma and delta to over-the-counter stocks.

more analysts, but this is the wrong approach. An good solution incorporates global networking and the implementation of AI.

Artificial intelligence constructs running on the bank's network must combine knowledge of options, futures, stock indices, and the underlying stock-market with computer-trading analysis. The result can be a powerful trading machine that prowls all the markets for price aberrations and imbalances it can exploit. The functionality offered by the global network must be able to point out changes that are already taking place and to flash missed opportunities and ignored challenges before the list becomes too long.

Such functionality should certainly sharpen any bank's ability to control costs, enabling management to carry out drastic cost-cutting programs. Determined to slash labor costs, financial institutions are discarding traditional notions about job security, compensation, and seniority. Many close branches, move operations, and eliminate levels of management and lines of business, but few are really determined to substitute networks and expert systems for costly labor—these few will be the survivors.

In a similar vein, networks and expert systems should help in *compliance*. One subject that banks cannot ignore is government regulations, and answers to problems caused by bureaucratic red tape can be increasingly given through AI and telecommunications. This is how, for instance, American banks are tooling up to face the Treasury Department's plans to require banks to keep information on international wire transfers in an effort to combat money laundering.

SOLUTIONS FOR A SOPHISTICATED CLIENT BASE

The instruments of debt and equity that flow across borders in realspace are so sophisticated—and the balances on which they rest so delicate—that it is easy to forget how conditional their continuation in time is, how exposed they may be to fraud, or how fragile is the layer of confidence on which they rest.

To create and sustain global markets, we need a tremendous amount of coordination, not only between different nations but also within the same economy and the same financial organization. Part of the problem lies in the fact that governments have not globalized as fast as markets have. This can be dangerous at a time when a single economy is being created in the First World, and when transborder financial, manufacturing, and trade links are growing in many dimensions.

The new financial instruments that are currently evolving do not recognize "borders." Throughout the First World, assets are being *equitized,* converted to *debt*, and *underwritten* for sale. Entities once considered too crucial to be subjected to market forces—for instance, government-owned telephone companies, nationalized banks, and water and energy monopolies—are also put up for sale.

Capital, currencies, and credit flood across formerly insulated national borders. This transborder flow of funds is now 30 times greater than merchandise trade. As I said in the beginning of this chapter, the automated clearinghouse in New York alone handles on the average more than two trillion dollars every day.

By the force of the transactions taking place, governmental, financial, manufacturing, and merchandising corporations are forced to learn how to manage their vast, distributed economic and other assets to take advantage of the opportunities before them. The ability to manage capital in a global sense has become nearly synonymous with controlling events around the globe—and it has also created levels of sophistication in financial dealing that never existed before.

There is today a dual emphasis on capital and networking, which changes some of the perspectives to which we have been accustomed in the past. Size alone may not be the only factor in market conquest, but, to counterbalance it, we have to become both wise and flexible. We need vision and speed of adaptation to the new conditions.

Speaking of size, in terms of market capitalization, Nomura Securities is about 20 times larger than Merrill Lynch—and its pretax profits greater than those of the entire American securities industry. One Japanese company—NTT—is worth more than IBM, AT&T, Exxon, GM, and GE combined. These statistics make clear the changes taking place.

Japanese banks, Daniel Burstein suggests, control nearly 10 percent of the American retail banking assets—and they did so in the decade of the 1980s.[6] Five of the top ten California banks are now Japanese. The Sumitomo Bank owns a minority interest in Goldman Sachs; Nippon Life holds a similar share of Shearson Lehman Hutton; Mutual Life has a bigger share of PaineWebber; and the Union Bank of California was bought by California First, where the majority owner is the Bank of Tokyo.

Combining this expanding capital base with realspace networking and the ingenious use of AI in financial operations gives credibility to the argument that, in 2000, the world will be dominated by a small group of mega financial institutions. If we believe this plausible hypothesis, we must assume that there will be many mergers and acquisitions along the way and that the solutions to be provided will be *globally networked.*

[6]D. Burstein, *Yen!* (Melbourne: Bantam/Schwarz, 1989).

The research laboratories of telecommunications companies are working fervently to meet that objective. In Japan, NTT's labs produce avant-garde telecommunications technology and intelligent building solutions to steadily upgrade the efficiency of the Japanese financial institutions in their operations. Such technological assistance is perceived to be vital as we move toward integrated capital markets and 24-hour trading.

These new policies call for significant investments. Figure 11.3 emphasizes the predominant trend. Data processing used to consume the lion's share of the information technology budget. This has radically changed, and it is expected that, by the mid-1990s, the number one player in budgetary allocations will be telecommunications—with the telecom executive getting more clout within the organization than his data processing counterpart.

These examples help document how the Japanese bet on the longer range rather than on immediate returns at the expense of a solid competitive condition. Many in Tokyo suggest that both the government and the major financial institutions have 30-year plans and that these plans are steadily reviewed to ensure that they meet the requirements of the international financial market as it develops.

As networks become the infrastructure of financial organization, steady training is the spearhead. The leaders of the Japanese financial industry appreciate that perfect practice makes the difference.

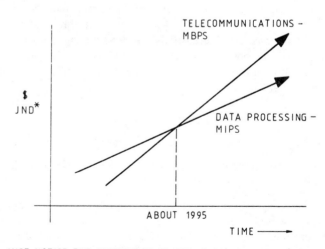

* JUST NOTICE THE DIFFERENCE: A SCALE OF MEASUREMENT

Figure 11.3 Trends in technology investments.

- A teacher is not there just to *acquaint* us with the tools of our trade.

- A teacher *is a tool of our trade.*

We never stop needing teachers—and this is true throughout the organization, at all levels and in all functions. As it cannot be repeated too often, our investments will be subutilized unless we train our personnel how to use them.

A trait of foremost financial organizations is ensuring that they are staffed by people who are still learning and who believe that *learning is a lifelong process.* Our success depends on the steady progress of human knowledge, which is instrumental in mastering change and in creating the preconditions for continuing success.

We must steadily raise our level of knowledge and find new opportunities for our customers. This means research, research, and research—which must be done increasingly online through expert systems that address global databases and through financial experts who can appreciate the work done by means of AI-assisted communications channels.

From human capital to financial resources and the mastering of networking technology, Japanese financial institutions are racing to the number one position. Being number one in Japan is very important. Chief executives who perceive themselves as number one in their own field want to do business only with those who are number one in theirs.

To this end, the Japanese have evolved planning capabilities and processes able to carry out systematic structural adjustments to evolving market conditions. These adjustments are economic, financial, managerial and technological. They employ communications and computers but also artificial intelligence, robotics, and increasingly powerful managerial tools.

Focus and astute choices are the keys to such strategies. Nomura gives a good example. It came out of nowhere in the early 1980s to dominate the Eurobond market in 1987:

- It assiduously stockpiled talent.

- It developed computers and network solutions.

- It waited and watched as American and European financial firms pulled back from market segments.

- And Nomura finally emerged as the number one underwriter.

While other financial institutions are licking wounds instead of reaping their inflated expectations for short-term profits, Nomura fills the empty seats that the others leave, with human capital and a network that has already taken on world dimensions.

12

Networks for Trading and Client Service

When it comes to high-technology investments, a financial institution is faced with significant constraints. First and foremost, in the majority of cases money spent on computers and communications is not linked to strategic planning; it is therefore rarely in line with the strategic directions of the firm.

Failure to conform to strategic guidelines often ends in technology investments being made at the wrong time and place through inopportune decisions, but this is only one of the reasons why less-than-expected results are being obtained. Besides the fact that software is often a mess, technology as a whole is rarely well-managed—let alone rationally investigated and justified:

- Competition usually sets the floor in spending.

- Cash flow and treasury reasons define the upper limit.

- Return on investment (ROI) is rarely taken as an objective criterion for choices.

Yet whether we speak of computers or of communications, and whether the network is done for cash management, trading, or customer service, it is very important to carefully cost-justify the investments we make.

If we have clear objectives in mind, it is not difficult to calculate return on investment. There are good reasons why financial institutions, exchanges, information providers, and manufacturing and merchandising organizations establish and maintain increasingly sophisticated networks:

- First and foremost, their networks assist them in maintaining account control.

- Online marketing, sales, and cash management help in obtaining more business from the same client population.

- Once established, networks make it feasible to channel auxiliary products—particularly those designed for online delivery.

Financial institutions have heard these arguments before, but they have reasons of their own for investing in networks: Though the budget is not trivial, networks still have a relatively low implementation cost compared to brick-and-mortar alternatives, and high technology ensures that there is no visible limit to the sophistication of services that can be offered to the clients—treasurers are a good example.

As time goes on, the relationship of the financial institution with its clients becomes indivisible from the network connection. This is shown in Figure

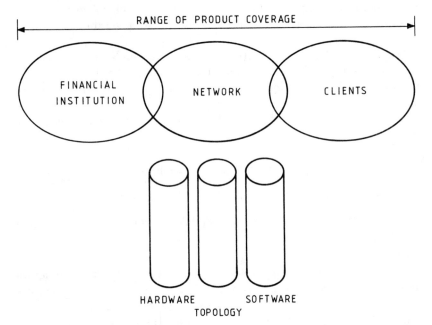

Figure 12.1 Network interface between providers and consumers of financial services.

12.1, which also suggests that the pillars on which network performance rests are the topology (that is, geographic coverage), hardware, and software, with the last item tending to be the weakest link in the chain.

AN ONLINE FOREX CLEARINGHOUSE

For some years, SWIFT,[1] a networking cooperative of about 2,000 banks worldwide, has tried to move into new competitive service sectors. One of these attempts involves providing networking services for an emerging European foreign exchange system. Such negotiations were done with a group of 25 European banks that intended to build a common clearinghouse for foreign exchange, known as the Exchange Clearing House Organization (ECHO).

The aim of ECHO—which never really succeeded in coming alive—has been to establish the first multilateral foreign exchange settlement system in the world. This was projected in an effort to reduce the administrative costs of financial institutions by replacing the bilateral arrangements through which they now settle foreign exchange transactions. However, not all banks endorse this idea. This case therefore constitutes a good example of the political problems that networking projects may encounter.

Looking at the fundamental concepts underlying the original proposal, the goal of the Exchange Clearing House Organization was to replace the mesh of bilateral agreements between banks for foreign exchange deals. A single common European system was supposed to be able to settle a day's foreign exchange deals across Europe in one batch using a set of common, predetermined rules for *netting*. But, as stated, this move has received mixed reactions from treasurers and financial institutions that presently carry out foreign exchange transactions under bilateral agreements. Two main issues underpin ECHO's failure and tend to characterize all similar endeavors in the future.

- The first involves politics and finance. Banks are not happy to forgo some of their profits from forex trading.

Banks tend to settle the deals one at a time, and although foreign exchange administrative costs across Europe add up to large sums each year, the business opportunity is great; the challenge is to reduce settlement costs without missing opportunities. According to calculations made by the ill-fated ECHO, the cost of forex settlements in Europe amounts to roughly

---

[1] Society for Worldwide Interbank Financial Telecommunications, established in 1973 and head-quartered in Brussels.

$400 million each day, and preliminary tests show that an umbrella system can reduce settlement costs by up to 20 percent—but that's a guess.

- The second issue is technical. Transaction and settlement rules differ from country to country in the European Community.

While the European Community's integration is moving ahead with its ups and downs, we are still a long way from uniform laws, norms, and regulations for all 12 countries—as the case should have been. Up to a point this is a negative, but for treasurers it also has positive aspects. They can optimize financial flows and investments between the 12 countries of the European Community, provided that they have the know-how and technology for doing so.

Practically everyone also expects that there will be many software challenges because no one has ever developed a multilateral exchanged netting system for foreign exchange. For the same reason, there will be technical challenges caused by political compromises that will take some time to reach.

Foreseen software hurdles and loose ends mean that nobody will venture to say how long it will take for the dust to settle, even after online operations might have started. But analogical reasoning with examples taken from similar efforts can be revealing. Traders at the New York Stock Exchange, for example, look forward to a 24-hour trading system in the United States and Europe to be truly functional only around the year 2000.

In its initial steps toward a 24-hour trading system, in September 1990 the board of the New York Stock Exchange (NYSE) approved the first form of after-hours trading in the Big Board. The move to establish an around-the-clock trading system came as the NYSE faced increased competition from other exchanges. The approved plans are intended to bring back business that the NYSE has lost. It was therefore not too difficult to get agreement, but political problems came to the foreground as such approval regarded the first two parts of a five-phase program for 24-hour trading.

Under the NYSE plan, trading would for the first time bypass the exchange's specialists, who keep orderly markets in assigned stocks. Rather, buyers and sellers would be matched by brokers or by the exchange electronically. The new rules essentially establish two additional trading sessions: One is designed to handle program trades, and the other to allow investors to trade after 4 P.M. at the closing price of each stock.

One problem with these plans is that these two trading periods, known as *crossing sessions*, would overlap. In the first, traders would be able to enter into the exchange's computer systems a single-sided order, such as a buy or a sell, or a matched buy and sell for execution. At 5 P.M., the exchange would attempt to match buy and sell orders and would execute matched trades. Wall Street executives said that orders that were not matched would be returned to customers—a procedure that in the long run, would prove to be quite counterproductive.

During the first session, if there was significant news about any individual company, trading in that company would be halted for the rest of the session. This is thought to be a measure to protect investors from buying securities at a price fixed at the 4 P.M. close of regular trading that could not respond to the new information.

However, in the second session, trading would not be halted. This second session is designed to handle certain forms of program trades now made in London, which means that it aims to reacquire settlement business that has been lost to competition—but does not necessarily fit well with the first session.

Although ECHO's and Big Board's after-hour goals are different, as trading deals with different commodities, there are similarities that lend themselves to case reasoning. When it comes to the implementation of technology, and most particularly of networking, we should never forgo the opportunity to learn from cases that are already being tested—particularly unsuccessful ones.[2]

TRADING THROUGH SCREENS

The National Association of Securities Dealers (NASD) operates the over-the-counter market—America's second largest stock market. Current plans involve a $30 million project to update its 20-year-old computerized trading network.[3]

Originally, NASD had hoped to share the costs with SEAQ of London's International Stock Exchange (ISE), but decided to bear them alone. The new system, which NASD hopes to phase in over three to five years, will still allow the two exchanges to jointly trade international stocks. However, different regulatory requirements affecting both markets have been an obstacle to integration of NASD and ISE, and this is not the only reason.

London's ISE has been conducting a strategic review of its own operations, whose results don't necessarily match the goals of NASD. From a

---

[2]An example of such a case is Project PIPE (Euroquote) of the Common Market's stock exchanges, which, after years of study, has been definitely dropped as of July 1991.

[3]*Wall Street Journal*, June 21–22, 1991.

strategic planning viewpoint, NASDAQ and SEAQ are today becoming the two major competitors in the rich North Atlantic equities market.

Britain's SEAQ and SEAQ International are being restructured into a unified and modernized network that will cover the whole of the European Community.[4] As of early 1993 it will be enriched by TAURUS, an online electronic settlements system. As a financial quotations, online trading, and settlements network, ISE's SEAQ is unmatched by any continental stock exchange. The real challenger will most likely be NASDAQ International.

NASDAQ has landed in western Europe and is actively seeking partners. There are reasons to believe that this will be the number two quotation, trading, and settlement network in the European Community, eventually fighting for first position. The third network with similar aims is that of the triple alliance: Reuters, Credit Swiss First Boston (CSFB), and Euroclear of Morgan Guaranty. Several West European banks collaborate, but the alliance dominates this third network.

It is still too early to say who will be the winner. Political, legal, and technological factors will determine the outcome—not just management and financing. In terms of regulatory rules, for instance, London's electronic SEAQ system has less stringent disclosure requirements than those of the NASD. SEAQ does not require immediate publication of transactions, but instead gives global figures on a next-day basis.

Technical factors may be less divergent. For instance, London's SEAQ uses a screen-based system for trading stocks that is similar to that of NASD, and each plans to modernize its trading computer platform to better operate in the domestic market, while being able to handle a true international stock market. Both for trading and for the management of financial assets, client companies have given these exchanges lots of hints.

In addition, classical exchanges face a possible erosion of their client base. Asset management companies with millions of dollars in equities and bonds, as well as administrators of money market funds and pension-fund portfolios, increasingly work through computer screens. They use networks known as *fourth-market* systems, such as Reuters' Instinet, which matches buyers with sellers, thus bypassing even SEAQ, NASDAQ, and Reuters/CSFB/Euroclear.

This changes the whole trading landscape in several ways. Institutions controlling large pools of capital are cutting back on services that once fed the bottom line of stockbrokers, including the following:

---

[4]See also D. N. Chorafas and H. Steinmann, *Financial Databases* (London and Dublin: Lafferty Publications, 1992).

- Research

- Trading

- Underwriting

- Money management

- Brokerage

These services are all being taken in-house, as treasurers find they can live without most of services supplied by Wall Street and London. And alternative trading systems may be more economical than traditional brokerages.

One conspicuous example is General Electric's in-house management of its $36 billion retirement fund. GE relies little on Wall Street research and trading systems, and it custom-designs its own domestic and foreign index funds. That makes the company its own broker, analyst, and rocket scientist—even though the GE empire includes an old-line Wall Street firm—Kidder, Peabody.[5]

The exchanges, of course, try to counterattack through the enlargement of financial horizons they can offer to corporations by means of networking. In June 1990, NASD started Portal, a closed-circuit computer terminal network that links dealers and institutions, particularly those that buy privately offered securities.

Among NASD's plans is one to expand the system to cover junk bond trading, and, most importantly, to be the first U.S. stock market to move toward round-the-clock operations by moving its opening bell to 3:30 A.M. Eastern Standard Time. The NASD is also pushing to make obsolete most "pink-sheet" listings of stocks—those whose prices are published once daily in paper lists. Another move is the development of advanced software to keep track of brokers in the fraud-riddled penny-stock market.

NASD is trying to cure pink-sheet problems by creating a separate NAS-DAQ market, which is known as the *electronic bulletin board.*

- For regular NASDAQ stocks, securities dealers post bids to buy and offers to sell securities on computer screens.

- An issue may have many dealers competing to attract orders from brokers.

[5] *Business Week*, November 5, 1990.

Displayed prices, NASD says, must be firm—that is, they must be honored when a broker calls to make a trade. No such discipline exists in the pink sheets.

GLOBEX AND ITS TRADING AMBITIONS

Globex is the computerized international financing trading system that Reuters plans to offer in partnership with the world's two largest futures exchanges, the Chicago Mercantile Exchange (the Merc) and the Chicago Board of Trade (the CBOT). First announced in early 1988 and set for a launching date in mid-1989, but subject to consequent slippage, it went alive in April 1992. This project is intended to perform the following functions:

- To act as an automated after-hours supplement to the exchange floors (pits), where each day traders shout and use hand signals to buy and sell financial futures contracts
- To be the world's biggest computer-based trading network for global around-the-clock trading in financial futures.

Financial futures are contracts in which traders bet whether the value of a financial commodity will rise or fall by a specified date.[6] Futures contracts for Eurodollar deposit rates, U.S. Treasury bills, Deutschemarks, and Japanese yen are among the products that would be traded through Globex.

Any company can subscribe, but a reasonable expectation is that the larger institutional investors will use Globex 6 P.M. to 6 A.M., Chicago time. That period will overlap with at least parts of the trading day in the money centers of Europe and Asia, which, rely heavily on the financial products available in Chicago, but currently can deal in them only when the trading floors of the Merc and CBOT are open.

The Merc and CBOT, however, are not alone in these plans. Other firms include the Chicago Board Options Exchange, the American Stock Exchange, and the Cincinnati Stock Exchange. All plan to offer after-hours computerized systems.

Although different exchanges are planning their networks individually, many experts believe that these systems will eventually merge into a unified global network, probably within a decade. Pressure by the ultimate users of the financial products will force them to merge, and there are economies of scale in developing one system that uses common software.

---

[6]See also D. N. Chorafas, *Treasury Operations and the Foreign Exchange Challenge* (New York: Wiley, 1992).

Precisely for software reasons and for economies of scale, Globex's potential customers—brokerage and other financial firms—have demanded that the Merc get together with the Chicago Board of Trade, which had developed its own global trading system, Aurora.

Brokers and other potential customers reckon that the new marketplace's liquidity will run deeper if trading is not divided between competing networks. And they want a broader market, rather than one split among competing financial networks.

If all the commodities exchanges in the First World run on the same network, a market of colossal potential with issues traded around the clock will ensue. Table 12.1 shows the total volume of futures contracts traded in 1990, by exchange.

But universal trading on one network is easier said than done. One European exchange already committed to participating in Globex is the five-year-old Paris futures exchange, the Marché à Terme International

Table 12.1 Yearly Volume of Futures Traded in 1990 Worldwide by the Globex Member Exchanges

Member	Number of Contracts
USA	
Chicago Board of Trade	120,770
Chicago Mercantile Exchange	84,838
New York Mercantile Exchange	36,358
Europe	
Germany, DTB	111,000
Britain, LIFFE	34,170
France, MATIF	28,858
Japan	
Osaka Securities Exchange	22,777
Tokyo Stock Exchange	21,623
Tokyo International Financial Futures Exchange	14,451
Australia	
Sydney Futures Exchange	11,563
Brazil	
BM&F	9,875
Singapore	
SIMEX	5,721
	502,004

de France (MATIF). Globex executives have reportedly received signs of interest from the London International Financial Futures Exchange (LIFFE) and the Singapore International Monetary Exchange.

This is small fry regarding the global trading ambitions; most importantly, after three years of talk. Cognizant people put the blame for the delays and slippages on the bureaucratic and technical complexities involved in developing such a project under the oversight of different partners, each of which brings new demands and requirements to the task.

The lesson is that, when it comes to common networking projects, we should not fail to appreciate the evolving complexity and moving targets. Neither should such projects underestimate the extent of services to be supported or the importance of making them appealing to the enduser—in order to ensure the project's profitability and survival.

A financial trading network designed to protect and enhance the investors' interests should allow them to trade any time at any exchange on any security without having to open a new account or use a different broker. That should make it attractive for a number of firms to participate.

The goal should also be to provide a seamless transition between normal hours and after-hours trading, attracting a whole new range of users. Value differentiation should take account of the fact that the fundamental concept of electronic trading is not new. Over the past dozen years, more than 15 financial exchanges in Europe, the United States, and Asia have adopted some form of computerized systems to match buyers with sellers. However, many of those systems do not operate in realtime. The trader who enters a *buy* bid through his computer terminal must wait.

Current systems take time to sift through all the offers to find a corresponding *sell*, or determine that no matching offer exists. What is needed in reality is high-performance computers allowing many traders to simultaneously interact in reviewing bids and offers. When traders decide to buy or sell, they must be able to execute the order and know within a few seconds whether a successful match has been made.

This immediacy can help create a liquidity that older forms of after-hours trading have often lacked. But realtime networks also have to be reliable. In a business where billions of dollars are continually in play, computer failures can be catastrophic.

A LEADING FINANCIAL NETWORK: PROJECT 2000 AT CITIBANK

One of the less appreciated consequences of networks at large—most particularly networks in the financial industry—is that information flows across national borders. Political borders do not stop the flow of information and knowledge moving through global networks—we saw beginning the 1960s with the "brain drain."

The opportunities and the challenge that information globility presents are incredible. Well-managed companies must therefore understand that decisions are made without loss of time and focus on where the bank is going in terms of market orientation, product design, human capital, and technological infrastructure, as well as what it wishes to do with the resources at its disposal.

The electronic delivery of financial services has many aspects: networks, terminals, databases, logic servers, and number crunchers. As I discussed in Chapter 5, large volumes of market data have to be filtered through AI, and Chapters 6 through 9 suggested that AI must be used for a wide variety of tasks from analytics to visualization, and from intelligent charting to pattern recognition.

The integration of information sources is one thing, the filtering of data flows another, and the visualization of digested information a third. These three processes are not distinct from one another, but highly interrelated. Together they become a productivity tool and a cutting edge against competition. As Figure 12.2 demonstrates, our goal should be actionable

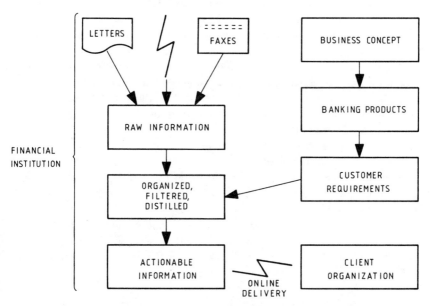

Figure 12.2   Electronic delivery of financial services.

information and knowledge; this is what gives *electronic banking* its distinct features.

To face the multifacted functionality the network of the 1990s, Citibank has established Project 2000 under top management directives. The board correctly considers its domain to define the direction of customer services and correspondent banking; and it believes that investments in technology should focus on this definition.

In the early 1970s, Citibank had already established a global network known as Marty; but with the introduction of Project 2000, Marty is being phased out. (Marty was Citibank's second financial network.) The reason for such fast substitution of networks and the resulting change in communications and computers is *sustained productivity increases* in the delivery mechanism of the bank.

Astute bank management understands that the delivery of financial services is today more important than plain old data processing, which deals mainly with production activities. Efficient networks must reach the client at his workplace, providing him online with the possibility of obtaining increasingly sophisticated financial functions—and each successive generation further enhances this endeavor.

For instance, services supported by the new network are characterized by electronic input, with business relating to corresponding banks, brokers, and large clients being done online. There are also online links to Swift, Fedwire, and Chips, and expert systems are widely used; one of them translates unformatted and telex-based money orders received from clients into the Swift format.

Funds transfers cost the bank money, which explains the interest in automating beyond classical data processing's reach. One of the most challenging tasks for the financial industry in the 1990s is the automation of the payments documents traffic, which, despite 35 years of computers in banking, is still done manually.

As the volume of payments documents has grown with financial activity, data processing has become increasingly incapable of curbing paper growth. As a result, banks hired more people to do the job, forgetting that, every time more people are hired, more problems, errors, delays—and higher costs—are created.

One of the reasons that the handling of payments documents still leaves much to be desired in the way of automation is the problem of *signature recognition*. It is no wonder that Citibank is actively working in this domain using one of the more advanced tools in AI: neural networks.[7]

[7]See also D. N. Chorafas and H. Steinmann, *Expert Systems in Banking* (London: Macmillan, 1990).

Table 12.2 Procedures Utilized among Financial Institutions to Manage Daily Cash Flow Liquidity

Manual[a]	65.5%[b]
Terminal or PC connected to host	40.3%
Stand-alone personal computer	18.6%

[a] It is significant that, by far, the largest operation is manual—in spite of the technological investments made.

[b] Some financial institutions participating in this survey have given multiple answers. The percentage points therefore do not add up to 100.

As many companies have discovered the hard way, throwing people at the problem is the wrong solution, just as throwing money at the problem gets no results. And even among the more successful automation efforts, where most paper has already been weeded out, quite often the labor component is still too strong.

At the same time, nobody said that this orientation toward greater effectiveness is widespread. Table 12.2 presents the results of the market survey done by the Italian Bankers' Association (ABI) on Cash Management. These are not the best results in a high-technology sense, but they are telling.

As Table 12.2 indicates, in spite of a significant use of terminals and PCs, the largest component of the work is still manual. This is as far as classical data processing can go. That is also why the foremost banks have understood that, if they stay at the level of traditional data processing, their operations will remain manual—and therefore costly, error-prone, inefficient, and noncompetitive.

As Citibank's answer to these challenges, Project 2000 is equipped with the best technology available. It is a smart network, ensuring access to optical disk (imaging) databases using not only expert systems but also more advanced AI tools, as indicated by the reference made to the neural network under the development for automatic signature recognition.

Within Citibank's new-generation global network, specific products supported by Project 2000 are funds transfer operations, cash letters, account reconcilement, client account management, and other advanced customer services. The overall concept is exemplified in Figure 12.3 and can be divided into three parts:

1. Electronic banking functionality supported end-to-end by the new financial network

2. Integration of the front desk and back office of the bank's brick-and-mortar network through shared communications and databases

3. Enrichment of the available computer power through artificial intelligence and supercomputers

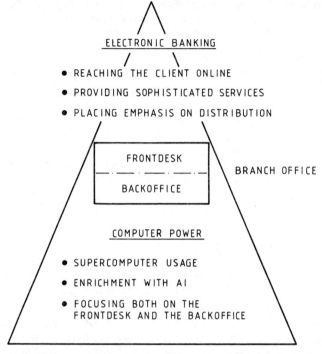

Figure 12.3   AI-supported online interfaces.

Part of the infrastructure of Project 2000 focuses on funds transfer mechanisms, with its first capacity goal being 100,000 funds transfers per day. Yet because of a sharp increase in funds transfer traffic at Citibank, this already seems to be too low a level, and new design objectives aim to bring it higher.

A significant percentage of resources devoted to the integration of computers and communications addresses itself to branch-office services. Project 2000 is also actively supported by Citibank's correspondent banking and investment services channels; both have taken an active interest in the system architecture, helped by the bank's software system development department.

The new financial network is also tuned to capitalize on and respond to the integrative perspectives regarding voice and data. Citibank did not provide statistics on this matter, but I discovered the following information during a study of large organizations that I made at the end of the 1980s:

- Some 20 to 25 percent of prevalent information flow took place with data, and 75 to 80 percent was done through voice.

- Voice traffic has been growing by only 4 percent a year, whereas data traffic was growing by 35 percent; data seems to have the upper hand.

- However, today *data* is a fuzzy notion because *text* is fast becoming the senior partner in the data flow.

- By the mid- to late 1990s, text is expected to represent at least 75 percent of the contents of databases, with a great deal of attention being paid to document handling.

It is estimated the in two to three years text and data will probably equal, then surpass, voice traffic. When this happens, instead of data operating as a guest on a voice network, voice will be the guest on a data network, with the traffic being both administered and controlled through AI constructs.

ELECTRONIC MESSAGE SERVICES WITH PROJECT 2000

From design to implementation, that most important point to consider is integration. Within this context, a study of Citibank's Project 2000 reveals some basic prerequisites regarding the evolution of electronic message services into the new landscape that must be serviced by the mid-1990s.

To learn how to use new technology and avoid rediscovering the wheel, we need a good case study on the methodological approach to follow. The work that has been done with Project 2000:

- Started by defining the current communications structure: telex, e-mail, fax, datacom

- Addressed itself to the bank's organizational units having the most pressing communications requirements

- Established the new service needs, as well as conversion possibilities

- Ensured an integrated logical network, using expert systems in the interfaces

- Found or developed adaptable software for message management, with a key role played by expert systems

- Established a cooperation factor involving channels (product lines), vendors, and internal and external people open to change

Although Project 2000 selected its system solution and associated software based on the foregoing criteria, attention has steadily been placed not only on current requirements but also on future *expansion*. Citibank now serves 6,000 customers directly and 30,000 customers indirectly through its network.

Attention was also given to the fact that an organization can adopt high technology only when it is able to change the culture of its system specialists and of its users. "If we fail in this effort we will have only ourselves to blame," said a Citibank executive.

Part of the restructuring of electronic message services has been the ability to offer a larger palette of effective client-oriented products on an integrative basis. Therefore, Project 2000 focused on *customer service roles*, helping the bank's own managers and professionals to track investigation queries and to understand large amounts of data.

The significant examples of AI implementation at Citibank suggest that the proper use of expert systems and the ongoing investments in AI fields such as pattern recognition permit continued reduction in cost, and they ensure sophisticated, decision-oriented solutions for Citibank's customers.

Although there are many practical examples in messaging and funds transfer, other AI implementations focus on *financial modeling*, recommending how to do funding. Rare are the financial organizations that can today provide support for financial modeling because this is both costly and ineffective if done with traditional computer systems and software.

As the leading financial institutions have found through experience, this point on value differentiation by means of expert systems particularly applies to customers who themselves have a sophisticated level of expertise. For a bank, meeting this level of sophistication means the ability to attract high–networth clients—hence competitiveness.

For instance, a value-added cash management implementation permits customers not only to track balances but also to reconcile. Similarly, within Project 2000, attention has been given to *trade services*. An example is letters of credit and collections, which represent 35 percent of Citibank's business; a further goal is to have this application integrated with funds transfer.

Research conducted in connection with Project 2000 now focuses on service issues such as the following:

1. Rapid response to a growing number of business needs

These needs have been caused by a large increase in customer requests. Priority has been given to answering the growing range of business require ments coupled with cost control procedures. This leads to the next goal:

2. Reduction of the cost of doing business

In terms of financial messages and of communications at large, electronic mail (e-mail) has resulted in a sharp reduction in telexes. But most of the management productivity that can come from e-mail has already been obtained. We need the next step.

"Every ounce of labor cost has been taken out with second-generation-type implementation," said a Citibank executive. Then he added, "Reducing costs is a tradition. The same is true about increasing productivity."

3. New business products and ventures

This is a subject presently put in third priority, but it will become the salient problem after the preceding two issues have been successfully addressed. In fact, at Citibank, developing new products is a top-priority objective, given the tight coupling of high technology and banking services.

Let me recapitulate; Top management directives at Citibank put emphasis on cost control and mental productivity. The standing guidelines state that the *competent* implementation of computers and communications should be *tuned to* and *judged by* its contribution to the increase in productivity of managers and professionals.

One can do nothing less than fully subscribe to these guidelines, which indicate good management. The Citibank strategy, in terms of cost reduction, has been tuned to the fact that by the mid-1980s, the simple things were already done: deliveries, and verifications were made online to the customer.

Since then, as it was stated during the meeting, paper has become practically nonexistent in Citibank operations, but this is not true of *people costs*. To control costs over the long term, top management therefore decided to focus on the reduction of people costs, also realizing the fact that it takes both sophisticated technology and appreciable investments to obtain substancial labor savings.

Capitalizing on the fact that his background is in industrial engineering, John Reed, Citibank's chief executive officer, has launched a major effort in industrial engineering, enriching this project with artificial intelligence. During our meeting, managers expressed the most interest in learning about the benefits they could derive from implementation of artificial intelligence. They believed that AI would permit them to address the actual human investment because that is where the opportunity is.

Citibank did not elaborate on what its top management is doing with executives and system specialists who cannot or will not live and work within the new policies. But, from a similar meeting with General Electric, I have a transcript of the management philosophy of John F. Welsh, Jr., which answers the query in the following terms:

1. "Employees who cannot adjust do not belong at the new GE."

2. "We now want to create an environment where employees are ready to go and eager to stay."

Since Welsh took the top job at GE, personnel has been reduced by 100,000 workers out of and original 400,000, and revenues have grown 48 percent. At the same time, GE's executive development center at Crontonville has been redirected to become the *change agent*. This is the wisest strategy for companies that wish to survive.

EMBEDDING ARTIFICIAL INTELLIGENCE IN THE FINANCIAL NETWORK

To the question "Are there any secrets for success in AI based on practical experience?" Citibank responded by outlining seven basic rules that seem to guide management's thinking:

1. AI is a technology you have to be *very comfortable* with to be successful, refocusing the allocation of your resources accordingly.

The budget presently allocated by Citibank to system software development (an *investment*) roughly falls into three groups: 38 percent to new systems (including major renewal); 38 percent to maintenance; and 24 percent to the development of *totally new products*, in which AI plays a key role.

2. Many factors are involved in being successful with new technology, not the least of which is *simplicity*.

Management must be very careful in evaluating an AI project's simplicity. The key questions to ask are "What is the level of complexity this project requires? Is this level understood? Do *we* have the needed experience?" If yes, then let's do it. If not, let's acquire the experience.

3. A critical role is played by the correct choice of *priorities*.

At Citibank, crucial queries include "Are we dealing with an issue worth dealing with? Is it a strategic question?" A senior executive commented that the availability or nonavailability of knowledge engineers is taken as secondary to this issue. Some are employed in bodyshop, and there is also internal personnel as well as more specialists in training. But it is competitiveness and priorities which will say whether a project is done and if it has a good payback.

4. Always account for the fact that the AI project to be chosen will have high *visibility*.

Not only are endusers today very knowledgeable and expectant of results, but the visibility of information systems work has also tremendously increased. Therefore, it is unwise to undertake AI projects in glamour areas, particularly subjects involving complex issues where there is a high probability of failure. "This means knowing what we do, and how much we can trust our human resources."

5. AI technology has great *potential* only if the questions of scope and domain are clearly defined, and if we understand the complexity of the system.

Vital to success in AI projects are understanding of the target application and limitations of the technology. One of the most frequent errors among financial organizations implementing AI is failure to look into the issue of complexity in the ill-fated hope that the new technology is limitless. Thus, they commit two failures in one act, subsequently rushing to the superficial conclusion that expert systems have not yet found a valid domain of application.

6. Lack of appropriate business *control* inevitably leads a project to failure.

A basic principle for the sound and efficient control of a business is the assignment of *one* primary role to the manager of a project and no more, thereby avoiding the problem of conflicting responsibilities. This principle has evolved after long and searching experience in business practice, yet it is often forgotten in the design of information systems implementation of AI.

7. People who can correct the failures that often occur in new projects are a vital component.

Setting unrealistic goals for a project guarantees that the AI application will go nowhere. But even if the scope is properly chosen, there is no way to eliminate risk in advanced projects.

Citibank took as an example of failure the automation of electronic letters of credit. In processing this application, the machine reads the letter (message), picks essential elements, and integrates them into another letter. This requires significant types of interpretation that involved unknown issues, and the application was not successful.

An example of successful AI implementation at Citibank is the use of AI in electronic funds transfer (EFT), specifically in telex structuring. The ongoing implementation of an expert system provides great benefits to the bank, and, though the application has been deliberately kept to a minimum, the labor savings are significant. Essential, for instance, is a name search: The expert system looks up the name; then it finds the *account number.* Even such simple constructs have given the bank first-class cost savings. This is the intended type of application of AI in its formative years in a financial organization: small, simple projects requiring ingenuity, projects that can be developed in a short time frame (two to three months) and immediately put into action.

Through AI, both the network and the banking services it supports can be kept dynamic. The Citibank executive gave evidence of prevailing management policy when he stated "Let's find out *how* the banking business is changing: Where is our business going? What will we be doing in the next 10 years? Then, let's prepare for that change using the best tools available."

Questions like these should be steadily asked because they motivate people. We need people who are motivated and knowledgeable as customers ask for increasingly sophisticated support. If the appropriate services are not provided, the customer base will erode, and return on investment will not be ensured. Is this our goal?

To summarize: We should emphasize satisfaction of the increasingly sophisticated requirements of our clients, before competitors have a chance to do so. For many years profitability has been very obscure—if not outright nonexistent—with traditional data processing. But as the Citibank example (among others) documents, profits can be quite impressive with intelligent networks and expert systems.

Customer response to the new AI-enriched financial network of Project 2000 has been overwhelming. Value-added services with AI permitted the bank to reduce cost and to keep competitive. Expert systems made it feasible to offer personalized services to the clients. A new generation of software technology provided the bank with timing advantages.

The AI approach permitted development of new financial services that could not be made in the past. This includes the ability to discover products and services needed for the coming market landscape, particularly in dealing with important customers. For the customer, the advantages gained include a new way of interacting with the bank. To satisfy the needs of the important customers, every inch of technological advantage has to be thought about in both technical and business terms. Once we have done our homework in both domains, we will be ready to realize its potential.

To keep our bank profitable, we have to be constantly alert. The target to shoot for with our intelligent financial network has three aspects: *any product at any time, anywhere in the world.*

This target should become the basis of our strategy, which must focus on developing a winning environment based on knowledgeable people, high technology, attractive products, and instrumental marketing. This means *hard work*, but hard work can also be fun. J. P. Morgan once wrote, "My job is more fun than being king, pope, or prime minister, for no one can turn me out of it, and I do not have to make any compromises with principles."

13
Services an Intelligent Network Can Provide

Networking technology changes quickly, and it thus affects all service indus-tries' products, from commercial banking and securities to airline passen-ger traffic and merchandising. Networking technology brings the producer closer to the customer, improves product appeal, reduces delivery costs, and increases profits.

The benefits we can obtain from networks show us that, if we wish to remain competitive, we should be steadily seeking new, more advanced, and highly effective ways of combining our products and services with tech-nology. It is precisely in this spirit that I am advising you to pay particular attention to realspace communications.

Intelligent networks provide us with the opportunity to link our opera-tions through gigastream channels, nationally as well as internationally, *as if* they were in the same geographical place, and at the same time ensure 24-hour servicing for our clients. I have already discussed the services intel-ligent networks can provide. Can we define these communications solutions in a way that is relevant for the 1990s?

The term *intelligent network* was coined in 1986 by Bellcore, the R&D laboratory of the former AT&T operating companies,[1] and it has become quite popular. Unfortunately, Bellcore only described the intelligent net-work concept—it did not define it. As a result, practically every telco today gives its own definition and interpretation.

Precisely for this reason, in this chapter we will examine the *facilities* that make up an intelligent network, its *functionality,* and the services it

[1]Ameritech, Bell Atlantic, BellSouth, Nymex Pacific Telesis, Southwestern Bell, and U.S. West.

should provide to its users. Subsequently, by the end of this chapter, I will discuss the wisdom of embedding artificial intelligence constructs in network applications, giving examples of practical experiences.

Compared with investments in people and machines required by traditional data processing, the implementation of knowledge engineering is highly economic. It is based on small teams of knowledgeable people who develop cost-effective solutions and provide immediate results.

There is, however, a catch with intelligent networks. They can neither be developed nor implemented by the data processing bureaucracy because their operation runs contrary to bureaucratic interests. At the beginning of his presidency, Richard Nixon lamented that the most frustrating problem he encountered upon becoming president was finding out how little control he had over the U.S. bureaucracy. Financial institutions have found the same with their data processing people.

NEW-GENERATION ONLINE SYSTEMS

The most widespread telecommunications service is telephony, and its capillarity is perceived by the user in terms of cost, availability, and quality of connection. During the first two decades of data communications (the 1960s and 1970s), service expectations were not very high, and new telecommunications features were not widely used. Telcos offered basic bit-stream features, and customers were generally undemanding and acquiescent.

However, during the 1980s this apparent passivity of telecommunications users was replaced by a rapid awakening of user awareness. New services were demanded that underlined the necessity of a strict research and development discipline. The users' awakening was not a chance event, but was led by demands posed by a growing range of applications.

The primary agent demanding quality of service and implying complexity of the newly networked applications was the financial market. This started a quarter century ago, but at that time the demands were posed by a growing number of simpler applications. The *first-generation* online systems (GOLS), which were installed in the late 1960s and early 1970s, were designed for the following applications:

- Interbranch transactions

- Demand deposits accounting

- Stand-alone general accounting

If this was the profile of the first-generation online system, by the mid-1970s the applications were succeeded by more extended approaches that added to the pallet of supported services, creating a *second-generation* system:

- Savings and time deposits
- Securities transactions
- Cash management
- Foreign exchange

With time, the applications characterizing the second-generation online system grew, and 10 years later they were restructured—and in some cases replaced—by the *third-generation* online systems, (3GOLS),[2] which featured integrated solutions:

- Electronic funds transfer (EFT)
- EFT associated with point of sale (EFT/POS)
- Business banking
- Provision of financial information
- Management databases
- Complete accounting solutions

Today, *fourth-generation* online systems are coming into the limelight, integrating most of the business applications of the third generation but also equipping them with expert systems; the carrier itself is an intelligent network.

Telemarketing by financial institutions is one example that helps demonstrate the change in the applications landscape. The key to telemarketing in banking is not just telephony; also needed is a unique integration with the client database that is enriched with profile analyzers, account management, and pattern recognition software.

Even in traditional fields such as accounting, change caused by integration comes in big steps. In the EFT/POS domain, for instance, the installation of checkout scanners in most supermarkets has brought with it an avalanche of data, more timely and specific than any available before.

---

[2]See also D. N. Chorafas and H. Steinmann, *Implementing Networks in Banking and Financial Services* (London: Macmillan, 1988).

As marketers are beginning to exploit this information, they are getting a better feel for exactly what a price cut, coupon blitz, or store display actually does for sales and profits. They also begin a new relationship with their bank, exploiting not only the EFT/POS end of networking but also other benefits such as online general accounting and valuation of inventories.

But for the bank as well the financial and the marketing departments, the consequences are significant. Online responses create great possibilities for investigating information, tracking it, and passing it immediately into data analysis.

The bank and the merchandising company have to work in synergy. Instead of receiving monthly or bimonthly reports with at best a regional breakdown of how a store is doing, treasurers of supermarket chains get steady cash management—just like the marketers who now have available 24-hour detailed data for every item and size, sometimes down to the individual store.

In America, Nestlé Foods Corp., using such data, learned that a combination of store displays and newspaper ads resulted in huge volume increases for its Quik chocolate drink. In Japan, the local subsidiary of 7-Eleven has achieved zero inventories, nearly doubling the available space to customer displays at each shop, sharply cutting down money tied up in inventories, and greatly increasing its profits.

Many marketers today exploit the possibility of using scanner data to analyze the effects of TV advertising and customer promotions such as coupons. Systems are being designed to provide reliable nationwide information linking which TV ads individual households watch with what they buy at the store. Packaged goods companies hope that such *single-source* data will allow them to hone their marketing more finely and thereby improve upon their performance.

If management knows how effective specific commercials or coupon programs are, then it can decide whether these are worth the trouble and expense. This requires taking the following steps:

- Making better use of the reams of information already available

- Transporting this information more efficiently through intelligent networks

- Using it more effectively to uncover patterns with the help of supercomputers and AI

- Presenting the results in a comprehensive, action-oriented manner through visualization

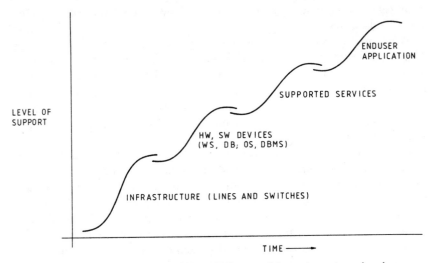

LEVEL OF
SUPPORT

ENDUSER
APPLICATION

SUPPORTED SERVICES

HW, SW DEVICES
(WS, DB; OS, DBMS)

INFRASTRUCTURE (LINES AND SWITCHES)

TIME ———►

Figure 13.1 Interlocking implementation and investment cycles in network solutions.

It is finally becoming a common idea among the foremost organizations that the exploitation of telecommunications services requires the existence of an infrastructure and the availability of terminals. Figure 13.1 illustrates the relationship of implementation and investment cycles, which over the years has allowed exploitation of networks and provided the ability to generate added value on supported services.

The steady improvement of supported services is a necessity not only because the market demands it but also because investment requirements for new infrastructure are extremely high. To achieve a positive return on those investments, it is necessary to have a forward-looking plan and to be able to take advantage of new service opportunities at the earliest possible stage.

We must design service features that make current and potential users aware of the existence of new possibilities. As I have emphasized, we must provide for appropriate user education. Another sound policy is to capitalize on state-of-the-art technology. This is the aspect of intelligent networks treated in the next section.

STRUCTURE OF AN INTELLIGENT NETWORK

Society and its *community intelligence* depend on effective communications. The emergence of an advanced telecommunications system therefore has significant consequences for society as a whole and for the nature of the work we do in particular.

When we say *telecommunications* we no longer mean only telephony. The regulatory and technological walls dividing telephony from data communications and entertainment communications have crumbled, and a new, integrated approach to telecommunications requirements has taken place. Chapter 10 demonstrated why, in the 1990s, we must deal with telecommunications as a *single* broad, dynamic field managed in a manner able to confront the challenges that arise.

In a knowledge society, further progress is greatly dependent on the means whereby both *information* and *knowledge* are captured, transmitted, stored, retrieved, manipulated, and used. An increasingly demanding marketplace, the accelerating pace of development, and a growing business diversification have caused business and technical information to grow rapidly in volume.

At the user side, the integrative capability of network intelligence can be visualized by means of a multilayered pyramid, where the data processing chores are enriched with a realtime communications discipline. This is a concept comprehensively presented in Figure 13.2, where the bottom layer focuses on transactions and the top layer on strategic issues.

A unified domain of communications, computers, and information technologies is the largest conglomerate of services the First World has ever experienced. Its market is and will increasingly be highly dynamic; its products are steadily evolving; and its jobs will shift from activities that rapidly become obsolete to new business opportunities.

- *More than half* of the economically active population of the First World works in communications and information occupations.

- *Two-thirds* of all economic activities are considered to be strongly dependent on the quality and competitiveness of the communications and information infrastructure.

The demands posed by this major shift in occupations oblige us to rethink our concepts and the approaches we have followed in the past. If we do not do so, we will not be able to provide workable solutions to our communications problems—but we will have only ourselves to blame.

Mismanaging resources is not a new phenomenon in human society. What is new is that such mismanagement happens today on a larger scale than ever before, and a fairly managed operation can turn into a badly managed one rather quickly. An example is the mismanagement of income among telephone companies.

Studies carried out in America and Europe indicate that more than 65 percent of revenue from *additional customers* is swallowed up by expenses

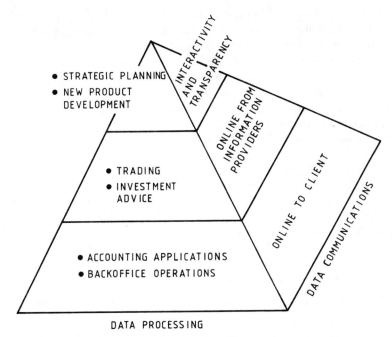

Figure 13.2 An integrative approach to network intelligence.

such as marketing, billing, collections, and added capital investments for traffic. Such capital investments, these studies suggest, are more intense the lower the technology being used.

It is, therefore, no wonder that telephone companies as well as financial organizations (for their own benefit) are very keen these days on developing intelligent network structures. We have to return to the fundamentals to clearly define what makes up a *network infrastructure*. In a plain-old-telephone-service sense, the answer is as follows:

- *Lines* for transmission
- *Nodes* for switching
- *Terminal equipment* (private branch exchange [PBX], sets)
- *Support equipment* (instrumentation)

Often, but not always, lines represent about 25 to 30 percent of the investments made by a telephone company; nodes (switching centers), 35 percent; and terminal equipment (telephone sets and private branch exchanges) installed at client sites, 10 to 12 percent. The balance is made up of a number of items, from building to installation and maintenance equipment.

At least in the United States, England, and Japan, after deregulation the equipment and software installed at client sites are, to a large extent, the client's own business. Hence, when we say that a given telco is keen on providing intelligent network capabilities, what we mean in a practical sense is that it is keen on providing added value to its lines, switching centers, and associated instrumentation. This value differentiation typically consists of the following items:

- *Artificial intelligence constructs* for switching, transmission, and maintenance
- *High quality* with low bit-error rate (BER)
- *High capacity* (broadband)
- *Nonblocking* solutions
- *Diagnostics* and a quality database
- *Forecasting* and load planning
- *Digitization* in channel transmission and switching
- *Innovation*, competitiveness, and corresponding investments

Intelligent network solutions do not come cheaply—but, when they are properly implemented, they can save a great deal of money and help increase service quality, customer satisfaction, and patronage. As telcos look for ways to cut costs while bettering their service, they find out that the competent implementation of the components of an intelligent network make a big difference in reaching this goal. Such components typically are as follows:

- Intelligent nodes
- Intelligent lines
- Quality databases
- Analytical tools (both algorithmic and heuristic)
- Simulators
- Schedulers

Clear-eyed telcos appreciate the value of each of these components. But not every telco is on this wavelength. Those stumbling backwards into the future have a total misconception about what an intelligent network is or what it can do. Asked about their definition of an intelligent network, some of the backward-leaning telco executives whom I interviewed gave "interesting" answers:

- Provide more services like telebanking.
- Organize shared databases to sell to user organizations.
- Put in place "high-level" service centers at some local exchanges.

No mention was made about cost-effectiveness; neither was there any idea about what these "high-level" services could or should be. These two points come together; based on American experience, Figure 13.3 demonstrates how it has been possible to cut costs by an appreciable share—from an inflation-adjusted 37 cents per minute for domestic dial calls—through stiffening competition and technology.

Among organizations that know how to read the future, intelligent networks are being deployed in order to enhance the post-industrial infrastructure. *Open networks* have been proposed as regulatory concepts but also as

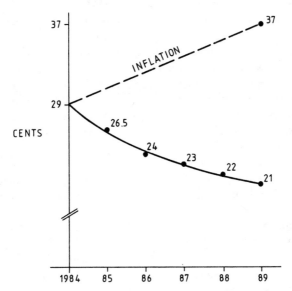

Figure 13.3 Long-distance prices in the United States (cents per minute, domestic dial calls).

technical initiatives. In the 1990s, the terms *open networks* and *intelligent networks* will tend to merge into one concept, as AI will make the difference between a monolithic structure and an open one.

TOWARD A BROADER SENSE OF NETWORK INTELLIGENCE

According to the Bellcore description, intelligent networks make available preprogrammed service logic programs that can be triggered by customer action. A number of such programs are in the network's repository, being selected according to the particular requirement by a trigger table in what has been called a *service switching point.*

In other words, according to this definition, an intelligent network will still be made up of nodes and links, but these nodes will be getting increasingly smart, which is a reasonable assumption, given that they are now computer based. To this Bellcore description, CCITT and other telcos have added that public and private databases will reside in the nodes. This is the *wrong* approach.

The telephone companies have no business running public databases, let alone private databases. Private databases are the domain of *information providers.* As for private databases, nobody will ever entrust a public authority (even a privatized telco) with his text and data. These are irrational concepts that only the non-businesslike telcos, and their bureaucracy, can understand—as they did in the early 1980s with the now defunct videotex.[3]

Of course, we should follow information systems and knowledge engineering in general, but our work in the 1990s should focus on *enduser functions;* the design and implementation of human windows, interactivity with private and public databases, and visualization are no business of the telco. This area of activity belongs to the user organization—and so do logic processing on workstations or number crunching on supercomputers, as shown in Figure 13.4.

The business of telcos *is* to provide the most reliable, wideband, failure-free, low-BER bitstream, and access to rich databases. These databases are typically owned and operated by the user organizations and by information providers.

Having explained questions of ownership, I should add that an appropriate definition of what should be done starts with *what needs to be fulfilled.* Intelligent networks are of vital interest to a post-industrial economy because they perform these functions:

---

[3]Videotex, in the late 1970s, linked television sets and phone lines in a new service, which was overpriced and undersupported by telephone companies, hence killed at the roots.

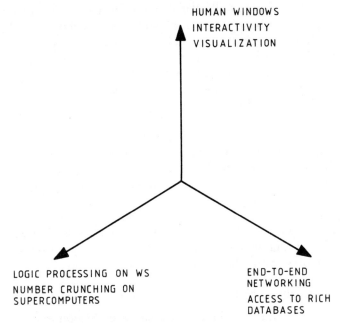

HUMAN WINDOWS
INTERACTIVITY
VISUALIZATION

LOGIC PROCESSING ON WS
NUMBER CRUNCHING ON
SUPERCOMPUTERS

END-TO-END
NETWORKING
ACCESS TO RICH
DATABASES

Figure 13.4 Emphasis on enduser functions.

1. *Influence the political, social, and business environment* within which they evolve

2. Are instrumental in unfolding *new opportunities* in the communications domain for manufacturing, merchandising, and financial companies

3. Provide a continuous stream of *multimedia* (text, data, graphics, voice, image) flowing between business centers as well as among consumers

4. Sweep over long distances at *gigastream* (gigabit per second, GBPS) channel capacity

5. Provide a single mechanism for integrated *service engineering,* which itself ensures significant competitive advantages.

6. Ensure an *agile layer* to which other services and databases can be attached through interconnected platforms

7. Are increasingly *cost-effective* in terms of the telecommunications services they provide, using high technology to swamp costs

Whenever we discuss cost-effective solutions, we must keep in mind that cost is one factor, and benefit is another. And these benefits should be tangible both to the network provider and to its clients. Precisely because of this duality of goals, which, to the superficial observer, may seem contradictory, intelligent networks include major *technical challenges*. To optimize the use of resources, they feature arbitration, dynamic traffic handling, and so on, creating through them preconditions for a liberal service provision environment.

Precisely for the same reasons, the new generation of networks includes artificial intelligence constructs applied to housekeeping services such as remote diagnostics, error detection and correction, reliability and uptime, quality histories—slowly covering through AI all *network control center* (NCC) functions.

Examples abound among the top telephone companies; the following three come from General Telephone and Electronics (GTE). The Proactive Rehabilitation of Output Plant (PROPHET) uses *heuristic* expert system techniques in order to do the following:

- Assist in trouble analysis

- Help control center staff in identification of local loop problems

- Address both cable and terminals

- Interface to GTE operating systems for preventive maintenance

Another expert system, Proactive Maintenance for Customer Access Facilities (CAF), identifies sections of cable that may need repair or replacement. Still another system, COMPASS, performs analysis of diagnostic messages of a telephone switching system. It examines maintenance logs from a central office and suggests maintenance action.

COMPASS is currently operational in many GTE branches. It provides guaranteed maintainability for existing switches by capturing expertise from the best telephone engineers of the firm.

The examples I have just given also help focus attention on the fact that *steady R&D* investments are producing new services for clients and new opportunities for the firms themselves. Although three-quarters of the Earth suffers from lack of adequate communication facilities, in the First World—America, Japan, and Western Europe—the exploration of communications frontiers is progressing toward new goals, and these goals seem reachable.

If we wish to achieve better cost-effectiveness, we must move toward more advanced organization of our resources, using new types of *protocols* and media solutions such as *photonics, supercomputers,* and *artificial intelligence* to maximize our advantages in the communications domain. This is the sense of developing and using intelligent networks.

Intelligent network solutions are evolving because the limited answers to telecommunications needs that were provided in the past simply cannot do the job. Just a few years ago, the feeling among telecom administrations was that the Integrated Services Digital Network (ISDN) would be the basis for future public networks. Today, most of the telcos are far from this view and are actively working on *new broadband technologies.*

Telcos at one time believed that intelligent networks were a subject for the mid- to late 1990s. But the timetable has been rapidly advanced, and the first intelligent network implementations are already beginning to appear; they will multiply in the early to mid-1990s.

User demand, particularly of the large corporate clients (who are the main income earners of telcos), and *a fast-paced technology* have changed both the expectations and the landscape. ISDN remains a major selling point for communications equipment manufacturers, but, propelled by demands of a fiercely competitive environment, the increasingly sophisticated needs of corporate clients have led telecom administrations to look for alternative methods of information delivery.

Emphasis is on fast, flexible, and economical provision of new services in a package attractive to the business user. Major trends include the advent of smart lines, switches enriched with expert systems, online diagnostics done through AI, and multimedia services that make up the intelligent network.

THE DRIVE TO CREATE NEW PRODUCTS AND SERVICES

Intelligent networks promise not only a host of significant communications facilities far beyond what has thus far been feasible, but also the option for users to create new services without the intervention of network operators. In addition, they provide the platform for a growing range of income-producing products.

The development and operation of intelligent networks is no one's exclusive province:

1. Telephone companies should steadily strive to incorporate more and more intelligence into their communications systems.

2. Value-added network (VAN) providers should increase the sophistication of services they offer to their clients.

3. The larger financial institutions, manufacturing industries, merchandising firms, and information providers should develop proprietary network solutions, although they may use the bitstream services of telcos and the value-differentiated offerings of VANs for channel capacity purposes.

Public databases are the only product of information providers, and private databases interest all enduser organizations. It is at this level that intelligent networks and databases come together.

By distributing high-level services in databases across a communications-intense structure, intelligent networks hold the promise to crack the software bottleneck that has delayed the introduction of new solutions to the problems of business, industry, and consumers. They are hence being heralded as the key that will unlock the economic doors of a knowledge society.

I must, however, state that, at the same time, intelligent networks blur the boundary between public and private telecommunications services through the provision of *virtual facilities*. Parallel to this, new flexible access systems are created by the deployment of fiber optics, the adoption of new protocols like frame relay and asynchronous transmission mode,[4] and the use of intelligent multiplexers in the local loop. These hold the potential to deliver true added value to customers at sharply decreased costs, and they provide the further advantage of almost limitless bandwidth, available on demand.

By offering both high quality and large capacity, fiber optics force a change in the way public telecommunications networks are designed and built. Optically based, connectionless switching schemes are doing away with the boundaries between *switching* and *transmission*, challenging long-held tenets about network planning, design, and implementation.

However, another effect of intelligent networks is a greater separation between *haves* and *have-nots*. The pace at which smart communications and flexible access systems are being deployed varies considerably from country to country. But differences are not caused by technology alone; the main impediment to modernization is political. It is not surprising that, given their revolutionary characteristics, intelligent networks have so far received the most favor in America, Japan, and England, which have deregulated telecommunications regimes.

The new telecommunications technologies hold interesting implications for everyone. But in practice, in the decade of the 1990s, the vested interests of the telco bureaucracy seriously block modernization and, by doing so, they keep the infrastructure of the whole country in a backwater condition.

---

[4]See D. N. Chorafas and H. Steinmann, *Intelligent Networks* (Los Angeles: CRC/Times Mirror, 1990).

FROM NETWORK INTELLIGENCE TO REALSPACE USAGE

During our meeting April 1991 in Tokyo, NTT's Dr. Fukuya Ishino underlined that the successful design of an intelligent network depends above all on the sophistication of the *internode protocol* and the software architecture being adopted. This is a direct reflection of the fact that the functions needed by the carriers are largely performed by means of software, from intelligent CAD to the management of heterogeneous databases and knowledge engineering–enriched diagnostics.

According to NTT, an intelligent network automates *fault administration*, detecting system or communication line faults and supporting recovery procedures. Knowledge engineering can also be of significant help to online *configuration management*.

An example of AI implementation by NTT is its Knowledge Base Management System (KBMS-2). Applications currently employing KBMS-2 include the following:

- Emergency fault handling for switching systems

- Fault diagnosis of crossbar switches

- Design of private networks

- Computer-aided training of network operators

- Trouble analysis of computer software

- Sales support for customer terminals

KBMS-2 is designed to run on various computer operating systems. It is being used with nine different architectures, including IBM 30XX, Vax-8000, MicroVax, Sun-3, Apollo Domain, and NEC PC-9800.

The NTT example is interesting because telcos often miss the fact that high-tech network implementations can give significant leverage. But, as successful cases help demonstrate, practical applications of knowledge engineering are not made for the sake of science; rather, they are made for the significant results they provide to their implementors.

The same is true of network development plans made by financial institutions and industrial corporations, as well as of the applications that follow such plans. As the more advanced implementors appreciate, intelligent networks are built to serve a purpose for the knowledge society. They promote the generation and propagation of community intelligence by serving consumers, national and multinational manufacturing concerns, financial institutions, merchandising organizations, and governments. Although such networks are widely distributed, they operate and exploit their resources *as if* they were concentrated at one point in *time* and *space*—which, as I have already explained, is the concept of *realspace*.

Both realspace and the facilities embedded in the new architectures lead toward structural changes in business and in society as a whole. Increasingly, user organizations find that *teleports* and *bypasses* are a better solution than depending completely on the telco; they are also discovering what they can achieve through *photonics*, the technology that will replace electronics by the end of the 1990s.

Nevertheless, far-reaching architectural approaches need a concept, knowledgeable people, and tools. These are the important elements for the following tasks:

- Steadily improving the quality of network design

- Focusing on the reliability of its implementation and operation

- Automating diagnostics and facilitating maintenance

- Providing quality histories to control the wares of different vendors

- Swamping the costs associated with networking to help extend the area of implementation

Management's role in *cost-effectiveness* should characterize any and every networking effort, and this is not just a matter of new software and hardware. The major part of the challenge is *architectural*.

One of the key decisions in telecommunications policy, and the investments it requires, is whether to proceed with an overlay on the current ossified network structures or with a full-blown replacement strategy. A great deal of future competitiveness is embedded in this decision. The whole procurement policy must be carefully reviewed, articulating a set of basic functional components that underlie the elements of all network services, and providing a means to combine and recombine these elements to create new services under the grand design of a systems architecture.

An open architecture should be chosen because it permits user organizations to switch vendors, developing solutions more quickly and at a lower cost. It should also be fairly simple to switch public network operators and manipulate third-party software houses, thus creating niche communications services for specific customer groups.

Another consequence of new departures is the possibility to uncouple the software control layer of public networks from underlying access and transport technologies. A properly planned network service logic would not depend on any single underlying technology, which would reduce the flexibility of the resulting solutions.

To make feasible such a strategy, a wise implementation of telecommunications services will use *the most advanced features*, grasping a new technology as soon as it becomes available. But only the leaders really know how to exploit such business opportunities in a timely and effective fashion.

The ingenious combination of design factors necessary to obtain commendable results requires the efforts of many specialists in telecommunications, databases, workstations, artificial intelligence, and supercomputers. Projects in these areas should not work independently of one another but in synergy; the effort should be interdisciplinary, combined into one technological aggregate.

The goals of the technology that we use, particularly the advanced technology, should include the following:

- To give our company a competitive edge

- To permit us to steadily improve our customer service

- To make it feasible to swamp costs, from the production to the distribution of services

- To ensure a reliable communication and computation platform with uninterrupted service

The solutions we adopt should definitely account for changes in the business environment, the diversification taking place, the growing competition, and internationalization, and for increasing deregulation and the rapid progress in technology which increasingly leads toward a knowledge society.

INTELLIGENT NETWORKS USED BY THE FINANCIAL INDUSTRY

The financial industry provides good examples of the developing perspective of intelligent network implementation, and is therefore a useful model for many other sectors. Within the financial industry itself, some areas need advanced network solutions more than others—with treasury, forex, and securities being at the top of the list.

Networks designed specifically for forex, treasury, and securities are made with globalization in mind. During the last 15 years, such international financial networks have made feasible realtime information services featuring financial reporting, stock quotations, interest rates, exchange rates, and payment orders. Payment functions started being executed online in a global sense, including payments made in connection to domestic and international operations, as well as integration with automated clearinghouse and netting systems.

However, what has not been always appreciated is that globalization of banking poses problems well beyond the technological issues. The core issue with the globalization of banking is that our thinking, our attitudes, our skills, and, consequently, our decisions must catch up with the networked realities.

The lag is primarily cultural. Many financial institutions have not yet changed their images and their approaches because the globalization of banking is *widely feared*—as a Peat Marwick study suggests. Yet globalization is an ongoing trend, and financial institutions that know how to capitalize on it reap the greatest profits.

Based on his research, Daniel Burstein comments on the role of realspace:[5] "In the year 2000, Nomura's headquarters will not be in Tokyo but on a satellite orbiting the Earth, uplinking and downlinking information and electronic transactions instantaneously across the globalized axis of London, New York, and Tokyo markets."

Such solution is a 1990s implementation of what Sun Tzu taught 2,500 years ago[6]—but *using technology as the weapon*. According to Burstein, Setsuya Tabuchi, Nomura's CEO, wields power strategically, borrowing from Sun Tzu's ancient writing on the art of war to steer his institution toward leadership of the global financial revolution.

Nomura is not just a direct competitor to other securities firms in America, Europe, or Japan; it is the largest and most profitable securities company in the world. It is clear that the strategic technological investments Nomura is doing aim to conquer market share—particularly the most lucrative segment of the market. No securities house, commercial bank, or other financial institution can afford to be insensitive to these developments.

Awareness should be followed by analysis, and analysis by action. Three basic aspects must be appreciated and acted upon simultaneously:

1. Globality is needed to underpin financial power.

2. Financial power is necessary to acquire and protect globality.

[5]D. Burstein, *Yen! The Threat of Japan's Financial Empire* (Melbourne: Bantam/Schwartz, 1989).

[6]Sun Tzu, *The Art of War* (New York: Delacorte Press 1983). This was the bible of Napoleon and Mao—as well as of many top bankers today.

3. Intelligent networks provide the linkage between financial centers, without which financial power cannot be successfully exercised—or even sustained over a long period of time.

The driving force behind the quest for *global, multifaceted* operations has naturally been profits. The motives, however, are more refined: expanding business opportunities; spreading risks; controlling settlements; examining market growth perspectives; and guaranteeing account control. The issue to be underlined at this point is that such goals can no more be successfully achieved without the proper networking solution.

Networks and databases help us provide integrated approaches, which are absolutely necessary to face the developing trends in the financial markets worldwide. Such approaches must account for the following factors:

- The growing *interdependence* of economies and, therefore, of financial markets

- The increasing *sophistication* of the client base, and the demands it poses on the banking system

- The *breaking down of barriers* between financial and other institutions, so far engaged in different lines of business

This is the viewpoint from which the impact of network technology on the financial industry should be studied. Upon investigation, we can see that such effects extend beyond the time-honored concept of a bank as financial intermediary.

For the modern, *post-deregulation* bank, realspace, online communication is indivisible from its means of doing business. It also influences the cultural change now taking place with the switch of focus from tangibles to intangibles, from procedures and formulas to conceptualization, from a structured to an unstructured environment. The facilities provided by networks are increasingly found to be the moving gear behind the

- Fast development of new financial products and services

- Rationalization of branch operations

- Control over costs and expenditures

- Improved client information capability

- Efficient operation and structure of computer systems

- Real automation in the handling of payment documents

The fundamental reason for pointing out such facts is to underline how close technology and marketing have come together in a practical, action-oriented sense. In finance, as in science, knowledge is not power until it is properly used.

The marketing of financial services, the proper use of artificial intelligence, network design, and supercomputer developments are issues that are coming closer together. The profitability of banking operations in the mid-1990s and beyond will depend on the effectiveness of such integration—as well as on imaginative solutions and fast implementation timetables.

Intellectual Capital and Strategic Planning

The knowledge that exists in an organization can be used to create advantage. *Intellectual capital* has always been a highly valued commodity on the leading edge of science—before 2000, this will also be true of the foremost companies in finance.

More than ever before, we must match our company's intellectual requirements and the technology we are using with our strategic plans. We must also appreciate that both our technology and our human resources are facing an accelerated obsolescence. At Westinghouse, according to research and development chief Dr. Isaac Barpal, the average technology becomes obsolete in five to seven years, and at the firm's electronic systems group, in just two to three years.

At the same time, a study by First Wachovia Bank demonstrated that, if not steadily trained, a banker loses 50 percent of his skill in five years. Another study has indicated that technologists can lose 50 percent of their skill in the short period of two to three years if they fail to follow a steady, lifelong learning program.

By contrast, through steady training and on-the-job experience, human resources can be made to *grow*. The more they become technology-literate the better they will perform the required tasks.

Each of the chapters of this book has been designed to meet this objective: contribute to *high-technology literacy*, particularly in the domains of treasury and forex.

Edmond Israel, chairman of the Luxembourg Stock Exchange, said during the May 4, 1992 dinner honoring him and his foundation: "The greatest danger we are facing today comes from the fact that people keep on thinking of the past rather than of the future. They try to solve *yesterday's problems*, rather than those of *today and tomorrow*."

This is true all the way from family planning and the population explosion to education, technology, corporate decisions, and the way the finance markets work. It is also true of the decision styles characterizing a significant number of bankers, treasurers, and technologists.

"Resistance to change comes from those people who stand to lose significant advantages from the inefficiencies of the current system," advises Gordon Macklin, former president of NASD. "But because of fast changes in technology all markets and all companies have to keep up—or they will lose their share." In order to adapt to the changing environment:

- Efficient organizations must develop within themselves an *entrepreneurial* approach, which permits dynamic and flexible response to market requirements.
- Inflexibility and red tape are the characteristics of financial and industrial companies that seem to exist only for themselves—and that sooner or later will be left in the dust in the technology race.

But survival requires brain power. It is estimated that by 2000, some 70 percent of all jobs in the First World will require *cerebral skills*, not just manual skills. The people we employ should learn how to use their grey matter. "People think I am intelligent because I use my brains twice a week," George Bernard Shaw once said. The top professionals today use their brains every day. What is manual and routine should be done by machines.

Because forex and treasury are demanding professions, we should seek to employ the best of the graduating class. It is no coincidence that Wall Street and the City of London have been primary destinations for the top graduates of business administration and finance schools: Prestige, glamour, and large bonuses, but also *high technology*, come with careers in treasury, banking, forex, and brokerage.

The best of the class have given the following reasons for choosing employment in the financial industry, as well as in the financial functions of other industries:

- New ideas
- New ways of thinking
- Personal contacts
- A growing body of knowledge
- Greater perspective
- Advanced tools to use in the daily job

High technology attracts able-brained people. When used in imaginative ways, these people make cost-effective solutions feasible. The emerging discipline of *knowledge engineering* is generating a number of techniques usefully applied to the industrialization of knowhow—and this process increasingly underpins treasury and foreign exchange operations.

Index

Security Pacific, 20, 73
Sensitivities, 11
Sensitivity analysis, 171
Service engineering, 273
Shannon, C. E., Dr., 90
Shaw, George Bernard, 284
Shearson Lehman Hutton, 15
Simulation, 146, 153, 169
  digital, 117
Simulator, 40, 152
Singapore International Monetary Exchange,
  250
Skandinaviska Enskilda Banken, 230
Software, 55, 73
Special drawing rights (SDR), 36
Spot trading facility, 135
SQL, 82
SQL Access Group, 87
Standard chartered, 20
State transition graph, 110, 111
Stock market prediction, 205
Strategic product, 59
Strategists, quantitative, 202
Studer, Robert, 225
Sumitomo Bank, 238
Sun Tzu, 229, 280
Supercomputer(s), 32, 70, 71, 74, 75, 77, 78,
  105, 211
Supercomputer-based solution, 37
Supercomputing, 75
SWIFT, 243
Synthesis, 40
System architecture, 231
System interconnection interface (SII), 84

Tabuchi, Setsuya, 280
Tactical asset allocation, 161
Takahashi, Johsen, 235
Taxation, 23
Tax consultation expert system, 42, 43
Technical analysis and trading assistant
  (TARA), 133–135
Technology, current, 77
Telecommunications, 268
Telecommunications Intelligent Network
  Architecture (TINA), 83
Telecommunications systems, advanced, 267

Telekurs, 76
Telemarketing, 265
Telerate, 76, 94, 97
Tera-FLIPS, 75
Terano, T., Dr., 186, 188–190, 214
Testing, 36, 102
Therblig timestamping, 104
Thinking Machines, 193
Third-generation online systems, 265
Time management, 229
Time-price data pointers, 104
Time-price index files, 104
Timestamping, 104
Tokyo Stock Exchange (TSE), 205, 206
Traders:
  derivative, 202
  proprietary, 201
  sales, 201
Trading programs, simulated, 151
Treasurer, 4–6, 13, 17
Treasury functions, 2, 3
Turing, Alan, Dr., 202
24-hour trading, 23

Ueberroth, Peter, 72
Uncertainty management, 33
Union Bank of Switzerland, 225
Utilitarian solutions, 84
Utilities library, 212
Utility communications architecture
  (UCA), 86

Value differentiation, 16, 54, 88, 270
Visualization, 176
Visualization strategy, 213
Voice-processing devices, 18
Von Clausewitz, Karl, 225
Von Neumann, John, Dr., 202

Wall Street, 77
Welsh, John F., 258
Westinghouse, 283
Wide area networks (WAN), 53
Workstations (WS), 52, 53

Yamaichi Securities, 112, 163
Yamamoto, K., 186